Dutch
phrase book

D0047791

**Berlitz Publishing / APA Publications GmbH & Co.
Verlag KG, Singapore Branch, Singapore**

Contacting the Editors
Every effort has been made to provide accurate information in this publication, but changes are inevitable. The publisher cannot be responsible for any resulting loss, inconvenience or injury. We would appreciate it if readers would call our attention to any errors or outdated information by contacting Berlitz Publishing, 95 Progress Street, Union, NJ 07083, USA. Fax: 1-908-206-1103
email: comments@berlitzbooks.com

Satisfaction guaranteed—If you are dissatisfied with this product for any reason, send the complete package, your dated sales receipt showing price and store name, and a brief note describing your dissatisfaction to: Berlitz Publishing, Langenscheidt Publishing Group, Dept. L, 46-35 54th Rd., Maspeth, NY 11378. You'll receive a full refund.

Cover photo: ©Getty Images/Ryan McVay
Developed and produced for Berlitz Publishing by:
G&W Publishing Services, Oxfordshire, U.K.
Dutch edition:Aletta Stevens and Maricke O'Connor

Printed in Singapore

Contents

Pronunciation

This section is designed to make you familiar with the sounds of Dutch by using our simplified phonetic transcription. You'll find the pronunciation of the Dutch letters and sounds explained below, together with their "imitated" equivalents. This system is used throughout the phrase book: simply read the pronunciation as if it were English, noting any special rules below.

In this phrase book we have used a friendly system to achieve a close approximation of the pronunciation, although this inevitably means some simplification of the more subtle aspects of Dutch pronunciation.

The Dutch language

Dutch is closer to English than any other major language. These are the countries where you can expect to hear Dutch spoken:

Nederland The Netherlands

Dutch is the national language and is spoken by practically all the population (15.5 million). In the northern province of Friesland a large percentage of the population speaks Frisian as a first language.

English is taught as the first foreign language at school, and is very widely spoken. In fact you might find that people are very anxious to practice their English, and make it difficult for you to practice your Dutch! However, your knowledge of the language will be greatly appreciated, and everyone will be pleasantly surprised to have found someone who is making the effort to speak Dutch.

België Belgium

Belgium has two official languages: Flemish and French. Flemish is spoken in the north of the country and has much in common with Dutch. Each is easily understood by the other. In fact, both Belgium and the Netherlands use a common literary language, Standard Dutch.

The southern part of Belgium is French-speaking, and Flemish isn't spoken. The capital, Brussels, is bilingual, and you should be able to use your *Berlitz Dutch Phrase Book* there. Flemish is also spoken in the northern part of France, on the Belgian border.

The former colonies and other Dutch-speaking areas

The Netherlands Antilles, which are self-governing island territories in the Caribbean, are part of the kingdom and have Dutch as an official language. Surinam is independent but is also a Dutch-speaking country.

In the former Dutch East Indies (including Indonesia) many Dutch words have been integrated into the local language. Cape Dutch, or Afrikaans, spoken in South Africa, is an offshoot of Dutch that is now considered a separate language.

Consonants

Letter	Approximate pronunciation	Symbol	Example	Phonetics
b,c,f,h,k,l,m, n,p,q,t,x,y,z	as in English			
ch	*ch* as in lo*ch*	kh	**nacht**	*nakht*
d	*d* as in English, but *t* if at the end of a word	d/t	**bed**	*bet*
g	*ch* as in lo*ch*, or	kh	**groot**	*khroat*
	rarely *zh* as in pleasure	zh	**genre**	*zhernrer*
j	*y* as in *y*es	y	**ja**	*ya*
r	*r* rolled in the front of the mouth at the beginning or in the middle of the word, but at the back of the mouth if at the end of a word	r	**rijst**	*reyst*
s	always hard as in pa*ss*	s	**stop**	*stop*
sch	*s* followed by *ch* as in lo*ch*	skh	**schrijven**	*skhrayvern*
v	as an English *f*	f	**vader**	*faader*
w	as an English *v*	v	**water**	*vaater*

Vowels and Dipthongs

Dutch has many vowel and dipthong (combined vowel) sounds and some will be unfamiliar to your ear. Below we give the best approximation, but try to listen to Dutch speakers to get a more accurate picture.

Letter	Approximate pronunciation	Symbol	Example	Phonetics
a	between *u* as in c*u*p and *a* as in c*a*t	a	**nacht**	*nakht*
aa	*ar* as in m*ar*ket	aa	**vader**	*faader*
i	*i* as in b*i*t	i	**kind**	*kint*
ie	*ee* as in s*ee*n	ee	**zien**	*zeen*
e	*e* as in r*e*d, or	e	**bed**	*bet*
	a is in b*a*d	eh	**er**	*ehr*
ei*	*ay* as in d*ay*	ay	**klein**	*klayn*
ij**	*er* as in moth*er* or	er	**lelijk**	*laylerk*
	ay as in d*ay*	ay	**wij**	*way*
o	*o* as in n*o*t	o	**pot**	*pot*
oe	*oo* as in t*oo*	oo	**hoeveel**	*hoofayl*
ou or	*ow* in n*ow*	ow	**koud**	*kowt*
au			**auto**	*owtow*
oo	*oa* as in b*oa*t	oa	**roos**	*roas*
eu	*u* as in p*u*re	u	**deur**	*dur*
u	*u* as in f*u*r or	uh	**bus**	*buhs*
	u as in n*ew*	uw	**nu**	*nuw*

* called **korte ei** (short "i")

** called **lange ij** (long "i")

8

Stress

Stress has been indicated in the phonetic transcription with underlining. Pronounce the underlined syllable with more emphasis (i.e. louder) than the others.

Pronunciation of the Dutch alphabet

A	*ah*		**N**	*en*
B	*bay*		**O**	*oa*
C	*say*		**P**	*pay*
D	*day*		**Q**	*kuw*
E	*ay*		**R**	*ehr*
F	*ef*		**S**	*es*
G	*khay*		**T**	*tay*
H	*hah*		**U**	*uw*
I	*ee*		**V**	*fay*
J	*yay*		**W**	*vay*
K	*kah*		**X**	*ix*
L	*el*		**Y**	*ehy*
M	*em*		**Z**	*zet*

Basic Expressions

ESSENTIAL

Yes.	**Ja.**	*yaa*
No.	**Nee.**	*nay*
Okay.	**Okee.**	*okay*
Please.	**Alstublieft.**	*alstuwbleeft*
Thank you.	**Dank u wel.**	*dangk uw vel*
Thank you very much.	**Hartelijk dank.**	*hartlayk dangk*

Greetings/Apologies Groeten/Excuses

Hello./Hi!	**Dag./Hallo!**	*daakh/haloa*
Good morning.	**Goedemorgen.**	*khoodermorkhern*
Good afternoon.	**Goedemiddag.**	*khoodermiddakh*
Good evening.	**Goedenavond.**	*khoodernaavont*
Good night.	**Goedenacht.**	*khoodernakht*
Good-bye.	**Dag.**	*daakh*
Excuse me! (to a man/woman) (*getting attention*)	**Meneer/Mevrouw!**	*mernayr/merfrow*
Excuse me. (*may I get past?*)	**Pardon.**	*pardon*
Sorry!	**Sorry!**	*sorree*
Don't mention it.	**Geen dank.**	*khayn dangk*
Never mind.	**Geeft niet.**	*gayft neet*

Communication difficulties
Communicatieproblemen

Do you speak English?	**Spreekt u Engels?** *spraykt uw <u>eng</u>-ils*
Does anyone here speak English?	**Is er hier iemand die Engels spreekt?** *is er heer <u>ee</u>mant dee <u>eng</u>-ils spraykt*
Could you speak more slowly?	**Kunt u iets langzamer spreken?** *kuhnt uw eets <u>langzaa</u>mer <u>spray</u>ken*
Could you repeat that?	**Kunt u dat herhalen?** *kuhnt uw dat hayr<u>haa</u>len*
Excuse me? [Pardon?]	**Pardon?** *par<u>don</u>*
What was that?	**Wat zegt u?** *vat zehkht uw*
Could you spell it?	**Kunt u dat spellen?** *kuhnt uw dat <u>spel</u>lern*
Please write it down.	**Kunt u het opschrijven?** *kuhnt uw het op<u>skhray</u>fern*
Can you translate this for me?	**Kunt u dit voor mij vertalen?** *kuhnt uw dit foar may fer<u>taa</u>lern*
What does this/that mean?	**Wat betekent dit/dat?** *vat be<u>tay</u>kernt dit/dat*
Can you point to the phrase in the book.	**Kunt u het zinnetje in het boek aanwijzen?** *kuhnt uw het <u>zin</u>nertyer in het book aan<u>vay</u>zern*
I understand.	**Ik begrijp het.** *ik be<u>khrayp</u> het*
I don't understand.	**Ik begrijp het niet.** *ik be<u>khrayp</u> het neet*
Do you understand?	**Begrijpt u het?** *be<u>khraypt</u> uw het*

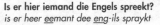

– *Dat is negen euro's vijfennegentig.*
(That's nine euros ninety-five.)
– Ik begrijp het niet. (I don't understand.)
– *Dat is negen euro's vijfennegentig.*
(That's nine euros ninety-five.)
– Kunt u het opschrijven?
(Can you write it down.)
– Ah. "Nine ninety-five." ... Alstublieft.
(Ah. "Nine ninety-five." ... Here you are.)

11

GRAMMAR

Questions can be formed in Dutch:

1. by inverting the subject and verb:
Kunt u me helpen?　Can you help me?

2. by using a question word + the inverted order:
Hoe wilt u betalen?　How do you want to pay?

Where? Waar?

Where is it?	**Waar is het?** *vaar is het*
Where are you going?	**Waar gaat u naar toe?** *vaar khaat uw naar too*
across the road	**naar de overkant** *naar de oaferkant*
at the meeting place	**op de ontmoetingsplaats** *op der ontmootingsplaats*
far from here	**ver hiervandaan** *fer heerfandaan*
from the U.S.	**uit Amerika** *oait amayrikaa*
here	**hier** *heer*
in the Netherlands	**in Nederland** *in nayderlant*
in the car	**in de auto** *in der owto*
inside	**binnen** *binnern*
into town	**de stad in** *der stat in*
near the bank	**dichtbij de bank** *dikhtbay der bank*
next to the post office	**naast het postkantoor** *naast het postkantoar*
opposite the market	**tegenover de markt** *taykhernoafer de markt*
on the left/right	**aan de linkerkant/rechterkant** *aan der linkerkant/rekhterkant*
on the sidewalk [pavement]	**op de stoep** *op de stoop*
outside the café	**buiten het café** *boaitern het kaffay*
there	**daar** *daar*
to the hotel	**naar het hotel** *naar het hotel*
towards Amsterdam	**richting Amsterdam** *rikhting amsterdam*
up to the traffic lights	**tot aan de stoplichten** *tot aan der stoplikhtern*

When? Wanneer?

When does the museum open?	**Wanneer gaat het museum open?** *van<u>nayr</u> khaat het moo<u>say</u>-um <u>oa</u>pern*
When does the train arrive?	**Wanneer komt de trein aan?** *van<u>nayr</u> komt der trayn aan*
10 minutes ago	**tien minuten geleden** *teen mi<u>nuw</u>tern kher<u>lay</u>dern*
after lunch	**na de lunch** *naa der luhnsh*
always	**altijd** *al<u>tayt</u>*
around midnight	**rond middernacht** *ront midder<u>nakht</u>*
at 7 o'clock	**om zeven uur** *om <u>zay</u>vern uwr*
before Friday	**vóór vrijdag** <u>*foar*</u> <u>*fray*</u>*daakh*
by tomorrow	**niet later dan morgen** *neet <u>laa</u>tir dan <u>mor</u>khern*
every week	**elke week** <u>*el*</u>*ker vayk*
for 2 hours	**voor twee uur** *foar tvay uwr*
from 9 a.m. to 6 p.m.	**van negen tot zes uur** *fan <u>nay</u>khern tot zes uwr*
in 20 minutes	**over twintig minuten** <u>*oa*</u>*fir <u>tvin</u>terkh mi<u>nuw</u>tern*
never	**nooit** *noait*
not yet	**nog niet** *nokh n<u>eet</u>*
now	**nu** *nuw*
often	**vaak** *faak*
on March 8	**op acht maart** *op akht maart*
on weekdays	**op weekdagen** *op <u>vayk</u>daakhern*
sometimes	**soms** *soms*
soon	**gauw** *khaw*
then	**dan** *dan*
within 2 days	**binnen twee dagen** <u>*binn*</u>*ern tvay <u>daa</u>khern*

13

What sort of …? Wat voor soort …?

I'd like something …	**Ik wil graag iets …**	*ik vil khraakh eets*
It's …	**Het is …**	*het is*
beautiful/ugly	**mooi/lelijk**	*moai/<u>lay</u>lerk*
better/worse	**beter/slechter**	<u>*bay*</u>*ter/*<u>*slekh*</u>*ter*
big/small	**groot/klein**	*khroat/klayn*
cheap/expensive	**goedkoop/duur**	*khoot*<u>*koap*</u>*/duwr*
clean/dirty	**schoon/vuil**	*skoan/foail*
dark/light	**donker/licht**	<u>*dong*</u>*ker/likht*
delicious/terrible	**heerlijk/walgelijk**	<u>*hayr*</u>*lerk/*<u>*vaal*</u>*khlerk*
early/late	**vroeg/laat**	*frookh/laat*
easy/difficult	**makkelijk/moeilijk**	<u>*mak*</u>*lerk/*<u>*mooy*</u>*lerk*
empty/full	**leeg/vol**	*laykh/fol*
good/bad	**goed/slecht**	*khoot/slekht*
heavy/light	**zwaar/licht**	*zvaar/likht*
hot/warm/cold	**heet/warm/koud**	*hayt/vaarm/kowt*
narrow/wide	**smal/breed**	*smal/brayt*
next/last	**volgend/laatst**	<u>*fol*</u>*khernt/laatst*
old/new	**oud/nieuw**	*owt/neeoo*
open/shut	**open/dicht**	<u>*oa*</u>*pern/dikht*
pleasant/nice/unpleasant	**prettig/fijn/vervelend**	<u>*pret*</u>*tikh/fayn/fir*<u>*fay*</u>*lernt*
quick/slow	**snel/langzaam**	*snel/*<u>*lang*</u>*zaam*
quiet/noisy	**rustig/lawaaierig**	<u>*ruh*</u>*stikh/la*<u>*vaay*</u>*ererkh*
right/wrong	**juist/verkeerd**	*yoaist/fer*<u>*kayrt*</u>
tall/short	**lang/kort**	*laang/kort*
thick/thin	**dik/dun**	*dik/duhn*
vacant/occupied	**vrij/bezet**	*fray/ber*<u>*zet*</u>
young/old	**jong/oud**	*yong/owt*

There are two types of nouns in Dutch: masculine-feminine and neuter. Masculine-feminine nouns take the definite article **de** (*the*), neuter nouns take **het**. All nouns take the indefinite article **een** (*a/an*). All plurals take the definite article **de.** For further details ➤ 169.

How much/many? Hoeveel?

How much is that?	**Hoeveel kost dat?** *hoofayl kost dat*
How many are there?	**Hoeveel zijn er?** *hoofayl zayn ehr*
1/2/3	**één/twee/drie** *ayn/tvay/dree*
4/5	**vier/vijf** *feer/fayf*
none	**geen** *khayn*
about 50 euros	**ongeveer vijftig euro's** *onkherfayr fayftikh uros*
a little	**een beetje** *ayn baytyer*
a lot of (traffic)	**veel (verkeer)** *fayl (ferkayr)*
enough	**genoeg** *khernookh*
few/a few of them	**weinig/een paar** *vaynikh/ayn paar*
more (than that)	**meer (dan dat)** *mayr (dan dat)*
less (than that)	**minder (dan dat)** *minder (dan dat)*
much more	**veel meer** *fayl mayr*
nothing else	**verder niets** *fehrder neets*
too much	**te veel** *ter fayl*

Why? Waarom?

Why is that?	**Waarom is dat?** *vaarom is dat*
Why not?	**Waarom niet?** *vaarom neet*
It's because of the weather.	**Dat komt door het weer.** *dat komt doar het vayr*
It's because I'm in a hurry.	**Dat komt omdat ik haast heb.** *dat komt omdat ik haast hep*
I don't know why.	**Ik weet niet waarom.** *ik vayt neet vaarom*

Who?/Which? Wie?/Welke?

Who is it for?	**Voor wie is het?** *foar vee is het*
(for) her/him	**(voor) haar/hem** *(foar) haar/hem*
(for) me	**(voor) mij** *(foar) may*
(for) you	**(voor) u** *(foar) uw*
(for) them	**(voor) hen** *(foar) hen*
someone	**iemand** *eemant*
no one	**niemand** *neemant*
Which one do you want?	**Welke wilt u?** *velker vilt uw*
this one/that one	**deze/die** *dayzer/dee*
one like that	**zo één** *zo ayn*
not that one	**niet die** *neet dee*
something	**iets** *eets*
nothing	**niets** *neets*

Whose? Van wie?

Whose is that?	**Van wie is dat?** *fan vee is dat*
It's ...	**Het is ...** *het is*
mine/ours/yours	**van mij/van ons/van u** *fan may/fan ons/fan uw*
his/hers/theirs	**van hem/van haar/van hen** *fan hem/fan haar/fan hen*
It's ... turn.	**Het is ... beurt.** *het is ... burt*
my/our/your	**mijn/onze/uw** *mayn/onzer/uwer*
his/her/their	**zijn/haar/hun** *zayn/haar/hern*

GRAMMAR

Here are the possessive adjectives

my	**mijn**
your (informal sing.)	**jouw**
your (formal sing.)	**uw**
his/her/its	**zijn/haar/zijn**
our	**onze (ons*)**
your (informal plural)	**jullie**
your (formal plural)	**uw**
their	**hun**

* **ons** is used with a neuter singular noun: **ons kind** (our child).

How? Hoe?

How would you like to pay?	**Hoe wilt u betalen?** *hoo vilt uw bertaalern*
by cash	**met contanten** *met kontantern*
by credit card	**met een creditcard** *met ayn kreditkaart*
How are you getting here?	**Hoe gaat u er naar toe?** *hoo khaat uw ehr naar too*
by car / bus / train	**met de auto/bus/trein** *met der owtow/buhs/trayn*
on foot	**lopend** *lowpent*
quickly	**snel** *snel*
slowly	**langzaam** *langzaam*
too fast	**te snel** *ter snel*
very	**heel** *hayl*
with a friend (man / woman)	**met een vriend/vriendin** *met ayn freent/freendirn*
without a passport	**zonder paspoort** *zonder paspoart*

Is it …? / Are there …? Is het …?/Zijn er …?

Is it free of charge?	**Is het gratis?** *is het khraatis*
It isn't ready.	**Het is nog niet klaar.** *het is nokh neet klaar*
Is there a shower in the room?	**Is er een douche op de kamer?** *is ehr ayn doosh op der kaamer*
Is there a bus into town?	**Is er een bus naar de stad?** *is ehr ayn buhs naar der stat*
There it is / they are.	**Daar is-ie/zijn ze.** *daar is ee/zayn zer*
Are there buses into town?	**Zijn er bussen naar de stad?** *zayn ehr buhssern naar der stat*
There aren't any towels in my room.	**Er zijn geen handdoeken op mijn kamer.** *ehr zayn khayn hantdookern op mayn kaamer*
Here it is / they are.	**Alstublieft.** *alstuwbleeft*

17

Can/May? Kunnen/Mogen?

Can I ...?	**Kan ik ...?** *kan ik*
May we ...?	**Mogen wij ...?** _moakhern_ *vay*
Can you show me ...?	**Kunt u mij ... laten zien?** *kuhnt uw may ..._laa_tern zeen*
Can you tell me ...?	**Kunt u mij vertellen ...?** *kuhnt uw may fer_tell_ern*
Can I help you?	**Kan ik u helpen?** *kan ik uw _help_ern*
Can you direct me to ...?	**Kunt u mij de weg wijzen naar ...?** *kuhnt uw may der vekh _vay_zern naar*
No, sorry.	**Nee, sorry.** *nay, _sorr_ee*

What do you want? Wat wenst u?

I'd like ...	**Ik wil graag ...** *ik vil khraakh*
Could I have ...?	**Mag ik ...?** *makh ik*
We'd like ...	**Wij willen graag ...** *vay _vill_ern khraakh*
Give me ...	**Mag ik ...** *makh ik*
I'm looking for ...	**Ik zoek naar ...** *ik zook naar*
I need to ...	**Ik moet ...** *ik moot*
go ...	**gaan ...** *khaan*
find ...	**... vinden** *_find_ern*
see ...	**... zien** *zeen*
speak to ...	**met ... spreken** *met ... _spray_kern*

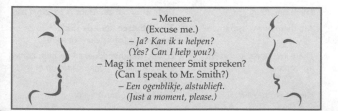

– Meneer.
(Excuse me.)
– *Ja? Kan ik u helpen?*
(Yes? Can I help you?)
– Mag ik met meneer Smit spreken?
(Can I speak to Mr. Smith?)
– *Een ogenblikje, alstublieft.*
(Just a moment, please.)

Other useful words
Andere handige woorden

fortunately	**gelukkig** *kherluhkerkh*
hopefully	**hopelijk** *hoaperlerk*
of course	**natuurlijk** *natuwrlerk*
perhaps	**misschien** *miskheen*
unfortunately	**helaas** *haylaas*
also/but	**ook/maar** *oak/maar*
and/or	**en/of** *en/of*

Exclamations Uitroepen

At last!	**Eindelijk!** *aynderlerk*
Go on.	**Gaat u verder.** *khaat uw fehrder*
Nonsense!	**Onzin!** *onzin*
That's true.	**Dat is waar.** *dat is vaar*
No way!	**Geen sprake van!** *khayn spraaker fan*
How are things?	**Hoe gaat het ermee?** *hoo khaat het ehrmay*
great/terrific	**prima/uitstekend** *preema/oaitstaykernt*
very good	**heel goed** *hayl khoot*
fine	**goed** *khoot*
not bad	**niet slecht** *neet slekht*
okay	**okee** *okay*
not good	**niet goed** *neet khoot*
fairly bad	**vrij slecht** *fray slekht*
terrible	**vreselijk** *frayserlerk*

Accommodations

Hotel (hotel)

Hotels are classified from one to five stars . Prices are per room and
include breakfast, service charges, and taxes (but are exclusive of an extra
five percent city tax in Amsterdam). Reservations can be made in Holland
through VVV Tourist Offices, the Netherlands Reservation Center, and
GWK offices.

Pension (pensyon)

Mostly family-run guesthouses offering full board (**vol pension**), half
board (**half pension**), or bed and breakfast (**logies-ontbijt**).

Motel (motel)

Efficient accommodations near highways and major roads.

Jeugdherberg (yught-hehrbehrgh)

There are 34 youth hostels around the country, some in interesting old
buildings. Many have rooms with 4–8 beds and are open to non-
members. NJHC (Nederlandse Jeugdherberg Centrale) is the Dutch Youth
Hostel Association.

Vakantiehuisje (fakanseehoaisyer)

Anything in the rental sector, from vacation cottages and apartments to
bungalows and houseboats.
The famous Centre Parcs, indoor vacation villages, originated in the
Netherlands and you may like to try them in their native environment.

Reservations Reserveringen

In advance Van te voren

Can you recommend a
hotel in …?

**Kunt u een hotel
aanbevelen in … ?** *kuhnt uw
ayn hotel aanberfaylern in …*

Is it near the center of town?

Is het dichtbij het stadscentrum?
is het dikhtbay het statsentrerm

How much is it per night?

Hoeveel kost het per nacht?
hoovayl kost het pehr nakht

Do you have a cheaper room?

Heeft u een goedkopere kamer?
hayft uw ayn khootkoaperer kaamer

Could you reserve a room for
me there, please?

**Kunt u daar een kamer voor mij
reserveren, alstublieft?** *kuhnt uw daar
ayn kaamer foar may rayzervayrern
alstuwbleeft*

At the hotel In het hotel

Do you have a room?

Heeft u een kamer? *hayft uw ayn kaamer*

I'm sorry, we're full.

Het spijt me, we zitten vol.
het spayt may, vay zittern fol

Is there another hotel nearby?

Is er een ander hotel in de buurt?
is ehr ayn aander hoatel in der buwrt

I'd like a single/double room.

**Ik wil graag een eenpersoonskamer/
tweepersoonskamer.** *ik vil khraakh ayn
aynpersoanskaamer/tvaypersoanskaamer*

Can I see the room, please?

Mag ik de kamer zien?
makh ik der kaamer zeen

I'd like a room with …

Ik wil graag een kamer met …
ik vil khraakh ayn kaamer met

a bath/shower

een bad/douche *ayn bat/doosh*

– Heeft u een kamer vrij? (Do you have a room?)
– Het spijt me, we zitten vol. (I'm sorry, we're full.)
– Oh. Is er een ander hotel in de buurt?
(Oh. Is there another hotel nearby?)
*– Ja, mevrouw/meneer. Het Ambassadeurshotel is heel dichtbij.
(Yes, ma'am/sir. The Ambassador Hotel is very near.)*

Reception Receptie

I have a reservation.	**Ik heb een reservering.** *ik hep ayn rayzervayring*
My name is …	**Mijn naam is …** *mayn naam is*
We've reserved a double and a single room.	**Wij hebben een tweepersoonskamer en een eenpersoonskamer gereserveerd.** *vay hepbern ayn tvaypersoons-kaamer en ayn aynpersoons-kaamer kherayzervayrt*
I've reserved a room for two nights.	**Ik heb een kamer voor twee nachten gereserveerd.** *ik hep ayn kaamer foar tvay nakhtern kherayzervayrt*
I confirmed my reservation by mail.	**Ik heb mijn reservering met de post bevestigd.** *ik heb mayn rayzervayring met der post berfestikht*
Could we have adjoining rooms?	**Mogen we kamers naast elkaar hebben?** *moakhen vay kaamers naast ehlkaar hepbern*

Amenities and facilities Gemakken en faciliteiten

Is there (a/an) … in the room?	**Is er (een) … op de kamer?** *is ehr (ayn) … op der kaamer*
air conditioning	**airconditioning** *air conditioning*
TV/telephone/fax	**tv/telefoon/fax** *tayvay/taylerfoan/faks*
Does the hotel have (a) …?	**Heeft het hotel (een) …?** *hayft het hoatel (ayn)*
laundry service	**wasservice** *vassehrvees*
satellite TV	**satelliet-tv** *satterleet-tayvay*
sauna/swimming pool	**sauna/zwembad** *sowna/svembat*
Could you put … in the room?	**Kunt u … op de kamer zetten?** *kuhnt uw … op der kaamer zettern*
an extra bed	**een extra bed** *ayn ekstra bet*
a crib [cot]	**een kinderbedje** *ayn kinderbetjer*
Do you have facilities for children/the disabled?	**Heeft u faciliteiten voor kinderen/gehandicapten?** *hayft uw fasilitaytern foar kinderen/kherhandikaptern*

How long …? Hoe lang …?

We'll be staying …	**We blijven …** *vay <u>blay</u>fern*
overnight only	**maar één nacht** *maar ayn nakht*
a few days	**een paar dagen** *ayn paar <u>daa</u>khern*
a week (at least)	**een week (minstens)** *ayn vayk (<u>min</u>sterns)*
I'd like to stay an extra night.	**Ik wil graag een extra nacht blijven.** *ik vil khraakh ayn <u>eks</u>tra nakht <u>blay</u>fern*

– Dag, ik heb een reservering. Mijn naam is John Newton.
(Hello, I have a reservation. My name's John Newton.)
– Dag. Meneer Newton. (Hello. Mr. Newton.)
– Ik heb een kamer voor twee nachten gereserveerd.
(I've reserved a room for two nights.)
– Dat is prima. Kunt u dit (inschrijf)formulier invullen?
(That's fine. Could you fill out this (registration) form?)

Mag ik uw paspoort zien, alstublieft?	May I see your passport, please?
Kunt u dit formulier invullen/ hier tekenen?	Please fill out this form / sign here.
Wat is het kenteken van uw auto?	What is your car license number?

ALLEEN KAMER: … GULDEN	room only: … gulden
ONTBIJT INBEGREPEN	breakfast included
MAALTIJDEN VERKRIJGBAAR	meals available
ACHTERNAAM/VOORNAAM	last name / first name
HUISADRES/STRAAT/NUMMER	home address / street / number
NATIONALITEIT/BEROEP	nationality / profession
GEBOORTEDATUM/-PLAATS	date / place of birth
PASPOORTNUMMER	passport number
KENTEKEN	car license number
PLAATS/DATUM	place / date
HANDTEKENING	signature

Price Prijs

How much is it ...?	**Hoeveel kost het ...?** *hoofayl kost het*
per night/week	**per nacht/week** *pehr nakht/vayk*
for bed and breakfast	**voor logies-ontbijt** *foar lozhees-ontbayt*
excluding meals	**exclusief maaltijden** *ekskluwseef mahltaydern*
for American Plan (A.P.) [full board]	**voor vol pension** *foar fol penshon*
for Modified American Plan (M.A.P.) [half board]	**voor half pension** *foar half penshon*
Does the price include ...?	**Is ... bij de prijs inbegrepen?** *is ... bay der prays inberkhraypern*
breakfast	**het ontbijt** *het ontbayt*
sales tax [VAT]	**BTW** *baytayvay*
Do I have to pay a deposit?	**Moet ik vooruitbetalen?** *moot ik foaroaitbertaalern*
Is there a discount for children?	**Is er korting voor kinderen?** *is ehr korting foar kinderen*

Decision De beslissing

May I see the room?	**Mag ik de kamer zien?** *makh ik der kaamer zeen*
That's fine. I'll take it.	**Dat is prima. Ik neem hem.** *dat is preema. ik naym hem*
It's too ...	**Het is te ...** *het is ter*
dark/small	**donker/klein** *dongker/klayn*
noisy	**lawaaierig** *lavaayererkh*
Do you have anything ...?	**Heeft u iets dat ... is?** *hayft uw eets dat ... is*
bigger/cheaper	**groter/goedkoper** *khroater/khootkoaper*
quieter/warmer	**rustiger/warmer** *ruhstikher/vaarmer*
No, I won't take it.	**Nee, ik neem hem niet.** *nay, ik naym hem neet*

Problems Problemen

The … doesn't work.	**… doet het niet.** *… doot het neet*
air conditioning	**de airconditioning** *de airconditioning*
fan	**de ventilator** *de ventilaator*
heating	**de verwarming** *der fervarming*
light	**het licht** *het likht*
There is no hot water/ toilet paper.	**Er is geen warm water/toiletpapier.** *ehr is khayn varm vaater/toiletpapeer*
The faucet [tap] is dripping.	**De kraan lekt.** *der kraan lekt*
The sink/toilet is blocked.	**De wastafel/het toilet is verstopt.** *der vastaafel/het toilet is ferstopt*
The window/door is jammed.	**Het raam/de deur zit vast.** *het raam/der dur zit fast*
My room has not been made up.	**Mijn bed is nog niet opgemaakt.** *mayn bet is nokh neet opkhermaakt*
The … is/are broken.	**… is/zijn gebroken.** *… is/zayn kherbroakern*
blinds/shutters	**de jaloezieën/luiken** *der zhaloozeeyern/loaikern*
lamp	**de lamp** *der lamp*
lock	**het slot** *het slot*
There are insects in our room.	**Er zijn insecten op onze kamer.** *ehr zayn insektern op onzer kaamer*

Action Actie

Could you have that taken care of?	**Kunt u daarvoor zorgen?** *kuhnt uw daarfoar zorkhern*
I'd like to move to another room.	**Ik wil graag een andere kamer.** *ik vil khraakh ayn anderer kaamer*
I'd like to speak to the manager.	**Ik wil graag met de manager spreken.** *ik vil khraakh met der manadzher spraykern*

Requirements Benodigdheden

British and American appliances will need an adapter, since 220-volt is standard with two-pin plugs and sockets.

About the hotel Informatie over het hotel

Where's the …?	**Waar is …?** *vaar is*
bar	**de bar** *der baar*
bathroom [toilet]	**het toilet** *het tvalet*
dining room	**de eetkamer** *der aytkaamer*
elevator [lift]	**de lift** *der lift*
parking lot [car park]	**de parkeerplaats** *der parkayrplaats*
shower room	**de douche** *der doosh*
swimming pool	**het zwembad** *het zwembat*
tour operator's bulletin board	**het mededelingenbord van de reisorganisator** *het mayderdaylingenbort fan der rays-orkhanisaator*
Does the hotel have a garage?	**Heeft het hotel een garage?** *hayft het hotel ayn garaazher*
Can I use this adapter here?	**Mag ik deze adaptor hier gebruiken?** *makh ik dayze adaptor heer kherbroaikern*

ALLEEN VOOR SCHEERAPPARATEN	razors [shavers] only
NOODUITGANG	emergency exit
BRANDUITGANG	fire door
NIET STOREN	do not disturb
DRUK OP … VOOR EEN BUITENLIJN	dial … for an outside line
DRUK OP … VOOR RECEPTIE	dial … for reception
HANDDOEKEN NIET UIT DE KAMER VERWIJDEREN	don't remove towels from the room

Personal needs Persoonlijke behoeften

The key to room …, please.	**Mag ik de sleutel van kamer …?** *makh ik der sloaiterl fan kaamer*
I've lost my key.	**Ik heb mijn sleutel verloren.** *ik hep mayn sloaiterl verloarern*
I've locked myself out of my room.	**Ik heb mezelf buitengesloten.** *ik hep mayzelf boaitern-kherssloatern*
Could you wake me at …?	**Kunt u me om … wakker maken?** *kuhnt uw mer om … vakker maakern*
I'd like breakfast in my room.	**Ik wil graag ontbijt op mijn kamer.** *ik vil khraakh ontbayt op mayn kaamer*
Can I leave this in the safe?	**Mag ik dit in de safe doen?** *makh ik dit in der sayf doon*
Could I have my things from the safe?	**Mag ik mijn spullen uit de safe hebben?** *makh ik mayn spuhlern oait der sayf heppern*
Where can I find (a) …?	**Waar vind ik (een) …?** *vaar fint ik (ayn)*
maid	**kamermeisje** *kaamermaysyer*
our tour guide	**onze reisgids** *onzer rayskhits*
May I have (an) extra …?	**Mag ik (een) extra … hebben?** *makh ik (ayn) ekstra … hepbern*
bath towel	**badhanddoek** *bat-handook*
blanket	**deken** *daykern*
hangers	**klerenhangers** *klayrernhangers*
pillow	**kussen** *kuhsern*
soap	**zeep** *zayp*
Is there any mail for me?	**Is er post voor me?** *is ehr post foar mer*
Are there any messages for me?	**Zijn er boodschappen voor me?** *zayn ehr boatskappern foar mer*
Could you mail this for me, please?	**Kunt u dit voor me posten?** *kuhnt uw dit foar mer postern*

BREAKFAST ➤ 43; CHANGING MONEY ➤ 138

Renting Huren

We've reserved an apartment/ a cottage	**We hebben een appartement/ vakantiehuisje gereserveerd …** *vay hepbern ayn apparterment/ fakanseehoaisye kherayzerfayrt*
in the name of …	**in naam van …** *in naam fan*
Where do we pick up the keys?	**Waar halen we de sleutels op?** *vaar haalern vay der sloaitels op*
Where is the…?	**Waar is …?** *vaar is*
electric meter	**de electriciteitsmeter** *der elektreeseetaytsmayter*
fuse box	**de zekeringkast** *der zaykeringskast*
valve [stopcock]	**de plugkraan** *der plagkraan*
water heater	**de geiser** *der kheyzer*
Are there any spare …?	**Zijn er reserve …?** *zayn ehr rersehrver*
fuses/sheets	**zekeringen/lakens** *zaykeringern/laakerns*
gas bottles	**gasflessen** *khasflessern*
When does the maid come?	**Wanneer komt de werkster?** *vannayr komt der verkster*
When do I put out the trash [rubbish]?	**Wanneer moet ik de vuilnis buitenzetten?** *vannayr moot ik der foailnis boaiternzettern*

Problems Problemen

Where can I contact you?	**Waar kan ik u bereiken?** *vaar kan ik uw beraykern*
How does the stove [cooker]/ water heater work?	**Hoe werkt het fornuis/de geiser?** *hoo verkt het fornois/der kheyzer*
The … is/are dirty.	**De … is/zijn vuil.** *der … is/zayn foail*
The … has broken down.	**De … is kapot.** *der … is kapot*
We accidentally broke/lost …	**We hebben per ongeluk … gebroken/ verloren.** *vay hepbern pehr onkherlerk … kherbroakern/ferloarern*
That was already damaged when we arrived.	**Dat was al beschadigd toen we aankwamen.** *dat vas al berskhaadikht toon vay aankvaamern*

Useful terms Handige termen

boiler	**de boiler** *der boiler*
dishes [crockery]	**het serviesgoed** *het sehrveeskhoot*
freezer	**de vrieskast** *der freeskast*
frying pan	**de koekepan** *der kookerpan*
kettle	**de ketel** *der kuyterl*
lamp	**de lamp** *der lamp*
refrigerator	**de koelkast** *der koolkast*
saucepan	**de steelpan** *der staylpan*
stove [cooker]	**het fornuis** *het fornoais*
utensils [cutlery]	**het bestek** *het berstek*
washing machine	**de wasmachine** *der vasmasheener*

Rooms De kamers

balcony	**het balkon** *het balkon*
bathroom	**de badkamer** *der batkaamer*
bedroom	**de slaapkamer** *der slaapkaamer*
dining room	**de eetkamer** *der aytkaamer*
kitchen	**de keuken** *der kukern*
living room	**de huiskamer** *der hoaiskaamer*
toilet	**het toilet** *het twalet*

Youth hostel De jeugdherberg

Do you have any places left for tonight?	**Heeft u plaatsen vrij voor vannacht?** *hayft uw plaatsern fray foar fannakht*
Do you rent out bedding?	**Verhuurt u beddegoed?** *ferhuwrt uw bedderkhoot*
What time are the doors locked?	**Hoe laat gaan de deuren op slot?** *hoo laat khaan der durern op slot*
I have an International Student Card.	**Ik heb een Internationale Studentenkaart.** *ik hep ayn internatshonaaler stuwdenternkaart*

REQUIREMENTS ➤ 26; CAMPING ➤ 30

Camping Kamperen

A campsite (**kampeerplaats**) may have facilities such as hot showers, camping shop, restaurant, laundromats, and cabins for hikers. The sites are spread around the country, in woods, near lakes, and on the coast.

Reservations can be made through the VVV and Stichting Vrije Recreatie (VVV Amsterdam: ☎ 0031 (0)900 400 4040).

Reservations De reserveringen

Is there a camp site near here?	**Is er een kampeerplaats in de buurt?** *is ehr ayn kampayrplaats in der buwrt*
Do you have space for a tent/trailer [caravan]?	**Heeft u ruimte voor een tent/caravan?** *hayft uw <u>roaim</u>ter foar ayn tent/<u>keh</u>rervern*
What is the charge …?	**Hoeveel kost het …?** *hoo<u>fayl</u> kost het*
per day/week	**per dag/week** *pehr daakh/vayk*
for a tent/car	**voor een tent/auto** *foar ayn tent/<u>ow</u>to*
for a trailer [caravan]	**voor een caravan** *foar ayn <u>keh</u>rervern*

Facilities Faciliteiten

Are there cooking facilities on site?	**Zijn er kookfaciliteiten op de kampeerplaats?** *zayn ehr <u>koak</u> faseelee<u>tay</u>tern op der kam<u>payr</u>plaats*
Are there any electric outlets [power points]?	**Zijn er stopcontacten?** *zayn ehr <u>stop</u>kont<u>ak</u>tern*
Where is/are the …?	**Waar is/zijn …?** *vaar is/zayn*
drinking water	**het drinkwater** *het <u>drink</u>vaater*
trashcans [dustbins]	**de vuilnisbakken** *der <u>foil</u>nisb<u>ak</u>kern*
laundry facilities	**de wasfaciliteiten** *der <u>vas</u>faseelee<u>tay</u>tern*
showers	**de douche** *der doosh*
Where can I get some propane gas?	**Waar kan ik butagas krijgen?** *vaar kan ik <u>buh</u>takhas <u>krayk</u>hern*

⊕	**NIET KAMPEREN**	no camping	⊖
	DRINKWATER	drinking water	
⊘	**GEEN KAMPVUREN/BARBECUES**	no fires/barbecues	⊗

Complaints Klachten

It's too sunny here.	**Er is hier te veel zon.** *ehr is heer ter fayl zon*
It's too shady here.	**Er is hier te veel schaduw.** *ehr is heer ter fayl <u>shaa</u>duw*
It's too crowded here.	**Het is hier te vol.** *het is heer ter fol*
The ground's too hard / uneven.	**De grond is te hard/ongelijk.** *der khront is ter hart/onkher<u>layk</u>*
Do you have a more level spot?	**Heeft u een plaats op gelijke grond?** *hayft uw ayn plaats op kher<u>lay</u>ker khront*
Why can't I camp here?	**Waarom mag ik niet hier kamperen?** *vaarom mach ik neet heer kam<u>pay</u>rern*

Camping equipment De kampeeruitrusting

butane gas	**het butagas** *het <u>buh</u>takhas*
campbed	**het kampeerbed** *het kam<u>payr</u>bet*
charcoal	**de houtskool** *der <u>howts</u>koal*
flashlight [torch]	**de zaklantaarn** *de <u>zak</u>lantaarern*
groundcloth [groundsheet]	**het grondzeil** *het <u>khront</u>zàyl*
guy rope	**de stormlijn** *der <u>storm</u>layn*
hammer	**de hamer** *der <u>haa</u>mer*
kerosene [primus] stove	**de primus** *der <u>pree</u>muhs*
knapsack	**de rugzak** *der <u>ruhkh</u>zak*
mallet	**de houten hamer** *der <u>how</u>tern <u>haa</u>mer*
matches	**de lucifers** *der <u>luw</u>sifers*
(air) mattress	**het luchtbed** *het <u>luhkht</u>bet*
paraffin	**de paraffine** *der parra<u>fi</u>ner*
sleeping bag	**de slaapzak** *der <u>slaap</u>zak*
tent	**de tent** *der tent*
tent pegs	**de haringen** *der <u>haa</u>ringern*
tent pole	**de tentstok** *de <u>tent</u>stok*

Checking out Uitchecken

What time do we have to check out?
Hoe laat moeten we uitchecken?
hoo laat mootern vay oaitchekkern

Could we leave our baggage here until …?
Mogen we onze bagage hier laten staan tot …? *moakhern vay onzer bakhaazher heer laatern staan tot*

I'm leaving now.
Ik vertrek nu. *ik fertrehk nuw*

Could you order a taxi for me, please?
Kunt u een taxi voor me bestellen? *kuhnt uw ayn taksee foar mer berstellern*

It's been a very enjoyable stay.
We hebben een prettig verblijf gehad. *vay hepbern ayn pretterkh ferblayf kherhat*

Paying Betalen

Service is included in hotel and restaurant bills, but you may leave a coin for the waiter or leave a tip (**fooi**) on your credit card voucher. Taxi fares are rounded up. Tipping guidelines: hotel porter €1 per bag, maid €7–8 per week, lavatory attendant 25 cents, nightclub cloakroom attendant €0.50–1 and nightclub doorman €1–1.50.

May I have my bill?
Mag ik de rekening?
makh ik der raykerning

How much is my telephone bill?
Hoeveel is mijn telefoonrekening?
hoofayl is mayn tellerfoan-raykerning

I think there's a mistake in this bill.
Ik geloof dat er een fout in deze rekening zit. *ik kherloaf dat ehr ayn fowt in dayze raykerning zit*

I've made … telephone calls.
Ik heb … telefoongesprekken gevoerd. *ik hep … tellerfoan-khersprekkern khefoort*

I've taken … from the mini-bar.
Ik heb … van de minibar gehaald. *ik hep … fan der minibaar kherhaalt*

Can I have an itemized bill?
Mag ik een gedetailleerde rekening? *makh ik ayn kherdayta-yayrder raykerning*

Could I have a receipt, please?
Mag ik een kwitantie?
makh ik ayn kvitansee

Eating Out

Restaurants

Café

Serves both coffee and alcohol. Amsterdam city center is famous for its **bruine café's** (brown cafés) – old, dark, and wood-panelled. You can play billiards too. They are often open from midday until 1–2 a.m.

Bar

There are many different kinds of bar, especially in Amsterdam (including gay bars). Opening hours are similar to the cafés.

Cafetaria

Self-service restaurant serving hot and cold food.

Broodjeswinkel

A kind of sandwich shop serving rolls (**broodjes**) with ham, cheese, and fish. A reasonably priced and quick place for lunch.

Hotel restaurant/Motel restaurant

Restaurant usually open to the public.

Koffieshop

Coffee in Holland is always brewed fairly strong and served with **koffiemelk**, a thick kind of evaporated milk sold in small bottles. Served with **gebak** (pastries) with or without **slagroom** (sweet whipped cream). Be aware that some **koffieshops** (especially in Amsterdam) sell stronger substances than caffeine!

Restaurant
There is a choice of Indonesian, French, Italian, Chinese, Japanese, Turkish, Indian, Thai, and international cooking.

Pannekoekhuisje
The Dutch are very fond of pancakes and the pancake houses offer a huge range of savory and sweet **pannekoeken** and the thinner variety, **flensjes**.

Proeflokaal
A place where you can taste and buy different kinds of **jenever** (Dutch gin), beer, and other alcoholic beverages.

Wegrestaurant
Highway or road restaurant, usually self-service.

Snackbar
Quick bites, including favorites such as **patat** (French fries), **kroketten** (croquettes) and **bitterballen** (small meatballs). Eat-in or take-out.

Theesalon
Tea shops serving different kinds of tea, often served in a glass, weak, and with or without lemon. Also delicious **gebak** (pastries) and coffee. Look for the cozy places at the back of bakeries.

Meal times Etenstijden

Breakfast (**ontbijt**, 7–10 a.m.). Tea or coffee, bread (brown, white, or currant bread, and **ontbijtkoek**, a sticky sweet ginger cake), sliced cheese and cold meats, jam, and perhaps a boiled egg (**gekookt eitje**).

Lunch (**lunch**, 12–2 p.m.). Bread (**boterhammen**) or rolls (**broodjes**) with cheese and cold meats, gherkins (**augurken**), salad, and fruit.

Dinner (**diner**, 6–8 p.m.). Soup, potatoes, meat, and vegetables followed by fruit, yogurt, etc.

Dutch cuisine Nederlandse keuken

Truly Dutch dishes are heavy winter fare, but menus now generally reflect the extent to which the Dutch have been open to foreign influences throughout the centuries. There is always a good choice of soups, meat, fish, potatoes, and vegetables. Many restaurants have a **menu van de dag** (set menu), a **toeristenmenu** (tourist menu), a **dagschotel** (dish of the day), or you can go **à la carte**.

Spicy dishes from Indonesia (a Dutch colony until 1949) are now part of Dutch eating habits. Characteristics are chili condiment (**sambal**), prawn crackers (**krupuk**), peanuts, coconut, and sweet soya sauce (**ketjap manis**).

A table for ..., please.	**Een tafel voor ..., alstublieft.**
	ern tahfel foar ... alstuwbleeft
1/2/3/4	**een/twee/drie/vier**
	ehn/tway/dree/feer
Thank you.	**Dank u.** *dank uw*
I'd like to pay.	**Ik wil graag betalen.**
	ik vil ghraaghbetaalern

Finding a place to eat Uit eten

Can you recommend a good restaurant?	**Kunt u een goed restaurant aanbevelen?** *kuhnt uw ayn khoot restoarant aanberfaylern*
Is there a/an ... near here?	**Is er een ... in de buurt?** *is ehr ayn ... in der buwrt*
Indonesian restaurant	**Indonesisch restaurant** *indoanaysees restoarant*
Chinese restaurant	**Chinees restaurant** *shinays restoarant*
fish restaurant	**visrestaurant** *fisrestoarant*
inexpensive restaurant	**redelijk geprijsd restaurant** *rayderlik kherprayst restoarant*
Italian restaurant	**Italiaans restaurant** *eetaliyaans restoarant*
French restaurant	**Frans restaurant** *fraans restoarant*
restaurant with local dishes	**restaurant met plaatselijke gerechten** *restourant met plaatserlayker kherehkhtern*
vegetarian restaurant	**vegetarisch restaurant** *vaykhertaarees restoarant*
Is there (a/an) ... nearby?	**Is er een ... in de buurt?** *is ehr ayn ... in der burt*
burger stand	**patatkraam** *patatkraam*
café	**eethuisje** *aythoaisyer*
café-restaurant	**café-restaurant** *kaffay-restoarant*
ice cream parlor	**ijssalon** *ayssalon*
pizzeria	**pizzeria** *pitseria*

DIRECTIONS ➤ 94

Reserving a table Reserveringen

I'd like to reserve a table ...	**Ik wil graag een tafel ... reserveren.** *ik vil khraakh ayn <u>taa</u>ferl ... rayzer<u>vay</u>rern*
for two	**voor twee personen** *foar tvay per<u>soa</u>nern*
for this evening/ tomorrow at ...	**voor vanavond/morgen om ...** *foar fan<u>aa</u>font/<u>mor</u>khern om*
We'll come at 8:00.	**We komen om acht uur.** *wer <u>koa</u>mern om aght uhr*
A table for two, please.	**Een tafel voor twee, alstublieft.** *ayn <u>taa</u>ferl foar tvay alstuw<u>bleeft</u>*
We have a reservation.	**We hebben gereserveerd.** *vay <u>hep</u>bern kherayzer<u>vayrt</u>*

Voor hoe laat?	For what time?
Welke naam is het?	What's the name, please?
Het spijt me. Het is erg druk./ We zitten vol.	I'm sorry. We're very busy./ We're full.
Er is over ... minuten een tafel vrij.	We'll have a free table in ... minutes.
Roken of niet-roken?	Smoking or non-smoking?

Where are we going to sit? Waar gaan we zitten?

Could we sit ...?	**Kunnen we ... zitten?** <u>kuh</u>nern vay ... <u>zit</u>tern
outside	**buiten** <u>boai</u>tern
by the window	**bij het raam** *bay het raam*

> – Ik wil graag een tafel voor vanavond reserveren.
>   (I'd like to reserve a table for this evening.)
> – *Voor hoeveel personen? (For how many people?)*
> – Voor vier personen. (For four.)
> – *Voor hoe laat? (For what time?)*
> – We komen om acht uur. (We'll come at 8:00.)
> – *En welke naam is het? (And what's the name, please?)*
> – Smit. (Smith.)
> – *Prima. Dan zien we u straks. (That's fine. See you then.)*

TIME ➤ 220; NUMBERS ➤ 216

Ordering Bestellen

Waiter! / Waitress!	**Meneer! / Mevrouw!** *mer<u>nayr</u> / me<u>frow</u>*
May I see the wine list, please?	**Mag ik de wijnkaart?** *makh ik der <u>vayn</u>kaart*
Do you have a set menu?	**Heeft u een dagmenu?** *hayft uw arn <u>dakh</u>menuw*
Can you recommend some typical local dishes?	**Kunt u wat typisch plaatselijke gerechten aanbevelen?** *kuhnt uw vat <u>tee</u>pish <u>plaats</u>lerker khe<u>rehkh</u>tern aanber<u>fay</u>lern*
Could you tell me what … is?	**Kunt u me vertellen wat … is?** *kuhnt uw mer fer<u>tell</u>ern vat … is*
What's in it?	**Wat zit erin?** *vat zit eh<u>rin</u>*
I'd like …	**Ik wil graag …** *ik vil khraakh*
I'll have …	**Ik neem …** *ik naym*
a bottle / glass / carafe of …	**een fles / glas / karaf …** *ayn fles / khlas / kar<u>raf</u>*

Wilt u al bestellen?	Are you ready to order?
Wat mag het zijn?	What would you like?
Wat wilt u drinken?	What would you like to drink?
Ik kan … aanbevelen.	I recommend …
We hebben geen …	We don't have …
Dat duurt … minuten.	That will take … minutes.
Eet smakelijk.	Enjoy your meal.

– *Wilt u al bestellen?* (*Are you ready to order?*)

– *Kunt u wat typisch plaatselijke gerechten aanbevelen?*
(*Can you recommend some typical local dishes?*)

– *Ja. Ik kan de erwtensoep aanbevelen.*
(*Yes. I recommend the pea soup.*)

– *Ok, dan wil ik dat graag.* (*OK, I'd like that.*)

– *Jazeker. En wat wilt u drinken?*
(*Certainly. And what would you like to drink?*)

– *Een karaf rode wijn, alstublieft.*
(*A carafe of red wine, please.*)

– *Jazeker.* (*Certainly.*)

DRINKS ➤ 49; *MENU READER* ➤ 52

Accompaniments Bijgerechten

Could I have … without the …?	**Mag ik de/het … zonder de/het …?** *makh ik der/het … zonder der/het*
Could I have salad instead of vegetables?	**Mag ik salade in plaats van groenten?** *makh ik salaader in plaats fan khroontern*
With a side order of …	**Met … erbij** *met … ehrbay*
Does the meal come with …?	**Wordt het geserveerd met …?** *vort het khersehrvayrt met*
vegetables/potatoes	**groenten/aardappelen** *khroontern/aardapperlern*
rice/pasta	**rijst/pasta** *rayst/pasta*
Do you have any …?	**Heeft u ook …?** *hayft uw oak*
ketchup/mayonnaise	**tomatenketchup/mayonaise** *toamaaternketshuhp/mayoanayzer*
I'd like … with that.	**Ik wil graag … erbij.** *ik vil khraakh … ehrbay*
vegetables/salad	**groenten/salade** *khroontern/salaader*
potatoes/French fries [chips]	**aardappels/patat** *aardapperls/patat*
sauce	**saus** *sows*
ice	**ijs** *ays*
May I have some …?	**Mag ik wat …?** *makh ik vat*
bread	**brood** *broat*
butter	**boter** *boater*
lemon	**citroen** *seetroon*
mustard	**mosterd** *mostert*
pepper	**peper** *payper*
salt	**zout** *zowt*
oil and vinegar	**olie en azijn** *oalee en asayn*
sugar	**suiker** *zoaiker*
artificial sweetener	**zoetjes** *zootyers*
vinaigrette [French dressing]	**slasaus** *slaasows*

General requests Algemene verzoeken

Could I/we have a(n) (clean) ..., please? | **Mag ik/Mogen we een (schoon/schone) ..., alstublieft?** *makh ik/ moakhern vay ayn (skhoan/ skhoaner) ..., alstuwbleeft*

ashtray | **asbak** *asbak*

cup/glass | **kopje/glas** *kopyer/khlas*

fork/knife | **vork/mes** *fork/mes*

plate/spoon | **bord/lepel** *bort/layperl*

napkin | **servet** *sehrfet*

I'd like some more ..., please. | **Ik wil graag nog wat ..., alstublieft.** *ik vil khraakh nokh vat ..., alstuwbleeft*

That's all, thanks. | **Dat is genoeg, dank u.** *dat is khernookh, dangk uw*

Where are the bathrooms [toilets]? | **Waar is het toilet?** *vaar is het toilet*

Special requirements Speciale vereisten

I can't eat food containing ... | **Ik mag geen ... eten.** *ik makh khayn ... aytern*

salt/sugar | **zout/suiker** *zowt/soaiker*

Do you have any dishes/ drinks for diabetics? | **Heeft u ook gerechten/drankjes voor diabetici?** *hayft uw oak kherehkhtern/ drankyers foar deeabayteesee*

Do you have vegetarian dishes? | **Heeft u vegetarische gerechten?** *hayft uw vaykhertaareeser kherehkhtern*

For the children Voor de kinderen

Do you have a children's menu? | **Heeft u een kindermenu?** *hayft uw ayn kindermenuw*

Could you bring a child's seat? | **Heeft u ook een kinderstoeltje?** *hayft uw oak ayn kinderstooltyer*

Where can I change the baby? | **Waar kan ik de baby verschonen?** *vaar kan ik der baybee ferskhoanern*

Where can I feed the baby? | **Waar kan ik de baby voeden?** *vaar kan ik der baybee foodern*

CHILDREN ➤ 113

Fast food/Café
Fast food/Eethuisje

I'd like (a) …	**Ik wil graag een …** *ik vil khraakh ayn*
beer	**biertje** *beertyer*
tea/coffee	**thee/koffie** *tay/koffee*
black/with milk	**zonder melk/met melk** *zonder melk/met melk*
I'd like red/white wine.	**Ik wil graag een rode/witte wijn.** *ik vil khraakh ayn roader/vitter vayn*
bottled/draft [draught] beer	**flessebier/getapt bier** *flesserbeer/khertapt beer*
A piece/slice of …, please.	**Een stuk/plakje …, alstublieft.** *ayn stuhk/plakyer …, alstuwbleeft*
I'd like two of those.	**Ik wil graag twee van die.** *ik vil khraakh tvay fan dee*
burger/fries	**burger/patat** *buhrger/patat*
breaded meat balls	**bitterballen** *bitterballern*
croquette	**kroket** *kroaket*
big gherkin	**zure bom** *zuwrer bom*
spring roll	**loempia** *loompeeya*
omelet/pizza	**omelet/pizza** *ommerlet/peetsa*
sandwich	**broodje** *broatyer*
cake	**cake** *kayk*
sausage roll	**saucijzebroodje** *soasayzerbroatyer*
frankfurter	**knakworst** *knakvorst*
chocolate/strawberry/vanilla ice cream	**chocolade/aardbeien/vanille ijs** *shoakoalaader/aardbayern/vaneeler ays*
A … portion, please.	**Een … portie, alstublieft.** *ayn … portsee, alstuwbleeft*
small/large	**kleine/grote** *klayner/khroater*
regular [medium]	**normale** *normaaler*
It's to go [take away].	**Het is om mee te nemen.** *het is om may ter naymern*
That's all, thanks.	**Dat is het, dank u.** *dat is het, dangk uw*

– Wat mag het zijn? (What would you like?)
– Twee koffie, alstublieft.
(Two coffees, please.)
– Met of zonder melk? (Black or with milk?)
– Met melk, alstublieft. (With milk, please.)
– Wilt u ook iets eten? (Anything to eat?)
– Dat is het, dank u. (That's all, thanks.)

Complaints Klachten

I have no knife/fork/spoon.	**Ik heb geen mes/vork/lepel.** *ik hep khayn mes/fork/layperl*
There must be some mistake.	**Er moet een vergissing zijn.** *ehr moot ayn ferkhissing zayn*
That's not what I ordered.	**Dat is niet wat ik heb besteld.** *dat is neet vat ik hep bersteld*
I asked for …	**Ik heb om … gevraagd.** *ik hep om … kherfraakht*
I can't eat this.	**Dit kan ik niet eten.** *dit kan ik neet aytern*
The meat is …	**Het vlees is …** *het flays is*
overdone	**overgaar** *oaferkhaar*
underdone	**niet gaar** *neet khaar*
too tough	**te taai** *ter taay*
This is too …	**Dit is te …** *dit is ter*
bitter/sour	**bitter/zuur** *bitter/zuwr*
The food is cold.	**Het eten is koud.** *het aytern is kowt*
This isn't fresh.	**Dit is niet vers.** *dit is neet fehrs*
How much longer will our food be?	**Hoe lang duurt het eten nog?** *hoo lang duwrt het aytern nokh*
We can't wait any longer. We're leaving.	**We kunnen niet langer wachten. We gaan weg.** *vay kuhnern neet langer vakhtern. vay khaan vehkh*
This isn't clean.	**Dit is niet schoon.** *dit is neet skhoan*
I'd like to speak to the manager.	**Ik wil de manager spreken.** *ik vil der manaydzher spraykern*

Paying Betalen

The bill, please.	**Mag ik de rekening?**
	makh ik der raykerning
We'd like to pay separately.	**We willen graag apart betalen.**
	vay villern khraakh apart bertaalern
It's all together, please.	**Alles bij elkaar, alstublieft.**
	allers bay elkaar, alstuwbleeft
I think there's a mistake in this bill.	**Ik geloof dat er een fout in deze rekening zit.** *ik kherloaf dat ehr ayn fowt in dayzer raykerning zit*
What is this amount for?	**Waar is dit bedrag voor?**
	vaar is dit berdrakh foar
I didn't have that. I had …	**Dat heb ik niet gehad. Ik had …**
	dat hep ik neet kherhat. ik hat
Is service included?	**Is de bediening inbegrepen?**
	is der berdeening inberkhraypern
Can I pay with this credit card?	**Kan ik met deze creditcard betalen?**
	kan ik met dayzer kredeetkaart bertaalern
I've forgotten my wallet.	**Ik ben mijn beurs vergeten.**
	ik ben mayn burs ferkhaytern
I don't have enough cash.	**Ik heb niet genoeg contanten.**
	ik hep neet khernookh kontantern
Could I have a receipt, please?	**Mag ik een kwitantie, alstublieft?**
	makh ik ayn kvitantsee, alstuwbleeft
That was a very good meal.	**Dat was een uitstekende maaltijd.**
	dat vas ayn oaitstaykernder maaltayt

– Meneer! Mag ik de rekening? (Waiter! The bill, please.)
  – *Jazeker. Alstublieft.* (Certainly. Here you are.)
– Is de bediening inbegrepen? (Is service included?)
  – *Ja.* (Yes.)
– Kan ik met deze creditcard betalen?
  (Can I pay with this credit card?)
  – *Ja, natuurlijk.* (Yes, of course.)
– Dank u. Dat was een uitstekende maaltijd.
  (Thank you. That was a very good meal.)

Course by course De gangen

Breakfast Ontbijt

I'd like …	**Ik wil graag …**
	ik vil khraakh
bread	**brood** *broat*
butter	**boter** *boater*
eggs	**eieren** *ayyerern*
boiled/fried/scrambled	**gekookte/gebakken/roereieren**
	kherkoakter/kherbakkern/roorayyerern
fruit juice	**vruchtensap** *fruhkhternsap*
grapefruit/orange	**grapefruit/sinaasappel**
	graypfroot/sinaasapperl
honey	**honing** *hoaning*
jam	**jam** *zhehm*
marmalade	**marmelade** *marmerlaader*
milk	**melk** *melk*
rolls	**broodjes** *broatyers*
toast	**toost** *toast*

Appetizers/Starters Hors d'oeuvre/Voorgerechten

Erwtensoep *ehrternsoop*
Thick green pea soup with smoked sausage and pork.

Russische eieren *ruhsseeser ayyerern*
Hard-boiled egg filled with mayonnaise, garnished with fish and salad.

Huzarensla *huhzaarernslaa*
Mixture of potato, raw vegetables, and meat with mayonnaise, garnished with salad, gherkins, and hard-boiled egg.

Nieuwe haring *neeoower haaring*
Freshly caught, salt-cured herring.

gerookte paling	*kheroakter paaling*	smoked eel
mosselen	*mosserlern*	mussels
oesters	*oosters*	oysters
pasteitje	*pastaytyer*	pastry filled with meat or fish (vol-au-vent)
zure haring	*zuwrer haaring*	pickled herring (rollmops)

Soups Soep

Groentensoep (met balletjes)
khroontersoop (met ballertyers)
Vegetable soup (with tiny meatballs).

Bruine bonen soep _broainer boanern soop_
Brown bean soup. Filling winter dish of kidney beans.

Erwtensoep _ehrternsoop_
The famous thick Dutch pea soup with pig's knuckle **(met kluif)**, pieces of
smoked sausage, and bacon – a meal in itself.

Sajur lodeh _saayoor lodder_
Indonesian fragrant soup of vegetables and coconut.

aardappelsoep	_aardapperlsoop_	potato soup
aspergesoep	_aspehrkhersoop_	asparagus soup
bouillon	_booyon_	consommé
gebonden soep	_kherbondern soop_	cream soup
heldere soep	_helderer soop_	broth (thin soup)
kippesoep	_kipersoop_	chicken soup
koninginnesoep	_koaninginnersoop_	cream of chicken
ossestaartsoep	_osserstaartsoop_	oxtail soup
tomatensoep	_toamaaternsoop_	tomato soup
uiensoep	_oaiyernsoop_	onion soup
vermicellisoep	_vehrmiselleesoop_	clear noodle soup
vissoep	_fissoop_	fish soup

Egg dishes Eiergerechten

boerenomelet	_boorernommerlet_	omelet with potatoes, vegetables, and bacon
gebakken ei	_kherbakkern ay_	fried egg
gekookt ei	_kherkoakt ay_	boiled egg
nasi goreng	_naasee khoareng_	Indonesian fried rice with spices, meat, and a fried egg on top
roereieren met gerookte zalm	_roorayyerern met kheroakter zalm_	scrambled eggs with smoked salmon
spiegeleieren met ham	_speekherlayyerern met ham_	fried eggs and ham
zachte eieren met saus en croutons	_zakhter ayyerern met sows en krootons_	soft-boiled eggs with sauce and croutons

Fish and seafood
Vis, schaal- en schelpdieren

forel	*foarel*	trout
garnalen	*kharnaalern*	shrimp [prawns]
haring	*haaring*	herring [whitebait]
inktvis	*inktfis*	squid
kabeljauw	*kaabelyow*	cod
krab	*krap*	crab
kreeft	*krayft*	lobster
makreel	*makreel*	mackerel
mosselen	*mosserlern*	mussels
octopus	*oktoapuhs*	octopus
oesters	*oosters*	oysters
paling	*paaling*	eel
sardientjes	*sardeentyers*	sardines
schelvis	*skhelfis*	haddock
schol	*skhol*	plaice
tong	*tong*	sole
tonijn	*toanayn*	tuna
venusschelpen	*veenuhsskhelpern*	clams
zalm	*zalm*	salmon

Gerookte paling *kheroakter paaling*
Smoked eel served on toast (appetizer) or with salad and potatoes (main course).

Nieuwe haring *neeoower haaring*
Fresh salted herring in season, best bought from a seaside stall and traditionally picked up by the tail with the fingers and held above the mouth for eating.

Haringsla *haaringslaa*
Salad of salted or marinated herring mixed with cold potato, cooked beetroot, apple, pickles, and mayonnaise.

Stokvisschotel *stokfisskhoaterl*
Oven stew of stockfish (dried cod), potatoes, rice, onions, and mustard.

Meat and poultry Vlees en gevogelte

biefstuk	*beefstuhk*	steak
duif	*doaif*	pigeon
eend	*aynt*	duck
fazant	*fasant*	pheasant
gans	*khaans*	goose
haas	*haas*	hare
houtsnip	*howtsnip*	woodcock
kalfsvlees	*kalfsflays*	veal
kalkoen	*kalkoon*	turkey
kip	*kip*	chicken
konijn	*koanayn*	rabbit
kuiken	*koaikern*	spring chicken
lamsvlees	*lamsflays*	lamb
parelhoen	*paarelhoon*	guinea fowl
patrijs	*patrays*	partridge
reebout	*raybowt*	venison
rundvlees	*ruhntflays*	beef
spek	*spek*	bacon
varkensvlees	*farkernsflays*	pork
worstjes	*vorstyers*	sausages

Blinde vinken *blinder finkern*
Veal slices stuffed with chopped veal, onion, and bacon.

Wiener Schnitzel *veener shnitserl*
Veal in breadcrumbs served with anchovy, capers, and lemon.

Goulash *goolash*
Hungarian goulash – cubes of beef, veal or pork in a sauce of tomato, onion, and paprika.

Hazepeper *haazerpayper*
Jugged hare – raw hare marinated in vinegar, wine, and herbs, stewed in gravy.

Jachtschotel *yakhtskhoaterl*
"Hunter's stew" – meat casserole with potatoes served with apple sauce.

Vegetables Groenten

aardappels	*aardapperls*	potatoes
andijvie	*andayvee*	endives
bietjes	*beetyers*	beetroot
Brussels lof	*bruhsserls lof*	chicory
champignons	*shampeenyons*	mushrooms
erwten	*ehrtern*	peas
knoflook	*knofloak*	garlic
knolraap	*knolraap*	rutabaga [swede]
komkommer	*komkommer*	cucumber
kool	*koal*	cabbage
paprika's	*papreekas*	peppers
(rode, groene)	*(roader, khrooner)*	(red, green)
rapen	*raapern*	turnips
rijst	*rayst*	rice
selderij	*selderay*	celery
sla	*slaa*	lettuce
sperziebonen	*spehrseeboanem*	green beans
uien	*oaiyern*	onions
wortels	*vorterls*	carrots

Stamppot van boerenkool met worst
Stamppot fan boorernkoal met vorst
One-pan dish of curly kale and potatoes, served with smoked sausage.

Hutspot met klapstuk *huhtspot met klapstuhk*
Mashed potatoes, carrots, and onions served with rib of beef (**klapstuk**).

Hete bliksem *hayter blikserm*
"Hot lightning" – potatoes, bacon, and apple with sugar and salt.

Bami goreng *baamee khoareng*
Indonesian fried noodles with spices, cabbage and other vegetables, onion, and meat, served with a fried egg.

Gado-gado *khaadoa-khaadoa*
Indonesian *al dente* mixture of vegetables, cucumber, and tofu (**tahu**), with peanut sauce and egg.

Cheese Kaas

Edammer kaas _aydammer kaas_
Mild, low fat cheese from Edam, sealed in red wax.

Goudse kaas _khowtser kaas_
Famous cheese from Gouda, softer than Edam and higher in fat.

Friese nagelkaas _freeser naakherlkaas_
From the province of Friesland, made with skimmed milk and cloves.

Komijnekaas _koamaynerkaas_
Mild, hard cheese with cumin seeds; also called **Leidse** or **Delftse kaas**.

Dessert Nagerecht

Appeltaart _apperltaart_
Dutch apple tart generously filled with mixed fruit and spices like cinnamon, and served with sweetened, whipped cream (**slagroom**). Also popular with morning coffee.

Haagse bluf _haakhser bluhf_
This "bluff from The Hague" is a fluffy dessert of sweetened, whipped egg whites with red currant sauce.

Pannekoeken _pannerkookern_
Thick pancakes, served in special pancake restaurants (**pannekoekhuisjes**). A traditional combination is pancake with bacon and syrup (**spekpannekoek met stroop**), substantial enough for a meal. There is a very popular thin variety of pancake, called **flensje**.

Poffertjes _poffertyers_
"Puffed up" tiny pancakes, sometimes served in a special eat-in stand (**poffertjeskraam**), piled on a plate and sprinkled with sugar icing.

Gebak _kherbak_
Look out for this custard slice, named after a cartoon character (**tompoes**), and a type of éclair (**moorkop**), often served with morning coffee ➤ 51.

Chipolatapudding _shipoalaatapuding_
Set pudding of eggs, biscuits and liqueur.

Kwarktaart _kvarktaart_
A light cheesecake.

Vla _flaa_
Custard is sold ready-made in the shops in different flavors.

Wafels _vaaferls_
Waffles, often served with ice cream and/or syrup.

Fruit Fruit

Appelmoes *apperlmoos*
Apple sauce, often served with children's meals.

Vruchtenvlaai *fruhkhternflaai*
Fruit flan from the province of Limburg, filled with different fruits, such as
cherries (**kersenvlaai**) or strawberries (**aardbeienvlaai**).

aardbeien	*aardbayern*	strawberries
appels	*upperls*	apples
bananen	*banaanern*	bananas
druiven	*droaivern*	grapes
frambozen	*framboazern*	raspberries
granaatappels	*khranaatapperls*	pomegranates
grapefruit	*graypfroot*	grapefruit
kersen	*kehrsern*	cherries
meloen	*meloon*	melon
perziken	*pehrzikern*	peaches
pruimen	*proaimern*	plums
sinaasappels	*sinaasapperls*	oranges
watermeloen	*vaatermeloon*	watermelon

Drinks Drankjes

Aperitifs Aperitieven

A popular aperitif (**aperitief** or **borreltje**) is beer or **jenever** (a kind of gin).
There is **jonge** (young) **jenever** and **oude** (mature) **jenever**, **bessenjenever**
(blackcurrant flavor), **citroenjenever** (lemon), and **berenburg** (Frisian gin).
Sherry, port, and vermouth are known by their English names.

Beer Bier/Pils

Heineken, Amstel, and Oranjeboom are the best-known Dutch beers. Ask
for **een pilsje** if you want a lager. Alternatively, you could try dark beer
(**een donker bier**), light beer (**een licht bier**), draft [draught] beer (**getapt
bier**), old brown (**oud bruin**) – a dark, slightly sweet stout – or orange-
flavored bitter (**oranjebitter**).

Do you have … beer?   **Heeft u … bier?** *hayft uw … beer*

bottled/draft [draught]   **flessebier/getapt**
                             flesserbeer/khertapt

Wine Wijn

The Netherlands is not a wine-growing country, but wines from other continental countries, such as France and Germany, are easily available and very reasonably priced.

Can you recommend a ... wine?	**Kunt u een ... wijn aanbevelen?** *kuhnt uw ayn ... vayn aanberfaylern*
red/white/blush [rosé]	**rode/witte/rosé** *roader/vitter/roasay*
dry/sweet/sparkling	**droge/zoete/mousserende** *droakher/zooter/moosserernder*
May I have the house wine?	**Mag ik de huiswijn?** *makh ik der hoaisvayn*

Spirits and liqueurs Sterke dranken en likeurs

Advocaat *adfoakaat*

The famous Dutch egg liqueur, served with a small spoon, and also combined with whipped cream, ice cream, cherry brandy, or a fizzy soft drink. Other Dutch liqueurs are **Half om half** (strong), **Parfait'amour** (fragrant) and **Curaçao** (orange flavor).

Brandewijn *brandervayn*

Brandy is served with the traditional **Brabantse koffietafel** (generous brunch in the province of Brabant). Popular varieties are **boerenjongens** (with raisins) and **boerenmeisjes** (with apricots).

(a double) whisky	**(een dubbele) whisky** *(ayn duhberler) wiskee*
straight [neat]	**puur** *puwr*
on the rocks [with ice]	**met ijs** *met ays*
with water/tonic water	**met water/tonic** *met vaater/tonnik*
I'd like a single/double ...	**Ik wil graag een enkele/dubbele ...** *ik vil khraakh ayn engkerler/duhberler*
brandy/gin/whisky/vodka	**cognac/jenever/whisky/wodka** *konyak/yernayver/wiskee/vodka*
gin and tonic	**gin-tonic** *zhintonnik*

Non-alcoholic drinks
Alcoholvrije dranken

Koffie _koffee_
Coffee is to the Dutch as tea is to the English. All coffee is
freshly made; instant coffee is only used in an emergency. Mid-
morning coffee with pastries (**een kopje koffie met gebak**) is a popular
time to ask friends to come around. Coffee is drunk with a little **koffiemelk**,
a kind of evaporated milk sold in small bottles, or **slagroom**, the sweetened
whipped cream also used as a topping on ice cream and to accompany
appeltaart.

Thee _tay_
Tea is drunk very weak and without milk, sometimes **met citroen** (with
lemon). Herb tea (**kruidenthee**) is also popular, for example mint tea
(**muntthee**), as is English tea (Earl Grey, English Breakfast tea, etc.).

I'd like …	**Ik wil graag …** _ik vil khraakh_
(hot) chocolate	**(warme) chocolade melk** _(varmer) shoakoalaader melk_
(cold, bottled) chocolate	**chocomel** _shoakoamel_
soft drink	**frisdrank** _frisdrank_
coke	**coke** _koak_
lemonade	**limonade** _limoanaader_
fruit juice	**vruchtensap** _fruhkhternsap_
orange	**sinaasappel** _sinaasapperl_
pineapple	**ananas** _annanas_
tomato	**tomaten** _toamaatern_
milkshake	**milkshake** _milkshayk_
mineral water	**mineraalwater** _mineraalvaater_
carbonated	**gazeus/met prik** _khasus/met prik_
non-carbonated [still]	**niet-gazeus/zonder prik** _neet-khasus/zonder prik_
buttermilk	**karnemelk** _karnermelk_

Menu Reader

gebakken	*gherbakkern*	baked/fried
gefrituurd	*gherfreetuwrt*	deep-fried
gegrilleerd	*gherghrilayrt*	grilled
gekookt	*gherkoakt*	boiled
gemarineerd	*ghermareenayrt*	marinated
gepaneerd	*gherpanayrt*	breaded
gepocheerd	*gherposhayrt*	poached
gerookt	*gherroakt*	smoked
geroosterd	*gherraostert*	roasted
gesauteerd	*ghersoatayrt*	sautéed
gesmoord	*ghersmoart*	braised
gestoofd	*gherstoaft*	stewed
gestoomd	*gherstoamt*	steamed
gevuld	*gherfuwlt*	stuffed
goed doorbakken	*ghoot doarbakkern*	well-done
in blokjes gesneden	*in blokyers ghersnaydern*	diced
in de oven gebruind	*in der oafern gherbroaint*	oven-browned
kort gebakken	*kort gherbakkern*	rare
met room bereid	*met roam berayt*	creamed
pikant	*peekant*	spicy
redelijk doorbakken	*rayderlayk doarbakkern*	medium
saignant	*saynyant*	rare

A **aalbessen** red currants

aan de kluif on the bone

aardappel potato

aardappelpuree mashed potato

aardappelsalade potato salad

aardappelsoep potato soup

aardbeien strawberries

abrikozen apricots

advocaat egg liqueur (➤ 50)

afgemaakt met ... seasoned with ...

alcoholische drank alcoholic drink

amandel almond

amandelgebak almond tart

Amsterdamse ui pickled onion

ananas pineapple

andijvie endive

andijviesla endive salad

anijs aniseed

anijslikeur aniseed liqueur

ansjovis anchovies

aperitief aperitif

appel apple

appelbol apple dumpling
appelflappen apple turnovers
appelmoes apple sauce (➤ 49)
appeltaart apple pie/tart (➤ 48)
artisjokken artichoke
asperge asparagus
aspergepunten asparagus tips
aspergesoep asparagus soup
au gratin au gratin
aubergine eggplant [aubergine]
augurken gherkins
avocado avocado
avondeten tea (*mealtime*)

B **baars** bass/perch
babyinktvis baby squid
babyoctopus baby octopus
balletjes tiny meat balls (in vegetable soup)
bami Chinese/Indonesian noodles
bami goreng fried Chinese/Indonesian noodles (➤ 47)
banaan banana
banketletter (almond) pastry letter
basilicum basil
bataat sweet potato
bavarois Bavarian cream
beignets fritters
beschuit Dutch toast
bessen currants
biefstuk steak (*pan-fried*)
biefstuk tartaar ground steak
biefstuk van de haas porterhouse steak

biefstuk van de rib T-bone steak
bier beer
bieslook chives
bieten beetroot
biscuitjes biscuits
bitterballen breaded meatballs
bladerdeeg puff pastry
blanc-manger blancmange
blankvoorn roach
blauwe druiven black grapes
bleekselderij celery
blikgroenten canned vegetables
blinde vinken meat rolls (*veal or beef*) (➤ 46)
bloedworst black pudding
bloem (plain) flour
bloemkool cauliflower
boerenjongens brandy with raisins (➤ 50)
boerenkool (curly) kale
boerenmeisjes brandy with apricots (➤ 50)
boerenomelet omelet with potatoes, vegetables, and bacon (➤ 44)
bolus Chelsea bun
bonen beans (*pulses*)
borrel aperitif
borreltjes drinks (*alcoholic*)
borst breast
borstplaat thick sugar slice
bosbessen blueberries
boter butter
boterbabbelaar butterscotch

boterham sandwich
boterhammen sliced bread
boterkoek butter biscuit
boterletter (almond) pastry letter
bouillon consommé
bourbon bourbon (whisky)
bout leg (*cut of meat*)
bowl punch
braadstuk roast
Brabantse koffietafel generous brunch (➤ 50)
bramen blackberries
brandewijn brandy (➤ 50)
brasem bream
brood bread
broodje bun / roll
broodkruimels breadcrumbs
bruidstaart wedding cake
bruine bonen brown beans
bruine bonen soep brown bean soup (➤ 44)
Brussels lof chicory

C **caffeïnevrij** decaffeinated
cake cake, sponge cake
caraf carafe
caramelpudding crème caramel (*caramel pudding*)
cep cep (*mushroom*)
champignons/champignonhoedjes button mushrooms
chanterelle champignons chanterelle mushrooms

chipolatapudding set pudding of eggs, biscuits and liqueur (➤ 48)
chocolade chocolate
chocomel (cold, bottled) chocolate
citroen lemon
citroengras lemon grass
citroensap lemon juice
cognac brandy
consommé consommé
contre-fillet sirloin steak
corned beef corned beef
courgette courgette
croquet croquette

D **dadels** dates
dagschotel dish of the day
dessert dessert
dessertwijn dessert wine
dille dill
diner dinner
dooier egg yolk
doperwten garden peas
doughnut doughnut
dragon tarragon
drilpudding jelly
droge wijn dry wine
droog dry
druiven grapes
dubbel double (a double shot)
duif pigeon

E **Edammer kaas** Edam cheese (➤ 48)
eend duck

eierdooier egg yolk
eieren eggs
eiergerechten egg dishes
eigengemaakt home-made
eiwit egg white
erwten peas
erwtensoep pea soup (➤ 43, 44)

F fazant pheasant
filet fillet
filterkoffie freshly brewed coffee
flamberen flaming [flambé]
flensjes thin small pancakes
fles bottle
flessebier bottled beer
foeli mace
forel trout
frambozen raspberries
fricandeau fricandeau (*meat with sauce*)
Friese nagelkaas cheese with cloves (➤ 48)
frisdrank soft drink

G gado-gado Indonesian mixture of vegetables, cucumber, and tofu (➤ 47)
gans goose
garnalen shrimps [prawns]
garnering garnish, trimming
gazeus carbonated (*drinks*)
gebak(jes) pastries (➤ 48)
gebakken (in de pan) fried

gebakken (oven) baked
gebakken kip fried chicken
gebarbecued barbecued
gebonden soep cream soup
gebraden braised
gecorseerd full-bodied (*wine*)
gedroogd dried
gedroogde dadels dried dates
gedroogde pruimen dried prunes
gedroogde vijgen dried figs
geflambeerd flaming [flambé]
gefrituurd deep-fried
gegratineerd gratin
gegrilleerd grilled
gegrilleerde kip grilled chicken
gehakt minced meat
gehaktballetjes meatballs
geit goat
geitenkaas goat cheese
gekoeld chilled (*wine, etc.*)
gekonfijte vruchten candied fruit
gekookt boiled
gekookt eitje boiled egg
gekookte aardappels boiled potatoes
gekruid seasoned
gele sperciebonen butter beans
gemarineerd marinated
gemarineerd in azijn marinated in vinegar
gember ginger
gemengd assorted, mixed
gemengde grill mixed grill

gemengde groenten mixed vegetables

gemengde kruiden mixed herbs

gemengde noten assorted nuts

gemengde salade mixed salad

gepaneerd breaded (*cutlet, etc.*)

gepocheerd poached

geraspt grated

gerookt cured

gerookt smoked

gerookte paling smoked eel (➤ 45)

gerookte zalm smoked salmon

geroosterd broiled [grilled]

geroosterd brood toast

geroosterde aardappels roast potatoes

geroosterde kip roast chicken

gesauteerd sautéed

gestoofd stewed

gestoofd fruit stewed fruit

gestoomd steamed

gestoomde vis steamed fish

getapt bier draft [draught] beer

gevogelte fowl

gevuld stuffed

gevuld met stuffed with

gevulde olijven stuffed olives

gezouten salted

gezouten pinda's salted peanuts

gin-tonic gin and tonic

glas glass

goelasj goulash (➤ 46)

granaatappelen pomegranates

griesmeelpudding semolina pudding

grill grill

groene erwten garden peas

groene paprika's green peppers

groene salade green salad

groentebouillon vegetable broth

groenten vegetables (*general*)

groentensoep vegetable soup (➤ 44)

grog grog, hot toddy

Goudse kaas Gouda cheese (➤ 48)

guave guava

H **Haagse bluf** dessert of whipped egg white with red currant sauce (➤ 48)

haan cock

haas hare

hachee hash

halve fles half bottle

hamlap pork steak

hanekammensoep chanterelle soup

hapjes snacks

hapjes vooraf appetizers

hard hard-boiled (*egg*)

harde kaas hard cheese

harder grey mullet

haring herring

haringsla salad of salted or marinaded herring (➤ 43, 45)

hart heart

hartig savory

havermoutpap porridge

hazelnoten hazelnuts
hazepeper jugged hare (➤ 46)
heet hot (*temperature*)
heet water hot water
heilbot halibut
heldere soep clear soup
hersens brains
hete bliksem dish of potatoes, bacon, and apple (➤ 47)
hete pepersaus hot pepper sauce
Hollandse biefstuk Dutch steak
honing honey
hoorntjes cream horn
hopjes coffee caramel/toffee
houtsnip woodcock
huiswijn house wine
hutspot stew made of mashed potatoes with carrots and onions or with curly kale (➤ 47)
hutspot met klapstuk mashed potatoes, carrots, and onions served with rib of beef (➤ 47)
huzarensla mixture of potato, raw vegetables, and meat with mayonnaise (➤ 43)

I **ijs** ice, ice cream
 ijsgekoeld iced (*drink*)
ijswater iced water
in beslag in batter
in beslag gebakken fried in batter
in de pan gebakken vis fried fish
in knoflook in garlic
in olie in oil
in oven gebakken vis baked fish

in plakjes gesneden sliced
ingeblikte vruchten canned fruit
inktvis squid
inwendige organen giblets

J **jachtschotel** meat casserole with potatoes (➤ 47)
jam jam
jenever gin (➤ 49)
jeneverbessen juniper berries
jong geitevlees kid (*goat*)
jonge eend duckling
jus gravy

K **kaas** cheese
 kaasplank cheese board
kabeljauw cod
kalfskarbonaden veal chops
kalfsoester scallop
kalfsvlees veal
kalkoen turkey
kammosselen scallops
kaneel cinnamon
kappertje caper
kapucijners marrowfat peas
karaf carafe
karbonades chops
karnemelk buttermilk
karwij caraway
kastanjes chestnuts (*sweet*)
katenspek smoked bacon
kaviaar caviar
kekers chickpeas

kersen cherries
kerstomaatje cherry tomato
kervel chervil
kievitsbonen kidney beans
kievitseieren lapwing's eggs
kip chicken
kip en gevogelte poultry
kippeborst breast of chicken
kippenlever chicken liver
kippensoep chicken broth, soup
kiwivrucht kiwi fruit
klapstuk beef rib
kluif pig's knuckle (*bone*)
knakworst frankfurter
knoedel dumpling
knoflook garlic
knoflookmayonaise garlic mayonnaise
knoflooksaus garlic sauce
knolraap rutabaga [swede]
knolselderij celeriac
koekjes cookies
koffie coffee (➤ 51)
kokkelschelp cockle
kokos coconut
kokosmakarons coconut macaroon
komijn cumin
komijnekaas cheese with cumin seeds (➤ 48)
komkommer cucumber
komkommersalade cucumber salad
konijn rabbit
koninginnesoep cream of chicken
kool cabbage

koolrabi kohlrabi (*turnip cabbage*)
koolsla coleslaw
koriander coriander
korstdeeg shortcrust pastry
koteletten chops, cutlets
koud cold
koud buffet cold buffet
koud gerecht cold dish
koude drankjes cold drinks
koude soep cold soup
krab crab
kreeft lobster
krentenbrood currant bread
kroepoek shrimp [prawn] crackers
krokant crisp
kroketten croquettes
kropsla lettuce
kruiden herbs
kruidnagels cloves
kruisbes gooseberry
kuiken spring chicken
kwarktaart light cheesecake (➤ 48)
kwartelvlees quail
kweegelei quince jelly
kwetsen damson

L lamsbout leg of lamb
lamsstoofschotel lamb stew
lamsvlees lamb
lamszadel saddle (*lamb*)
laurierblad bay leaf
lekkerbekje fried breaded fillet of haddock

lende loin
lendebiefstuk fillet, rump steak
lendevlees loin (*pork, etc.*)
lente-uitjes spring onions
lever liver
licht light (*sauce, etc.*)
likeur liqueur
limoen lime
limoensap lime juice
limonade lemonade
limonadesiroop fruit drink [squash]
linzen lentils
loempia spring roll
lofsla salad of raw chicory rings
lopend buffet buffet

M **machtig** rich (*sauce*)
maïs sweet corn
makreel mackerel
mandarijn tangerine
marmelade marmalade
marsepein marzipan
mayonaise mayonnaise
melk milk
meloen melon
menu menu
menu van de dag set menu of the day
met balletjes with tiny meat balls (*in vegetable soup*)
met citroen with lemon
met ijs on the rocks [with ice]
met koolzuur carbonated

met melk white/with milk (*coffee*)
met prik carbonated (*drinks*)
met suiker with sugar
met water/tonic with water/tonic water
mie noodles
mierikswortel horseradish
milkshake milk shake
mineraalwater mineral water
moerbei mulberry
moorkop chocolate éclair
mosselen mussels
mosterd mustard
mousserend sparkling
mousserende wijn sparkling wine
munt mint
muntthee mint tea

N **nasi goreng** Indonesian rice dish with egg (➤ 44)
nectarine nectarine
niertjes kidneys
niet-alcoholische dranken non-alcoholic drinks
nieuwe haring freshly caught, salt-cured herring (➤ 43, 45)
noga nougat
nootmuskaat nutmeg

O **octopus** octopus
oesters oysters

oesterzwammen oyster mushrooms
oliebollen doughnut ball [lardy cake]
olijven olives
omelet omelet
ontbijt breakfast
ontbijtgranen cereal
op houtskool geroosterd charcoal-grilled
op ijs on the rocks
ossehaas tenderloin
ossestaart ox
ossestaartsoep oxtail soup

P **paddestoelen** field mushrooms
paling eel
pannekoeken pancakes (➤ 48)
paprika's peppers
parelhoen guinea fowl
passievrucht passion fruit
pastei pie
pasteideeg pastry
pasteitje vol-au-vent
pastinaken parsnips
patat French fries [chips]
patates frites French fries [chips]
pâté pâté
patrijs partridge
peer pear
pekelvlees sliced salted meat
pens tripe
peper pepper

perzik peach
peterselie parsley
peultjes sugar peas
pikant hot (*spicy*)
pikant worstje spicy sausage
pils lager
pinda's peanuts
pindasaus peanut sauce
pittabrood pita bread
pittig sharp (*flavor*)
plaatselijke specialiteit local speciality
plak slice
poffertjes tiny puffed-up pancakes (➤ 48)
pompoen pumpkin
poon sea robin [gurnard fish]
portie portion
prei leeks
prinsessenbonen haricot beans
pruimen plums, prunes
pure whisky straight [neat] whisky
puur straight [neat]

R **raap** turnip
rabarber rhubarb
radijs radish
rammenas winter radish
rapen turnips
rauw raw
reebout venison
rettich rettich (*white radish-related, carrot-shaped vegetable*)

ribstuk rib
rijp ripe
rijst rice
risotto risotto
rivierkreeft crayfish
rode kool red cabbage
rode peper chili pepper
roerei scrambled egg
rog ray
roggebrood rye bread
rollade rolled meat
romig creamy
rood red (*wine*)
rookvlees sliced smoke-dried beef
room cream
roomijs ice cream
roomsoep cream soup
rosbief roast beef
rosé blush [rosé] (*wine*)
rozemarijn rosemary
rozijnen raisins
rum rum
rundvlees beef
russische eieren hard-boiled egg filled with mayonnaise (➤ 43)

S **saffraan** saffron
sajur lodeh Indonesian soup of vegetables and coconut (➤ 44).
salade salad
salie sage
sap juice
sardientjes sardines
saté meat on skewers

saucijzebroodje sausage roll
saucijzen sausages
saus sauce
savooiekool savoy cabbage
schaaldieren crustaceans
schapekaas ewe's milk cheese
schapevlees mutton
schelpdieren shellfish
schelvis haddock
schenkel shank (*top of leg*)
schimmelkaas blue cheese
schnitzel veal/pork cutlet
schol plaice
schorseneer salsify, oyster plant
schotel dish
Schotse Whisky Scotch whisky
schouderstuk shoulder (*cut of meat*)
schuimgebak meringue
schuimig foamy
selderij celery
sinaasappel orange
sinaasappelsap orange juice
siroop syrup
sjalots shallots
sla lettuce
slagroom sweet whipped cream
slakken snails
slasaus vinaigrette [French dressing]
snijbonen sliced green beans
snoepjes candy [sweets]
soep soup
soesjes choux pastry
specerijen spices

specialiteiten van de chef-kok specialities of the house
speenvarken suckling pig
spek bacon
spekpannekoeken bacon pancakes
spelletje game
sperziebonen French / green beans
spiegelei fried egg
spiesjes met skewered
spijkerrog skate
spinazie spinach
spitskool oxheart cabbage
sprits Dutch short biscuit
sprotten sprats
spruitjes Brussel sprouts
spuitwater soda water
stamppot one-pan dish with vegetables and mashed potatoes (➤ 47)
sterk strong (*flavor*)
sterk gekruid highly seasoned
sterke dranken spirits
stervrucht star fruit
stokbrood French bread, baguette
stokvis hake
stokvisschotel oven stew of stockfish (dried cod) (➤ 45)
stoofschotel casserole, stew
strandgapers clams
stroop treacle, molasses
stuk van de rib T-bone steak
suiker sugar
suikerglazuur icing

sultanarozijnen sultanas

T **taart** tart (*sweet, savory*)
taartje tartlette (*sweet, savory*)
tafelwijn table wine
tafelzuur pickles
tahoe tofu, soya bean curd
tarbot turbot
tartaartje ground steak
tarwebloem wholewheat flour
taugé bean spouts
thee tea (*beverage*) (➤ 51)
tijm thyme
timbaaltje timbale (*chopped meat or fish in a pastry shell*)
tomaten tomatoes
tomatenketchup tomato ketchup
tomatensaus tomato sauce
tomatensoep tomato soup
tompoes custard slice
tong tongue, sole (*fish*)
tonic tonic water
tonijn tuna
toost toast
tostie toasted sandwich
touristenmenu tourist menu
tournedos fillet steak (*thick, round*)
truffels truffles
tuinbonen broad beans
tuinkers cress
tulband turban-shaped fruit cake

uien onions

    uiensoep onion soup

uitsmijter lunchtime snack of bread, ham and fried eggs (➤ 47)

 van de haas tenderloin (*cut of meat*)

vanille vanilla

varkenshaasje pork tenderloin

varkenskarbonaden pork chops

varkenspootjes trotters (*pigs' feet*)

varkensvlees pork

varkensworstjes pork sausages

veenbes cranberry

vegetarisch vegetarian

venkel fennel

venusschelpen clams

vermicellisoep clear noodle soup

vermout vermouth

vers fresh

vers fruit fresh fruit

verse dadels fresh dates

verse kwark fresh-curd cheese

verse vijgen fresh figs

vet fatty

vijgen figs

vis fish

viskroketten fish fingers

vissoep fish soup

vla custard (➤ 48)

vlaai fruit tart

vlees meat (*general*)

vleesbouillon meat broth

vogelnestje bird's nest (*edible*)

vruchtendrank fruit drink

vruchtensap fruit juice

vruchtenvlaai fruit flan from the province of Limburg (➤ 49)

wafels waffles (➤ 48)

    walnoten walnuts

warme chocolademelk hot chocolate

waterkastanjes water chestnuts

waterkers watercress

watermeloen watermelon

wentelteefjes French toast

Wiener Schnitzel breaded veal slices (➤ 46)

wijn wine

wijnkaart wine list

wijting whiting

wild zwijn wild boar

wilde eend wild duck (*mallard*)

witlof chicory

witlofsla chicory salad

witte bonen white/baked beans

witte druiven white grapes

witte kool white cabbage

witte saus white sauce

worstjes sausages

wortelsalade raw grated carrot

worteltjes carrots

yoghurt yogurt

zacht mild (*flavor*)

63

zacht gekookt soft-boiled (*eggs*)
zachte kaas soft cheese
zalm salmon
zandgebak shortbread, shortcake
zeebaars sea bass
zeebarbeel red mullet
zeebliek whitebait
zeebrasem sea bream
zeeduivel monkfish
zeekat cuttlefish
zeepaling conger eel
zeer droog very dry (*wine, etc.*)
zeevis, schaal- en schelpdieren seafood
zelfrijzend bakmeel self-raising flour
zoet sweet
zoet-zure saus sweet and sour sauce
zoete rode paprika's sweet red peppers
zoete wijn sweet wine
zoetjes sweetener
zoetwatervis freshwater fish
zonder plain
zonder melk black (*coffee*)
zonder prik non-carbonated [still] (*drinks*)
zout salt
zoutwatervis salt-water fish
zult brawn
zure bom big gherkin
zure haring pickled herring, rollmops
zuring sorrel

zuur sour (*taste*)
zuurkool sauerkraut
zwaardvis swordfish
zwarte bessen black currants
zwezeriken sweetbreads

64

Travel

ESSENTIAL

1/2/3 ticket(s) to ...	**één/twee/drie kaartje(s) naar ...** *ayn/tvay/dree <u>kaar</u>tyer(s) naar*
To ..., please.	**Naar ..., alstublieft.** *naar ..., alstuw<u>bleeft</u>*
one-way [single]	**een enkeltje** *ayn <u>engkerl</u>tyer*
round-trip [return]	**een retourtje** *ayn re<u>toor</u>tyer*
How much ...?	**Hoeveel ...?** *hoo<u>fayl</u>*

Safety <u>Veiligheid</u>

Can you come with me to the bus stop?	**Kunt u met me meegaan naar de bushalte?** *kuhnt uw met mer <u>may</u>khaan naar der <u>buhs</u>halter*
I don't want to ... on my own.	**Ik wil niet op mijn eentje ...** *ik vil neet op mayn <u>eyn</u>tyer*
stay here	**hier blijven** *heer <u>blay</u>fern*
walk home	**naar huis lopen** *naar hoais <u>loa</u>pern*
I don't feel safe here.	**Ik voel me hier niet veilig.** *ik fool mer heer neet <u>fay</u>likh*

Arrival Aankomst

Citizens of the UK, the US, Canada and Eire require only a valid passport for entry to The Netherlands. Citizens of Australia and New Zealand also require a visa. This should be checked with the embassy.

No visa is necessary for citizens of European countries staying up to three months, only a passport. No passport is required for accompanied children entered in the passport of their parents or a guardian of the same nationality.

Duty-free into:	Cigarettes	Cigars	Tobacco	Spirits	Wine
Canada	200 and	50 and	400g.	1l. or	1l.
UK	200 or	50 or	250g.	1l. and	2l.
US	200 and	100 and	discretionary	1l. or	1l.

There are virtually no export restrictions. Plants, flowers, and fruit may be imported in small quantities for personal use.

Suggested maximum for items for personal consumption bought duty-paid within the EU: 90l. wine or 60l. sparkling wine, 20l. fortified wine, 10l. spirits and 110l. beer.

Passport control Paspoortcontrole

We have a joint passport.	**We hebben een gezamelijk paspoort.** *vay hepbern ayn kherzaamerlerk paspoart*
The children are on this passport.	**De kinderen staan op dit paspoort.** *der kinderern staan op dit paspoart*
I'm here on vacation [holiday]/business.	**Ik ben hier met vakantie/voor zaken.** *ik ben heer met fakansee/foar zaakern*
I'm just passing through.	**Ik ben op doorreis.** *ik ben op doarrays*
I'm going to …	**Ik ga naar …** *ik khaa naar*
I'm on my own.	**Ik ben op mijn eentje.** *ik ben op mayn eyntyer*
I'm with my family.	**Ik ben met mijn gezin.** *ik ben met mayn kherzin*
I'm with a group.	**Ik ben met een groep.** *ik ben met ayn khroop*

WHO ARE YOU WITH? ➤ 120

Customs Douane

I have only the normal allowances.

Ik heb alleen de normale toegestane hoeveelheid.
ik hep allayn der normaaler tookherstaaner hoofaylhayt

It's a gift.

Het is een cadeau. *het is ayn kadow*

It's for my personal use.

Het is voor mijn persoonlijk gebruik.
het is foar mayn persoanlerk kherbroaik

Heeft u iets aan te geven?	Do you have anything to declare?
Hierop moet u accijns betalen.	You must pay duty on this.
Waar heeft u dit gekocht?	Where did you buy this?
Kunt u deze tas even openmaken?	Can you open this bag?
Heeft u nog meer bagage?	Do you have any more luggage?

I'd like to declare ...

Ik wil graag ... aangeven.
ik vil khraakh ... aankhayfern

I don't understand.

Ik begrijp het niet. *ik berkhrayp het neet*

Does anyone here speak English?

Is er hier iemand die Engels spreekt?
is ehr heer eemant dee eng-ils spraykt

PASPOORTCONTROLE	passport control
GRENSOVERGANG	border crossing
DOUANE	customs
NIETS AAN TE GEVEN	nothing to declare
AANGIFTE GOEDEREN	goods to declare
BELASTINGVRIJE GOEDEREN	duty-free goods

Duty-free shopping Belastingvrij winkelen

What currency is this in?

In welke valuta is dit?
in velker valuwta is dit

Can I pay in ...?

Mag ik in ... betalen?
makh ik in ... bertaalern

dollars

dollars *dollars*

euros

euro's *uros*

pounds

ponden *pondern*

Plane Vliegtuig

In a country as small as the Netherlands, the excellent road and rail networks are used more than the internal flight routes. However, in addition to the main Schiphol Airport, there are small airports at Rotterdam, Eindhoven, and Maastricht.

Tickets and reservations Tickets en reserveringen

When is the … flight to New York?	**Wanneer is de … vlucht naar New York?** *van<u>nayr</u> is der … fluhkht naar nu york*
first/next/last	**eerste/volgende/laatste** <u>ayr</u>ster/<u>fol</u>khernder/<u>laat</u>ster
I'd like two … tickets to …	**Ik wil graag twee … tickets naar …** *ik vil khraakh tvay … <u>tik</u>kerts naar*
one-way [single]	**enkeltjes** <u>eng</u>kerltyers
round-trip [return]	**retourtjes** re<u>toor</u>tyers
first class	**eerste klas** <u>ayr</u>ster klas
business class	**"business class"** <u>biz</u>nis klas
economy class	**"economy class"** ekono<u>mee</u> klas
How much is a flight to …?	**Hoeveel kost een vlucht naar …?** *hoo<u>fayl</u> kost ayn fluhkht naar*
Are there any supplements/ discounts?	**Is er toeslag/korting?** *is ehr <u>toos</u>lakh/<u>kor</u>ting*
I'd like to … my reservation for flight number 123.	**Ik wil graag mijn reservering … voor vluchtnummer 123.** *ik vil khraakh mayn rayzer<u>vay</u>ring foar <u>fluhkht</u>nuhmer*
cancel	**cancellen** <u>kan</u>serlern
change	**veranderen** fer<u>an</u>derern
confirm	**bevestigen** ber<u>fes</u>terkhern

Inquiries about the flight Informatie over de vlucht

How long is the flight?	**Hoe lang is de vlucht?** *hoo lang is der fluhkht*
What time does the plane leave?	**Hoe laat vertrekt het vliegtuig?** *hoo laat fer<u>trehkt</u> het <u>fleekht</u>toaikh*
What time will we arrive?	**Hoe laat komen we aan?** *hoo laat <u>koa</u>mern vay aan*
What time do I have to check in?	**Hoe laat moet ik inchecken?** *hoo laat moot ik <u>in</u>chekkern*

Checking in Inchecken

Where is the check-in desk for flight ...?	**Waar is de check-in desk voor vlucht ...?** *vaar is der chekin desk foar fluhkht*
I have ...	**Ik heb ...** *ik hep*
three cases to check in	**drie koffers voor inchecken** *dree koffers foar inchekkern*
two pieces of hand luggage	**twee stukken handbagage** *tvay stuhkern hantbagaazher*
How much hand luggage is allowed free?	**Hoeveel handbagage mag ik gratis meenemen?** *hoofayl hantbagaazher makh ik khraatis maynaymern*

Uw paspoort, alstublieft.	Your passport, please.
Wilt u bij het raam of bij het gangpad zitten?	Would you like a window or an aisle seat?
Roken of niet-roken?	Smoking or non-smoking?
U mag nu door naar de vertrekhal.	Please go through to the departure lounge.
Hoeveel stukken bagage heeft u?	How many pieces of baggage do you have?
U heeft overgewicht.	You have excess baggage.
U moet een toeslag van ... euro's betalen.	You'll have to pay a supplement of ... euros.
Dat is te zwaar/groot voor handbagage.	That's too heavy/large for hand baggage.
Heeft u deze tassen zelf ingepakt?	Did you pack these bags yourself?
Zitten er scherpe of electronische dingen in?	Do they contain any sharp or electronic items?

AANKOMST	arrivals
VERTREK	departures
VEILIGHEIDSCONTROLE	security check
TASSEN NIET ZONDER TOEZICHT ACHTERLATEN	do not leave bags unattended

BAGGAGE ➤ 71

Information Informatie

Is there any delay on flight …?	**Is vlucht … vertraagd?** *is fluhkht … fertraakht*
How late will it be?	**Hoeveel is hij vertraagd?** *hoofayl is hay fertraakht*
Has the flight from … landed?	**Is de vlucht uit … geland?** *is der fluhkht oait … kherlant*
Which gate does flight … leave from?	**Van welke gate vertrekt vlucht …?** *fan velker gayt fertrehkt fluhkht*

Boarding/In-flight Boarding/In-flight

Your boarding card, please.	**Uw boarding-kaart, alstublieft.** *uwer boardingkaart, alstuwbleeft*
Could I have a drink/ something to eat, please?	**Mag ik iets te drinken/eten hebben, alstublieft?** *makh ik eets ter drinkern/ ayten hepbern, alstuwbleeft*
Please wake me for the meal.	**Kunt u me wakker maken voor de maaltijd?** *kuhnt uw mer vakker maakern foar der maaltayt*
What time will we arrive?	**Hoe laat komen we aan?** *hoo laat koamern vay aan*
An airsickness bag, please. I'm airsick.	**Ik ben luchtziek, mag ik een papieren zak?** *ik ben luhkhtzeek, makh ik ayn papeerern zak*

Arrival Aankomst

Where is/are (the) …?	**Waar is /zijn …?** *vaar is/zayn (der/het)*
buses	**de bussen** *der buhssern*
car rental	**het autoverhuurbedrijf** *het owtoferhuwrberdrayf*
currency exchange	**het geldwisselkantoor** *het kheltvisserlkantoar*
exit	**de uitgang** *der oaitkhang*
taxis	**de taxi's** *der taksees*
Is there a bus into town?	**Is er een bus naar de stad?** *is ehr ayn buhs naar der stat*
How do I get to the … hotel?	**Hoe kom ik bij hotel …?** *hoo kom ik bay hoatel*

Baggage Bagage

Porters (**kruiers**) at airports and stations and airports have largely been replaced by free luggage carts [trolleys].

Where is/are the …?	**Waar is/zijn …?** *vaar is/zayn (der/het)*
luggage carts [trolleys]	**de bagagewagentjes** *der bagaazhervaakherntyers*
baggage check [left-luggage office]	**het bagagedepot** *het bagaazherdepo*
baggage claim	**de bagage-claim** *der bagaazher-klaym*
Could you take my luggage to …?	**Kunt u mijn bagage meenemen naar …?** *kuhnt uw mayn bagaazher maynaymern naar*
a taxi/bus	**een taxi/bus** *ayn taksee/buhs*
Where is the luggage from flight …?	**Waar is de bagage van vlucht …?** *vaar is der bagaazher fan fluhkht*

Loss, damage, and theft Verlies, schade en diefstal

I've lost my baggage.	**Ik ben mijn bagage kwijtgeraakt.** *ik ben mayn bagaazher kvaytkheraakt*
My baggage has been stolen.	**Mijn bagage is gestolen.** *mayn bagaazher is kherstoalern*
My suitcase was damaged.	**Mijn koffer is beschadigd.** *mayn koffer is berskhaadikht*
Our baggage has not arrived.	**Onze bagage is niet aangekomen.** *onzer bagaazher is neet aankherkoamern*

Hoe ziet uw bagage eruit?	What does your baggage look like?
Heeft u het reclaim-kaartje?	Do you have the claim check [reclaim tag]?
Uw bagage …	Your luggage …
is misschien naar … gestuurd	may have been sent to …
kan later vandaag nog aankomen	may arrive later today
Kunt u morgen terugkomen?	Can you come back tomorrow.
Bel dit nummer om te controleren of uw bagage is aangekomen.	Call this number to check if your baggage has arrived.

POLICE ➤ 159; COLOR ➤ 143

Train Trein

The Dutch blue and yellow trains are punctual, fast, and comfortable, and the excellent network reaches even the tiniest places and into neighboring Germany, Belgium and Luxembourg. The fast through-trains are called **sneltrein**, the others **stoptrein**. HST, the Dutch high-speed train, is not yet completed, but the TGV runs between Paris and Amsterdam, stopping in Rotterdam and the Hague. This links with the Channel Tunnel. Be careful to choose the right station in cities with several, e.g. **Den Haag Centraal Station** and **Den Haag Hollands Spoor**.

Eurostar

With the Eurostar, Brussels is just 2 hours 40 mins from London's Waterloo station, and with the intercity connections to the Netherlands, Rotterdam is less than 5 hours and Amsterdam less than 6 hours from London.

Holland Rail Pass

This pass allows you to travel for any three or five days within one month. The days don't need to be consecutive, as you date the pass on the days when you're using it. Everywhere in Holland is a day trip away. Proof of age and a valid passport are required.

Fares

Children under four travel free. Children 4–11 traveling with an adult can travel for a nominal fee. There are no discounts for senoir citizens on the rail network within Holland, but you can purchase a *Rail Europa Senior* (*RES card*), which gives you 30 percent off international fares.

Other tickets

There are numerous other tickets available, like the *Summer Tour Rover* (in July and August, giving two people three days of unlimited travel within ten days), the *1-Day Rover Ticket* and the *Group Travel Multi Rover*, (giving a group of 2–6 one day of unlimited travel). The Benelux *Tourrail Card* gives you five days of unlimited travel within one month in Holland, Belgium, and Luxembourg. The *Euro Domino* gives you 3–5 days of unlimited travel in Belgium within one month.

Bicycle rental from train stations

You can rent bicycles direct from many Dutch stations. Rail passengers qualify for a discount. It is advisable to book in advance because of the high demand, especially during vacation. I.D. is required when you pick up your bicycle and you will be asked to pay a refundable deposit.

To the station Naar het station

How do I get to the train station? | **Hoe kom ik bij het station?**
hoo kom ik bay het stashion

Do trains to Rotterdam leave from ... station? | **Vertrekken de treinen naar Rotterdam van station ...?**
fertrehkkern der traynern naar rotterdam fan stashion

How far is it? | **Hoever is het?** *hoofehr is het*

Can I leave my car there? | **Kan ik mijn auto hier achterlaten?**
kan ik mayn owto heer akhterlaatern

At the station Op het station

Where is/are the ...? | **Waar is/zijn ...?** *vaar is/zayn*

baggage check
[left-luggage office] | **het bagagedepot**
het bagaazherdepo

currency exchange | **het geldwisselkantoor**
het kheltvisserlkantoor

information desk | **de informatiebalie**
der informateebaalee

lost and found
[lost property office] | **gevonden voorwerpen**
kherfondern foarverpern

platforms | **de perronnen** *der perronnern*

snack bar | **de snackbar** *der snehkbaar*

ticket office | **het loket** *het loket*

waiting room | **de wachtkamer** *der vakhtkaamer*

INGANG	entrance
UITGANG	exit
NAAR HET PERRON	to the platforms
INFORMATIE	information
RESERVERINGEN	reservations
AANKOMST	arrivals
VERTREK	departures

DIRECTIONS ➤ 94

Tickets and reservations
Kaartjes en reserveringen

There are many special tickets (**kaartjes**), including the Holland Rail Pass (➤ 72). Note that most stations do not accept credit cards, but many have ticket machines. A conductor (**conducteur**) usually checks tickets on the train.

I'd like a ... ticket to Amsterdam.	**Ik wil graag een ... (kaartje) naar Amsterdam.** *ik vil khraakh ayn ... (kaartyer) naar amsterdam*
one-way [single]	**enkeltje** *engkerltyer*
round-trip [return]	**retourtje** *retoortyer*
first/second class	**eersteklas/tweedeklas** *ayrsterklas/tvayderklas*
concessionary	**met korting** *met korting*
I'd like to reserve a/an ...	**Ik wil graag een ... reserveren.** *ik vil khraakh ayn ... rayservayrern*
aisle seat	**plaats bij het gangpad** *plaats bay het khangpat*
window seat	**plaats bij het raam** *plaats bay het raam*
Is there a sleeping car [sleeper]?	**Is er een slaapwagon?** *is ehr ayn slaapvaagon*
I'd like a(n) ... berth.	**Ik wil graag een couchette ...** *ik vil khraakh ayn koosheter*
upper/lower	**boven/onder** *boafern/onder*

Price Prijs

How much is that?	**Hoeveel kost dat?** *hoofayl kost dat*
Is there a discount for ...?	**Is er korting voor ...?** *is ehr korting foar*
children/families	**kinderen/gezinnen** *kinderern/kherzinnern*
senior citizens	**zestig-plussers** *zestikhpluhsers*
students	**studenten** *stuhdentern*

Questions Vragen

Do I have to change trains?	**Moet ik overstappen?** *moot ek <u>oa</u>ferstappern*
Is it a direct train?	**Is het een rechtstreekse verbinding?** *is het ayn <u>rehkht</u>straykser fer<u>bin</u>ding*
You have to change at …	**U moet overstappen in …** *uw moot <u>oa</u>ferstappern in*
How long is this ticket valid for?	**Hoe lang is dit kaartje geldig?** *hoo lang is dit <u>kaar</u>tyer <u>khel</u>dikh*
Can I take my bicycle on the train?	**Kan ik mijn fiets meenemen op de trein?** *kan ik mayn feets <u>may</u>naymern op der trayn*
Can I return on the same ticket?	**Kan ik op hetzelfde kaartje terugkomen?** *kan ik op het<u>zelf</u>der <u>kaar</u>tyer tru<u>hkh</u>koamern*
In which car [coach] is my seat?	**In welke wagon is mijn plaats?** *in <u>vel</u>ker vaa<u>gon</u> is mayn plaats*
Is there a dining car on the train?	**Is er een restauratiewagon?** *is ehr ayn restoa<u>raat</u>seevaa<u>gon</u>*

– Ik wil graag een kaartje naar Amsterdam, alstublieft.
(I'd like a ticket to Amsterdam, please.)
– Een enkeltje of een retourtje? (One-way or round-trip?)
– Een retourtje, alstublieft. (Round-trip, please.)
– Dat is achttien euro's vijftig. (That's 18.50 euros.)
– Moet ik overstappen? (Do I have to change trains?)
Ja, u moet overstappen in Utrecht.
(Yes, you have to change at Utrecht.)
– Dank u wel. Dag. (Thank you. Good-bye.)

Train times Treintijden

Could I have a timetable, please?	**Mag ik een spoorwegboekje?** *makh ik ayn <u>spoor</u>vehkhbookyer*
When is the … train to Amsterdam?	**Wanneer gaat de … trein naar Amsterdam?** *van<u>nayr</u> khaat der … trayn naar amster<u>dam</u>*
first/next/last	**eerste/volgende/laatste** *<u>ayr</u>ste/<u>fol</u>khernder/<u>laat</u>ster*

How frequent are the trains to …?	**Hoe vaak gaan de treinen naar …?** *hoo faak khaan der <u>tray</u>nern naar*
once/twice a day	**één/twee keer per dag** *ayn/tvay kayr pehr daakh*
five times a day	**vijf keer per dag** *fayf kayr pehr daakh*
every hour	**om het uur** *om het uwr*
What time do they leave?	**Hoe laat vertrekken ze?** *hoo laat fer<u>treh</u>kkern zer*
on the hour	**op het hele uur** *op het <u>hay</u>ler uwr*
20 minutes past the hour	**twintig minuten over het hele uur** *<u>tvin</u>tekh mi<u>nuw</u>tern <u>oa</u>fer het <u>hay</u>ler uwr*
What time does the train stop at …?	**Hoe laat stopt de trein in …?** *hoo laat stopt der trayn in …*
What time does the train arrive in …?	**Hoe laat komt de trein aan in …?** *hoo laat komt der trayn aan in*
How long is the trip [journey]?	**Hoe lang is de reis?** *hoo lang is der rays*
Is the train on time?	**Is de trein op tijd?** *is der trayn op tayt*

Departures Vertrek

Which platform does the train to … leave from?	**Van welk perron vertrekt de trein naar …?** *fan velk per<u>ron</u> fer<u>trehkt</u> der trayn naar*
Where is platform 4?	**Waar is perron vier?** *vaar is per<u>ron</u> veer*
over there	**daar** *daar*
on the left/right	**aan de linkerkant/rechterkant** *aan der <u>lin</u>kerkant/<u>rehkh</u>terkant*
Where do I change for …?	**Waar stap ik over voor …?** *vaar stap ik <u>oa</u>fer foar*
How long will I have to wait for a connection?	**Hoe lang moet ik op een verbinding wachten?** *hoo lang moot ik op ayn fer<u>bin</u>ding <u>vakh</u>tern*

Boarding Instappen

Is this the right platform for …?	**Is dit het juiste perron voor …?** *is dit het juaister perron foar*
Is this the train to …?	**Is dit de trein naar …?** *is dit der trayn naar*
Is this seat taken?	**Is deze plaats bezet?** *is dayzer plaats berzet*
That's my seat.	**Dat is mijn plaats.** *dat is mayn plaats*
Here's my reservation.	**Hier is mijn reservering.** *heer is mayn rayzervayring*
Are there any seats/ berths available?	**Zijn er plaatsen/couchettes beschikbaar?** *zayn ehr plaatsern/koosheters berskhikbaar*
Do you mind if …?	**Is het goed als …?** *is het khoot als*
I sit here	**ik hier zit** *ik heer zit*
I open the window	**ik het raam opendoe** *ik het raam oaperndoo*

On the trip Op reis

How long are we stopping here for?	**Hoe lang stoppen we hier?** *hoo lang stoppern vay heer*
When do we get to …?	**Wanneer zijn we in …?** *vannayr zayn vay in*
Have we passed …?	**Zijn we al langs … gekomen?** *zayn vay al langs … kherkoamern*
Where is the dining/ sleeping car?	**Waar is de restauratie-/slaapwagen?** *vaar is der restoaraatsee-/slaapvaagon*
Where is my berth?	**Waar is mijn couchette?** *vaar is mayn kooshetter*
I've lost my ticket.	**Ik ben mijn kaartje kwijtgeraakt.** *ik ben mayn kaartyer kvaytkheraakt*

NOODREM	emergency brake
ALARM	alarm
AUTOMATISCHE DEUREN	automatic doors

TIME ➤ 220

Long-distance bus [Coach]
Reisbus

There are many bus tours (**excursies**) to the classic tourist sights, such as the bulb fields (**bollenvelden**), windmills (**molens**), cheese markets (**kaasmarkt**), traditional villages near the IJsselmeer ("IJssel Lake," formally the **Zuyderzee**), and reclaimed land (**polders**). The VVV offices provide information and reservations.

Where is the bus [coach] station?	**Waar is het busstation?** *vaar is het buhs-stashion*
When's the next bus [coach] to …?	**Wanneer is de volgende bus naar …?** *vannayr is der folkhernder buhs naar*
Where does it leave from?	**Waar vandaan vertrekt hij?** *vaar fandaan fertrehkt hay*
Where are the bus [coach] bays?	**Waar zijn de bushaltes?** *vaar zayn de buhs-halters*
Does the bus [coach] stop at …?	**Stopt de bus in …?** *stopt der buhs in*
How long does the trip [journey] take?	**Hoe lang duurt de reis?** *hoo lang duwrt der rays*

Bus/Streetcar [Tram] Bus/Tram

In buses and trams you use the national **strippenkaart** which you buy at newsstands, stations, and VVV offices before traveling. Always have at least two strips stamped: one for the trip and one for each zone you travel through. The stamp is valid for an hour and you can change bus or tram within that time. Amsterdam also has a *Circle Tram* for tourists.

Where can I get a bus/ streetcar [tram] to …?	**Waar kan ik op de bus/tram stappen naar …?** *vaar kan ik op der buhs/tram stappern naar*
What time is the bus to …?	**Hoe laat gaat de bus naar …?** *hoo laat khaat buhs … naar*

U heeft die bushalte daar nodig.	You need that stop over there.
U heeft bus nummer … nodig.	You need bus number …
U moet overstappen in …	You must change buses at …

BUSHALTE	bus stop
NIET ROKEN	no smoking
UITGANG/NOODUITGANG	exit/emergency exit

DIRECTIONS ➤ 94; TIME ➤ 220

Buying tickets Kaartjes kopen

Where can I buy tickets?	**Waar kan ik kaartjes kopen?** _vaar kan ik kaartyers koapern_
A ... ticket to the ..., please.	**Een ... (karte) naar ..., alstublieft.** _ayn ... (kaartyer) naar ... alstuwbleeft_
one-way [single]	**enkeltje** _engkerltyer_
round-trip [return]	**retourtje** _retoortyer_
A booklet of tickets, please.	**Een strippenkaart, alstublieft.** _ayn strippernkaart, alstuwbleeft_
How much is the fare to ...?	**Hoeveel is het naar ...?** _hoofayl is het naar_

Traveling Rondreizen

Is this the right bus / streetcar [tram] to ...?	**Is dit de juiste bus/tram voor ...?** _is dit der yoaister buhs/tram foar_
Could you tell me when to get off?	**Kunt u me waarschuwen wanneer ik moet uitstappen?** _kuhnt uw mer yaarskhuwvern vannayr ik moot oaitstappern_
Do I have to change buses?	**Moet ik overstappen?** _moot ik oaferstappern_
How many stops are there to ...?	**Hoeveel haltes is het naar ...?** _hoofayl halters is het naar_
Next stop, please!	**Volgende halte, alstublieft!** _folkhernder halter, alstuwbleeft_

LOKET	ticket office
KAARTJESAUTOMAAT	ticket vending machine

– Pardon. Is dit de juiste bus voor het stadhuis?
(Excuse me. Is this the right bus for the town hall?)
– Ja, nummer acht. (Yes, number 8.)
– Een enkeltje naar het stadhuis, alstublieft.
(One one-way ticket to the town hall, please.)
– Dat is twee euro's. (That's two euros.)
– Kunt u me waarschuwen wanneer ik moet uitstappen?
(Could you tell me when to get off?)
– Het is nog vier haltes. (It's four stops from here).

NUMBERS ➤ 216; DIRECTIONS ➤ 94

Subway Metro

The subway (**metro**), a feat of engineering in largely clay and marshy soil, is mostly found in the **Randstad**, the metropolitan region which runs along the west coast and includes the major cities, Amsterdam and Rotterdam.

You can use the **strippenkaart** (➤ 78) or the automatic ticket dispensers. The network closes just after midnight.

General Inquiries Algemene inlichtingen

Where's the nearest subway [metro] station?
> **Waar is het dichtstbijzijnde metrostation?**
> *vaar is het dikhtstbayzaynder metroastashion*

Where can I buy a ticket?
> **Waar kan ik een kaartje kopen?**
> *vaar kan ik ayn kaartyer koapern*

Could I have a map of the subway [metro], please?
> **Mag ik een kaart van de metro?**
> *makh ik ayn kaart fan der metroa*

Traveling Rondreizen

Which line should I take for ...?
> **Welke lijn moet ik nemen voor ...?**
> *velker layn moot ik naymern foar*

Is this the right train for ...?
> **Is dit de juiste trein voor ...?**
> *is dit der yoaister trayn foar*

Which stop is it for ...?
> **Welke halte is het voor ...?**
> *velker halter is het foar*

How many stops is it to ...?
> **Hoeveel haltes is het naar ...?**
> *hoofayl halters is het naar*

Is the next stop ...?
> **Is de volgende stop ...?**
> *is der folkhernder stop*

Where are we?
> **Waar zijn we?** *vaar zayn vay*

Where do I change for ...?
> **Waar stap ik over voor ...?**
> *vaar stap ik oafer foar*

What time is the last train to ...?
> **Hoe laat is de laatste trein naar ...?**
> *hoo laat is der laatster trayn naar*

NAAR ANDERE LIJNEN/ OVERSTAPPEN   to other lines/transfer

NUMBERS ➤ 216; BUYING TICKETS ➤ 74, 79

Ferry Veerboot

Ferry companies (**veerboot**) operating services from the UK to the Netherlands include the Stena Line (Harwich–Hook of Holland), P & O North Sea Ferries (Hull–Rotterdam) and Scandinavian Seaways (Newcastle–IJmuiden-Amsterdam). There are inland ferries to the Frisian Wadden Islands (**Waddeneilanden**), in Zeeland, across the "IJssel Lake" (**IJsselmeer**), and on many small rivers.

When is the … ferry to …?	**Wanneer gaat de … veerboot naar …?** *van_nayr_ khaat der _ayr_boat naar*
first/next/last	**eerste/volgende/laatste** *_ayr_ster/_folk_hernder/_laat_ster*
A round-trip [return] ticket for …	**Een retourtje voor …** *ayn re_toor_tyer foar*
one car and one trailer [caravan]	**één auto en één caravan** *ayn _ow_to en ayn _keh_rervern*
two adults and three children	**twee volwassenen en drie kinderen** *tvay fol_vas_sernern en dree _kin_derern*
I want to reserve a … cabin.	**Ik wil een … hut reserveren.** *ik vil ayn … huht ray_zer_vayrern*
single/double	**eenpersoons/tweepersoons** *_ayn_pehrsoans/_tvay_pehrsoans*

REDDINGSBOEI	life preserver [life belt]
REDDINGSBOOT	lifeboat
VERZAMELPLAATS	muster station
GEEN TOEGANG	no access

Boat trips Boottochten

There are boat trips on the canals (**rondvaart**) in Amsterdam and cruises on the Meuse in Rotterdam towards Europort, the world's biggest port.

Is there a …?	**Is er een …?** *is ehr ayn*
boat trip/river cruise	**boottocht/rondvaart** *_boat_tokht/_ront_faart*
What time does it leave?	**Hoe laat vertrekt hij?** *hoo laat fer_trehkt_ hay*
What time does it return?	**Hoe laat komt hij terug?** *hoo laat komt hay truhkh*
Where can we buy tickets?	**Waar kunnen we kaartjes kopen?** *vaar _kuhn_nern vay _kaart_kyers _koa_pern*

TIME ➤ 220; BUYING TICKETS ➤ 74, 79

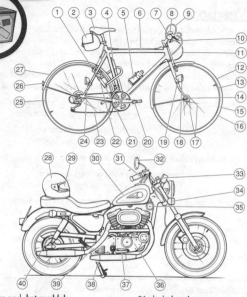

1 brake pad **het remblok**
2 bicycle bag **de fietstas**
3 saddle **het zadel**
4 pump **de pomp**
5 water bottle **de veldfles**
6 frame **het frame**
7 handlebars **het stuur**
8 bell **de bel**
9 brake cable **de remkabel**
10 gear shift [lever]
   de versnellingshandgreep
11 gear control cable **versnellingskabel**
12 inner tube **de binnenband**
13 front/back wheel **het voorwiel/**
   achterwiel
14 axle **de as**
15 tire [tyre] **de band**
16 wheel **het wiel**
17 spokes **de spaken**
18 bulb **de lamp**
19 headlamp **het voorlicht**
20 pedal **het pedaal**

21 lock **het slot**
22 generator [dynamo] **de dynamo**
23 chain **de ketting**
24 rear light **het achterlicht**
25 rim **de velg**
26 reflectors **de reflectoren**
27 fender [mudguard] **het spatbord**
28 helmet **de helm**
29 visor **het vizier**
30 fuel tank **de brandstoftank**
31 clutch lever **het koppelingspedaal**
32 mirror **de spiegel**
33 ignition switch **de contactschakelaar**
34 turn signal [indicator]
   de richtingaanwijzer
35 horn **de claxon**
36 engine **de motor**
37 gear shift [lever]
   de versnellingshandgreep
38 kick stand [main stand] **de standaard**
39 exhaust pipe **de uitlaatpijp**
40 chain guard **de kettingbeschermer**

REPAIRS ➤ 89

Bicycle/Motorbike
Fiets/Motorfiets

Bicycles (**fiets**) can be hired from most train stations (valid rail ticket and deposit required). Cycling is part of everyday life in the Netherlands. You can take your bicycle on a train or follow the cycle tracks through town and country.

I'd like to rent a …	**Ik wil graag een … huren.**
	ik vil khraakh ayn … huwren
bicycle/moped	**fiets/brommer**
	feets/brommer
motorbike	**motorfiets** *moaterfeets*
How much does it cost per day/week?	**Hoeveel kost het per dag/week?**
	hoofayl kost het pehr daakh/vayk
Do you require a deposit?	**Moet ik vooruitbetalen?**
	moot ik foaroaitbertaalern
The brakes don't work.	**De remmen doen het niet.**
	der remmern doon het neet
There are no lights.	**Er zijn geen lampen.**
	ehr zayn khayn lampern
The front/rear tire [tyre] has a flat [puncture].	**Ik heb een platte voorband/achterband.**
	ik hep ayn platter foarband/akhterbant

Hitchhiking Liften

Hitchhiking is quite common, but carries the usual risks.

Where are you heading?	**Waar gaat u naar toe?**
	vaar khaat uw naar too
I'm heading for …	**Ik ga naar …** *ik khaa naar*
Is that on the way to …?	**Is dat op weg naar …?**
	is dat op vehkh naar
Could you drop me off …?	**Kunt u me … afzetten?**
	kuhnt uw mer … afzettern
at the … exit	**bij de uitgang voor …**
	bay der oaitkhang foar
Thanks for giving me a lift.	**Bedankt voor de lift.**
	berdankt foar der lift

DIRECTIONS ➤ 94; NUMBERS ➤ 216

Taxi/Cab Taxi

Taxis are not usually hailed in the street. You can call for one or go to a taxi stand (**taxistandplaats**). Use the tip to round up the fare. The **treintaxi** is economical when you arrive by train in a town, but buy a **treintaxi** ticket on departure and be prepared to wait until the driver has enough passengers. There are water taxis on the canals in Amsterdam.

Where can I get a taxi?	**Waar kan ik een taxi krijgen?** *vaar kan ik ayn taksee kraykhern*
Do you have the number for a taxi?	**Heeft u het nummer voor een taxi?** *hayft uw het nuhmer foar ayn taksee*
I'd like a taxi …	**Ik wil … graag een taxi.** *ik vil … khraakh ayn taksee*
now/in an hour	**nu/over een uur** *nuw/oafer ayn uwr*
for tomorrow at 9:00	**voor morgen om 9 uur** *foar morkhern om naykher uwr*
The address is …	**Het adres is …** *het adres is*
I'm going to …	**Ik ga naar …** *ik khaa naar*

⊙ TE HUUR	for hire ⊕

Can you take me to (the) …	**Kunt u me naar … rijden?** *kuhnt uw mer naar … raydern*
airport	**de luchthaven/het vliegveld** *der luhkhthaafern/het fleeghfelt*
train station	**het station** *het stashion*
this address	**dit adres** *dit adres*
How much will it cost?	**Hoeveel gaat het kosten?** *hoofayl khaat het kostern*
Keep the change.	**Houdt u het wisselgeld maar.** *howt uw het visserlkhelt maar*

– Kunt u me naar het station rijden?
(Please take me to the station.)
– *Jazeker.* (Certainly.)
– Hoeveel gaat het kosten? (How much will it cost?)
– *Negen euro's vijftig. … We zijn er.*
(Nine euros fifty. … Here we are.)
– Dank u. Houdt u het wisselgeld maar.
(Thank you. Keep the change.)

NUMBERS ➤ 216; DIRECTIONS ➤ 94

Car/Automobile Auto

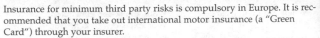

To drive a car (**autorijden**) in the Netherlands it is essential to have a valid national or international driver's license (**rijbewijs**), car registration papers (**kentekenbewijs**), a nationality plate/sticker on the back of the car and a red warning triangle for breakdowns. The minimum driving age is 18.

Insurance for minimum third party risks is compulsory in Europe. It is recommended that you take out international motor insurance (a "Green Card") through your insurer.

Driving is on the right. Traffic from the right has priority, as have streetcars [trams] and buses leaving their stops.

Be careful of the numerous cyclists who do not always watch out themselves or have lights at night. Their large numbers make them rule the road in many cases.

Your driver's license can be taken away or you may incur a heavy fine for more than 0.5 milliliters of alcohol in your bloodstream (two beers or the equivalent).

Seat-belts (**veiligheidsgordels**) are compulsory in the front and, if fitted, in the back.

Conversion Chart

km	1	10	20	30	40	50	60	70	80	90	100	110	120	130
miles	0.62	6	12	19	25	31	37	44	50	56	62	68	74	81

Road network

National speed limit: 120 kilometers per hour (approximately 75 mph); 120 or 100 kmph (75 or 60 mph) on the (**auto**)**snelweg**, the Dutch highway [motorway]. In built-up areas the speed limit is 50 kmph (30 mph) and outside built-up areas on main roads 80 kmph (50 mph).

The speed limit for cars towing a trailer [caravan] is 70 kmph (44 mph) in built-up areas and 80 kmph (50 mph) outside built-up areas on main roads.

There are virtually no toll roads.

Car rental Autoverhuur

You will need a valid national or international driver's license, held for at least 12 months, a passport, and credit card. CDW (Collision Damage Waiver) insurance is reasonably priced. There are rental offices (**autoverhuurbedrijven**) at Schiphol Airport and in the center of Amsterdam; or you might treat yourself to a chauffeur-driven car.

Where can I rent a car?	**Waar kan ik een auto huren?** *vaar kan ik ayn <u>ow</u>to <u>huw</u>rern*
I'd like to rent a/an …	**Ik wil graag een …** *ik vil khraakh ayn*
2-/4-door car	**tweedeurs/vierdeurs auto** *t<u>vay</u>durs/<u>veer</u>durs <u>ow</u>to*
automatic	**auto met automatische versnelling** *<u>ow</u>to met ow<u>toomaa</u>teeser fer<u>snel</u>ling*
car with 4-wheel drive	**auto met vierwielaandrijving** *<u>ow</u>to met feer<u>veelaandray</u>fing*
car with air conditioning	**auto met airconditioning** *<u>ow</u>to met "airconditioning"*
I'd like it for a day/week.	**Ik wil hem graag voor een dag/week.** *ik vil hem khraakh foar ayn daakh/vayk*
How much does it cost per day/week?	**Hoeveel kost het per dag/week?** *hoo<u>fayl</u> kost het pehr daagh/vayk*
Is insurance included?	**Is de verzekering inbegrepen?** *is der fer<u>zay</u>kering inber<u>khray</u>pern*
Are there special weekend rates?	**Zijn er speciale weekendtarieven?** *zayn ehr spay<u>shiaa</u>ler "weekend" ta<u>ree</u>evern*
Can I return the car at …?	**Kan ik de auto weer inleveren in …?** *kan ik der <u>ow</u>to vayr in<u>lay</u>ferern in*
What sort of fuel does it take?	**Wat voor brandstof gebruikt hij?** *vat foar <u>brant</u>stof kher<u>broa</u>ikt hay*
Where are the high [full]/low [dipped] beams?	**Waar zijn de grote lichten/dimlichten?** *vaar zayn der <u>khroa</u>ter <u>likh</u>tern/ <u>dim</u>likhtern*
I would like full insurance.	**Ik wil graag een volledige verzekering.** *ik vil khraakh ayn fol<u>lay</u>dikher fer<u>zay</u>kering*

Gas [Petrol] station Benzinestation

Where's the next gas [petrol] station, please?	**Waar is het volgende benzinestation?** *vaar is het folkhernder benzeenerstashion*
Is it self-service?	**Is het zelfbediening?** *is het zelfberdeenerng*
Fill it up, please.	**Volgooien, alstublieft.** *folkhoiyern, alstuwbleeft*
… liters, please.	**… liter, alstublieft.** *liter, alstuwbleeft*
premium [super]/regular	**super/normaal** *suwper/normaal*
unleaded/diesel	**loodvrij/diesel** *loatfray/deesel*
I'm at pump number …	**Ik sta bij pomp nummer …** *ik staa bay pomp nuhmer*
Where is the air pump/water?	**Waar is de luchtpomp/het water?** *vaar is der luhkhtpomp/het vaater*

PRIJS PER LITER	price per liter
PARKEREN	parking

Parking Parkeren

Parking in Amsterdam is very restricted and extremely expensive. Visitors are encouraged to park in the suburbs and travel in by public transportation. Parking meters and booting [clamping] are widely used.

Is there a parking lot [car park] nearby?	**Is er een parkeerplaats in de buurt?** *is ehr ayn parkayrplaats in der buwrt*
What's the charge per hour/day?	**Hoeveel kost het per uur/dag?** *hoofayl kost het pehr uwr/daakh*
Do you have some change for the parking meter?	**Heeft u wisselgeld voor de parkeermeter?** *hayft uw visserlkhelt foar der parkayrmayter*
My car has been booted [clamped]. Who do I call?	**Er is een wielklem op mijn auto gezet. Wie moet ik bellen?** *ehr is ayn veelklem op mayn owto kherzet. vee moot ik bellern*

NUMBERS ➤ 216; DIRECTIONS ➤ 94

Breakdown Pech

Where is the nearest garage?	**Waar is de dichtstbijzijnde garage?** *vaar is der dikhtstbayzaynder kharaazher*
My car broke down.	**Ik heb pech.** *ik hep pekh*
Can you send a mechanic/tow [breakdown] truck?	**Kunt u een monteur/takelwagen sturen?** *kuhnt uw ayn montur/taakerlvaagern stuwrern*
I'm a member of ...	**Ik ben lid van ...** *ik ben lit fan*
My registration number is ...	**Mijn kenteken is ...** *mayn kentaykern is*
The car is ...	**De auto staat ...** *der owto staat*
on the highway [motorway]	**op de snelweg** *op der snelvehkh*
2 km from ...	**twee kilometer van ...** *tvay keelomayter fan*
How long will you be?	**Hoe lang doet u erover?** *hoo lang doot uw ehroafer*

What is wrong? Wat is er aan de hand?

My car won't start.	**Mijn auto wil niet starten.** *mayn owto vil neet startern*
The battery is dead.	**De accu is leeg.** *der akkuw is laykh*
I've run out of gas [petrol].	**Ik heb geen benzine meer.** *ik hep khayn benzeener mayr*
I have a flat [puncture].	**Ik heb een platte band.** *ik hep ayn platter bant*
There is something wrong with ...	**Er is iets mis met ...** *ehr is eets mis met*
I've locked the keys in the car.	**Ik heb de sleutels in de auto gesloten.** *ik hep der sloaiterls in der owto khersloatern*

TELEPHONING ➤ 127; CAR PARTS ➤ 90–91

Repairs Reparaties

Do you do repairs?	**Doet u reparaties?** *doot uw rayparaatsees*
Can you repair it?	**Kunt u het repareren?** *kuhnt uw het rayparayrern*
Please make only essential repairs.	**Graag alleen essentiële reparaties.** *khraakh allayn essentsiayler rayparaatsees*
Can I wait for it?	**Kan ik erop wachten?** *kan ik ehrop vakhtern*
Can you repair it today?	**Kunt u het vandaag nog repareren?** *kuhnt uw het fandaakh nokh rayparayrern*
When will it be ready?	**Wanneer is het klaar?** *vannayr is het klaar*
How much will it cost?	**Hoeveel gaat het kosten?** *hoofayl khaat het kostern*
That's outrageous!	**Dat is belachelijk!** *dat is berlakhlayk*
Can I have a receipt for my insurance?	**Mag ik een kwitantie voor mijn verzekering?** *makh ik ayn kvitantsee foar mayn ferzaykering*

De ... doet het niet.	The ... isn't working.
Ik heb de nodige onderdelen niet.	I don't have the necessary parts.
Ik zal de onderdelen moeten bestellen.	I'll have to order the parts.
Ik kan het alleen tijdelijk repareren.	I can only repair it temporarily.
Uw auto kan niet meer gerepareerd worden.	Your car is beyond repair.
Het kan niet gerepareerd worden.	It can't be repaired.
Het zal ... klaar zijn.	It will be ready ...
later vandaag	later today
morgen	tomorrow
over ... dagen	in ... days

DAYS OF THE WEEK ➤ 218; NUMBERS ➤ 216

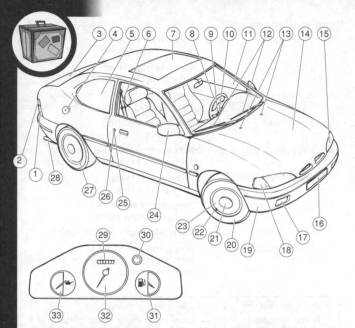

1 taillights [back lights] **de achterlichten**
2 brakelights **de remlichten**
3 trunk [boot] **de achterbak**
4 gas tank door [petrol cap]
   de benzinedop
5 window **het autoraampje**
6 seat-belt **de veiligheidsriem**
7 sunroof **het zonnedak**
8 steering wheel **het stuur**
9 ignition **de ontsteking**
10 ignition key **het contactsleuteltje**
11 windshield [windscreen] **de voorruit**
12 windshield [windscreen] wipers
    de ruitewissers
13 windshield [windscreen] washer
    de ruitesproeier
14 hood [bonnet] **de motorkap**
15 headlights **de koplampen**

16 license [number] plate **het nummerbord**
17 fog lights **de mistlamp**
18 turn signals [indicators]
    de richtingaanwijzers
19 bumper **de bumper**
20 tires [tyres] **de banden**
21 hubcap **de wieldop**
22 valve **het ventiel**
23 wheels **de wielen**
24 outside [wing] mirror **de buitenspiegel**
25 automatic locks
    de centrale deurvergrendeling
26 lock **het slot**
27 wheel rim **de velg**
28 exhaust pipe **de uitlaatpijp**
29 odometer [milometer] **de kilometerteller**
30 warning light **het waarschuwingslampje**

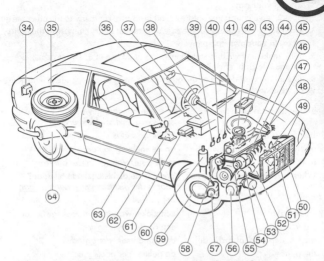

31 fuel gauge **de brandstofmeter**
32 speedometer **de snelheidsmeter**
33 oil gauge **het oliepeil**
34 backup [reversing] lights
   de achteruitrijlichten
35 spare tire [wheel] **het reservewiel**
36 choke **de choke**
37 heater **de verwarming**
38 steering column **de stuurkolom**
39 accelerator **het gaspedaal**
40 pedal **het pedaal**
41 clutch **de koppeling**
42 carburetor **de carburateur**
43 battery **de accu**
44 air filter **de luchtfilter**
45 camshaft **de nokkenas**
46 alternator **de wisselstroomdynamo**
47 distributor **de verdeler**
48 points **de bougies**

49 radiator hose (top/bottom)
   de radiatorslang (boven/onder)
50 radiator **de radiator**
51 fan **de ventilator**
52 engine **de motor**
53 oil filter **de oliefilter**
54 starter motor **de startmotor**
55 fan belt **de ventilatorriem**
56 horn **de claxon**
57 brake pads **de remblokken**
58 transmission [gearbox]
   de versnellingsbak
59 brakes **de remmen**
60 shock absorbers **de schokbrekers**
61 fuses **de zekeringen**
62 gear shift [lever] **de pook**
63 emergency brake **de handrem**
64 muffler [silencer] **de knalpot**

Accidents Ongelukken

In the event of an accident (**ongeluk**):

1. put your red warning triangle about 100 meters behind your car;
2. give your name, address, and insurance company to the other party;
3. if considered necessary (in the case of personal injury), report to the police;
4. report to your own company;
5. don't make any written statement without advice of a lawyer or automobile club official;
6. note all relevant details of the other party, and any independent witnesses of the accident.

There has been an accident.	**Er is een ongeluk geweest.** *ehr is ayn onkherluhk khervayst*
It's …	**Het is …** *het is*
on the highway [motorway]	**op de snelweg** *op der snelvehkh*
near …	**in de buurt van …** *in der burt fan*
Where's the nearest telephone?	**Waar is de dichtstbijzijnde telefoon?** *vaar is der dikhtstbayzaynder telerfoan*
Call …	**Bel …** *bel*
an ambulance	**een ziekenwagen** *ayn zeekernvaagern*
a doctor	**een dokter** *ayn dokter*
the fire department [brigade]	**de brandweer** *der brandvayr*
the police	**de politie** *der poaleetsee*
Can you help me please?	**Kunt u me alstublieft helpen?** *kuhnt uw mer alstuwbleeft helpern*

Injuries Verwondingen

There are people injured.	**Er zijn mensen gewond.** *er zayn mensern khervont*
No one is hurt.	**Niemand is gewond.** *neemant is khervont*
He's seriously injured.	**Hij is ernstig gewond.** *hay is ehrnstikh khervont*
She's unconscious.	**Ze is bewusteloos.** *zer is berusterterloas*
He can't breathe.	**Hij kan niet ademhalen.** *hay kan neet aadermhaalern*
He can't move.	**Hij kan zich niet bewegen.** *hay kan zikh neet bervaykhern*
Don't move him.	**Verplaats hem niet.** *verplaats hem neet*

INJURIES/DOCTOR ➤ 162; DIRECTIONS ➤ 94

Legal matters Juridische kwesties

What's your insurance company?	**Wat is uw verzekerings-maatschappij?** *vat is uw ferzaykeringsmaatskappay*
What's your name and address?	**Wat is uw naam en adres?** *vat is uwer naam en adres*
The car ran into me.	**De auto reed op me in.** *der owto rayt op mer in*
The car was going too fast.	**De auto reed te snel.** *der owto rayt ter snel*
The car was driving too close.	**De auto reed te dichtbij.** *der owto rayt ter dikhtbay*
I had the right of way.	**Ik had voorrang.** *ik hat foarrang*
I was (only) driving ... kmph.	**Ik reed (maar) ... kilometer per uur.** *ik rayt (maar) ... keelomayter pehr uwr*
I'd like an interpreter.	**Ik wil graag een tolk.** *ik vil khraag ayn tolk*
I didn't see the sign.	**Ik zag het verkeersbord niet.** *ik zakh het terkayrsbort neet*
This person saw it happen.	**Deze persoon heeft het gezien.** *dayze persoan hayft het kherzeen*
The registration number was ...	**Het kenteken was ...** *het kentaykern vas*

Mag ik uw ... zien, alstublieft?	Can I see your ..., please?
rijbewijs	driver's license
verzekeringskaart	insurance card
het kentekenbewijs	vehicle registration
Hoe laat is het gebeurd?	What time did it happen?
Waar is het gebeurd?	Where did it happen?
Was er nog iemand anders bij betrokken?	Was anyone else involved?
Zijn er getuigen?	Are there any witnesses?
U reed te snel.	You were speeding.
Uw lichten doen het niet.	Your lights aren't working.
U zult een boete moeten betalen.	You'll have to pay a fine (on the spot).
U moet een verklaring afleggen op het politiebureau.	You have to make a statement at the station.

Asking directions De weg vragen

Excuse me, please.	**Pardon.** *par<u>don</u>*
How do I get to …?	**Hoe kom ik in …?** *hoo kom ik in*
Where is …?	**Waar is …?** *vaar is*
Can you show me on the map where I am?	**Kunt u me op de kaart laten zien waar ik ben?** *kuhnt uw mer op der kaart <u>laa</u>tern zeen vaar ik ben*
I've lost my way.	**Ik ben de weg kwijt.** *ik ben der vehkh kvayt*
Can you repeat that, please?	**Kunt u dat herhalen?** *kuhnt uw dat hayr<u>haa</u>lern*
More slowly, please.	**Iets langzamer, alstublieft.** *eets <u>lang</u>zaamer, alstuw<u>bleeft</u>*
Thanks for your help.	**Bedankt voor uw hulp.** *ber<u>dankt</u> foar uw huhlp*

Traveling by car Rondreizen met de auto

Is this the right road to …?	**Is dit de juiste weg voor …?** *is dit der <u>yoais</u>ter vehgh foar*
Is it far?	**Is het ver?** *is het fehr*
How far is it to … from here?	**Hoe ver is het hiervandaan naar …?** *hoo fehr is het heerfan<u>daan</u> naar*
Where does this road lead?	**Waar gaat deze weg naar toe?** *vaar khaat <u>day</u>zer vehgh naar too*
How do I get onto the highway [motorway]?	**Hoe kom ik op de snelweg?** *hoo kom ik op der <u>snel</u>vehkh*
What's the next town called?	**Hoe heet de volgende plaats?** *hoo hayt der <u>folg</u>hernder plaats*
How long does it take by car?	**Hoe lang duurt het met de auto?** *hoo lang durt het met der <u>ow</u>to*

– Pardon. Hoe kom ik op het station?
(Excuse me, please. How do I get to the train station?)
– *Neem de derde straat rechts en dan is het recht voor u uit.*
(Take the third right and it's straight ahead.)
– De derde straat rechts. Is het ver?
(Third right. Is it far?)
– *Het is tien minuten lopen. (It's ten minutes on foot.)*
– Bedankt voor uw hulp. (Thanks for your help.)
– *Graag gedaan. (You're welcome.)*

Location Lokatie

Het is ...	It's ...
rechtdoor	straight ahead
aan de linkerkant	on the left
aan de rechterkant	on the right
aan het eind van de straat	at the end of the street
op de hoek	on the corner
om de hoek	around the corner
in de richting van ...	in the direction of ...
tegenover .../achter ...	opposite .../behind ...
naast .../na ...	next to .../after ...
Ga door de ...	Go down the ...
zijstraat/hoofdstraat	side street/main street
Steek de/het ... over	Cross the ...
het plein/de brug	square/bridge
Neem de derde straat rechts.	Take the third right.
Sla links af ...	Turn left ...
na de eerste stoplichten	after the first traffic lights
bij het tweede kruispunt	at the second intersection [crossroad]

By car Met de auto

Het is ... van hier.	It's ... of here.
ten noorden/ten zuiden	north/south
ten oosten/ten westen	east/west
Neem de weg voor ...	Take the road for ...
U bent op de verkeerde weg.	You're on the wrong road.
U moet terug naar ...	You'll have to go back to ...
Volg de borden voor ...	Follow the signs for ...

How far? Hoe ver?

Het is ...	It's ...
dichtbij/ver weg	close/a long way
vijf minuten lopen	5 minutes on foot
tien minuten met de auto	10 minutes by car
ongeveer honderd meter verder	about 100 meters down the road
ongeveer tien kilometer van hier	about 10 kilometers away

TIME ➤ 220; NUMBERS ➤ 216

Road signs Verkeersborden

WEGOMLEGGING	detour [diversion]
EENRICHTINGSSTRAAT	one-way street
WEG GESLOTEN	road closed
SCHOOLKINDEREN	school children crossing
STOPPEN	stop
NIET INHALEN	no passing [overtaking]
LANGZAAM RIJDEN	drive slowly
KOPLAMPEN GEBRUIKEN	use headlights

Town plans Stadsplattegrond

bank	bank
bioscoop	movie theater [cinema]
bushalte	bus stop
busroute	bus route
hoogstraat	main [high] street
informatiebureau	information office
kerk	church
luchthaven/vliegveld	airport
metrostation	subway [metro] station
park	park
parkeerplaats	parking lot [car park]
politiebureau	police station
postkantoor	post office
school	school
sportterrein	playing field [sports ground]
stadion	stadium
station	train station
taxistandplaats	taxi stand [rank]
theater	theater
u bevindt zich hier	you are here
verkeersvrij gebied	pedestrian zone [precinct]
voetgangersoversteekplaats	pedestrian crossing
warenhuis	department store
winkelstraat	shopping street
ziekenhuis	hospital

Sightseeing

The local tourist offices have signs with the blue letters "VVV" on a white background. They also provide lists of places to stay, and sell road and cycling maps. Information is also available at **Grens Wisselkantoren** (**GWK**: money exchange bureaus at train stations), and at border crossings.

Tourist information office VVV

Where's the tourist information office?	**Waar is de VVV?** *vaar is der fay fay fay*
What are the main points of interest?	**Wat zijn de belangrijkste bezionswaardigheden?** *vat zayn der berlangraykster berzeensvaardikhhaydern*
We're here for …	**We zijn hier voor …** *vay zayn heer foar*
a few hours	**een paar uur** *ayn paar uwr*
a day	**een dag** *ayn daakh*
a week	**een week** *ayn vayk*
Can you recommend …?	**Kunt u … aanbevelen?** *kuhnt uw … <u>aan</u>berfaylern*
a sightseeing tour	**een rondrit** *ayn <u>ron</u>trit*
an excursion	**een excursie** *ayn eks<u>kuhr</u>see*
a boat trip	**een rondvaart** *ayn <u>ron</u>tfaart*
Do you have any information on …?	**Heeft u ook informatie over …?** *hayft uw oak infor<u>maat</u>see <u>oa</u>fer*
Are there any trips to …?	**Zijn er ook tochtjes naar …?** *zayn ehr oak <u>tokh</u>tyers naar*

Excursions Excursies

How much does the tour cost?	**Hoeveel kost de rondrit?** *hoofayl kost der rontrit*
Is lunch included?	**Is de lunch inbegrepen?** *is der luhnsh inberkhraypern*
Where do we leave from?	**Waar vandaan vertrekken we?** *vaar fandaan fertrehkkern vay*
What time does the tour start?	**Hoe laat begint de rondrit?** *hoo laat berkhint der rontrit*
What time do we get back?	**Hoe laat komen we terug?** *hoo laat koamern vay truhkh*
Do we have free time in …?	**Hebben we tijd vrij in …?** *hepben vay tayt fray in*
Is there an English-speaking guide?	**Is er een Engelstalige gids?** *is ehr ayn engilstaalikher khits*

On tour Op rondreis

Are we going to see …?	**Zien we ook …?** *zeen vay oak*
We'd like to have a look at the …	**We willen graag de/het … bekijken.** *vay villern khraakh der/het … berkaykern*
Can we stop here …?	**Kunnen we hier stoppen …?** *kuhnen vay heer stoppern*
to take photographs	**om foto's te nemen** *om foatoas ter naymern*
to buy souvenirs	**om souvenirs te kopen** *om sooverneers ter koapern*
to use the bathrooms [toilets]	**om het toilet te gebruiken** *om het toilet ter kherbroaikern*
Would you take a photo of us, please?	**Zou u een foto van ons willen nemen?** *zoa uw ayn foatoa fan ons villern naymern*
How long do we have here/in …?	**Hoe lang hebben we hier/in …?** *hoo lang hepbern vay heer/in*
Wait! … isn't back yet.	**Wacht even! … is nog niet terug.** *vakht ayfern! … is nokh neet truhkh*

Sights Bezienswaardigheden

Maps can be bought at VVV offices, gas stations, and bookstores. (A city map is **plattegrond**; a road map is **wegenkaart**.)

Where is the …?	**Waar is …?** *vaar is*
art gallery	**de kunstgalerie** *der kuhnstkhaaleree*
battle site	**het slagveld** *het slakhfelt*
botanical garden	**de botanische tuin** *der boat__aan__isher toain*
castle	**het kasteel** *het kast__ayl__*
cathedral	**de kathedraal** *der katter__draal__*
cemetery	**de begraafplaats** *der berkhr__aaf__plaats*
church	**de kerk** *der kerk*
downtown area	**het stadscentrum** *het stats__en__trerm*
fountain	**de fontein** *der font__ayn__*
historic site	**de historische plaats** *der hist__oa__risher plaats*
~~market~~	~~**de markt**~~ ~~*der markt*~~
monastery	**het klooster** *het kl__oa__ster*
museum	**het museum** *het muhz__ay__erm*
old town	**het oude stadsgedeelte** *het __owd__er statskherd__ay__lter*
opera house	**het operagebouw** *het __oa__perakherbow*
palace	**het paleis** *het pal__ays__*
park	**het park** *het park*
parliament building	**het parlementsgebouw** *het parler__ments__kherbow*
ruins	**de ruïnes** *der ruh__wi__ners*
shopping area	**het winkelcentrum** *het vinkerls__en__trerm*
statue	**het standbeeld** *het __stant__baylt*
theater	**het theater** *het tay__aa__ter*
tower	**de toren** *der __toa__rern*
town hall	**het stadhuis** *het stath__ois__*
viewpoint	**het uitkijkpunt** *het __oait__kaykpuhnt*
war memorial	**het gedenkteken** *het kherd__enk__taykern*
Can you show me on the map?	**Kunt u dat op de kaart laten zien?** *kuhnt uw dat op der kaart __laat__ern zeen*

Admission Entree

Museums are often closed on Mondays and major holidays.

Is the ... open to the public?	**Is de/het ... open voor het publiek?** *is der/het ... <u>oa</u>pern foar het puh<u>bleek</u>*
What are the opening hours?	**Wat zijn de openingstijden?** *vat zayn der <u>oa</u>perningstaydern*
Is ... open on Sundays?	**Is ... op zondag geopend?** *is ... op <u>zon</u>dakh kher<u>oa</u>pernt*
When's the next guided tour?	**Wanneer is de volgende rondleiding?** *van<u>nayr</u> is der <u>folk</u>hernder <u>ront</u>layding*
Do you have a guide book (in English)?	**Heeft u een gids (in het Engels)?** *hayft uw ayn khits (in het <u>engils</u>)*
Can I take photos?	**Mag ik foto's nemen?** *makh ik <u>foa</u>toas <u>nay</u>mern*
Is there access for the disabled?	**Is er toegang voor gehandicapten?** *is ehr <u>too</u>khang foar kher<u>handi</u>kaptern*

Tickets Kaartjes

How much is the entrance fee?	**Hoeveel kost de entree?** *<u>hoo</u>fayl <u>kos</u>tern de en<u>tray</u>*
Are there any discounts for ...?	**Zijn er ook kortingen voor ...?** *zayn ehr oak <u>kor</u>ting for*
children	**kinderen** <u>kin</u>derern
handicapped	**gehandicapten** ghe<u>handi</u>captern
groups	**groepen** <u>ghroo</u>pern
senior citizens	**zestig-plussers** <u>ses</u>tigh pluhssers
students	**studenten** stuw<u>den</u>tern
... tickets, please.	**... kaartjes, alstublieft.** *... <u>kaar</u>tyers alstuw<u>bleeft</u>*
Two adults and three children, please.	**Twee volwassenen en drie kinderen, alstublieft.** tway fol<u>va</u>sernern en free <u>kin</u>derern
I've lost my ticket.	**Ik ben mijn kaartje kwijt.** *ik ben mayn <u>kaar</u>tyer kwayt*

– Vijf kaartjes, alstublieft. Zijn er ook kortingen?
(Five tickets, please. Are there any discounts?)

– Ja. Voor kinderen is het vier euro's vijftig en voor zestig-plussers zes euro's.
(Yes. Children are four euros and fifty cents and senior citizens are six euros.)

– Twee volwassenen en drie kinderen, alstublieft.
(Two adults and three children, please.)

– Dat is negenentwintig euro's vijftig, alstublieft.
(That's twenty-nine euros fifty, please.)

TOEGANG VRIJ	admission free
GESLOTEN	closed
MUSEUMWINKEL	museum shop
LAATSTE TOEGANG OM 17.00 UUR	latest entry at 5 p.m.
VOLGENDE RONDLEIDING OM ...	next tour at ...
GEEN TOEGANG	no entry
NIET FLITSEN	no flash photography
NIET FOTOGRAFEREN	no photography
GEOPEND	open
OPENINGSTIJDEN	visiting hours

Impressions Indrukken

It's ...	**Het is ...** *het is*
amazing	**verbazingwekkend** *ferbaazingvekkernt*
beautiful	**prachtig** *prakhtikh*
boring	**saai** *saay*
breathtaking	**adembenemend** *aadermbernaymernt*
incredible	**ongelooflijk** *onkherlooflerk*
interesting	**interessant** *interrersant*
magnificent	**magnifiek** *manyerfeek*
romantic	**romantisch** *roamantees*
stunning	**verbluffend** *ferbluhffernt*
superb	**schitterend** *skhitterernt*
ugly	**lelijk** *laylerk*
It's a good value.	**Het is waar voor je geld.** *het is vaar foar yer khelt*
I (don't) like it.	**Ik vind het (niet) mooi.** *ik fint het (neet) moy*
It's a rip-off.	**Het is afzetterij.** *het is afzetteray*

101

altaar altar(piece)
ambachten crafts
apsis apse
badhuis baths
baksteen brick
balk beam
beeldhouwwerk sculpture
begonnen in ... started in ...
bibliotheek library
binnenplaats courtyard
crypte crypt
dak roof
detail detail
deur door
deurpost doorway
doek canvas
doopvont font
door ... by ... (*person*)
edelsteen gemstone
eeuw century
email enamel
ets etching
expositie display
foyer foyer
fresco fresco
fries frieze
gargouille gargoyle
gebladerte foliage
geboren in ... born in ...
gebouw building
gebouwd in ... built in ...
geëxposeerd stuk exhibit
geometrisch aangelegde tuin
  formal garden
geschilderd door ... painted
  by ...

geschonken door ... donated
  by ...
gestorven in ... died in ...
gevel gable
gewelf vault
glas-in-lood raam stained-glass
  window
goud(en) gold(en)
gracht moat
graf grave
grafsteen headstone
gravure engraving
half in vakwerk half-timbered
heerschappij reign
hek gate
herbouwd in ... rebuilt in ...
hersteld in ... restored in ...
hoeksteen cornerstone
hoogte height
hout wood
houtskool charcoal
houtsnijwerk carving
ijzerwerk ironwork
in bruikleen on loan
in opdracht van ...
  commissioned by ...
in stijl van ... in the style of ...
kanteel battlement
keizer emperor
keizerin empress
kerkhof churchyard
klei clay
klok clock
koning king
koningin queen
koor choir (stall)

kroon crown
kunstwerken works of art
lambrizering panelling
landschap landscape
landschapschilderij landscape
  (*painting*)
leefde lived
lezing lecture
lijstwerk molding
marmer marble
meester master
meesterwerk masterpiece
meubilair furniture
model model
munt coin
muur wall
muurschildering mural
nis alcove
olieschilderijen oils
ontdekt in ... discovered in ...
ontwerp design
ontworpen door designed
  by ...
opgericht in ... erected in .../
  founded in ...
ophaalbrug drawbridge
orgel organ
overhangend overhanging
paneel panel
pilaar pillar
plafond ceiling
podium stage
praalgraf tomb
preekstoel pulpit
raam window
schaal één op honderd scale
  1:100
schaduw shadow
schets sketch
schilder painter

schilderij
  painting/picture
schip nave
schone kunsten fine
  arts
school van school of ...
sieraden jewelry
staatsvertrek stateroom
steen stone
steunbeer buttress
stilleven still life
tableau tableau
tekening drawing
tentoonstelling exhibition
terracotta terra cotta
tijdelijk geëxposeerd stuk
  temporary exhibit
tombe tomb
toren tower
torenspits spire
torentje turret
trap stairs
trappenhuis staircase
uitstalkast display cabinet
verguld gilded
vernietigd door destroyed by
vertrekken (koninklijke) apartments (royal)
visgraat herringbone
vleugel wing (*building*)
voetstuk pediment
voltooid in ... completed in ...
wandtapijt tapestry
wapen weapon
wapenzaal armory
wassen beeld waxwork
waterverf schilderij watercolor
zeetafereel seascape
zilver silver
zilverwerk silverware

What's that building?	**Wat is dat gebouw?** *vat is dat kher<u>bow</u>*
When was it built?	**Wanneer is het gebouwd?** *van<u>nayr</u> is het kher<u>bowt</u>*
Who was the artist/architect?	**Wie was de kunstenaar/architect?** *vee vas der <u>kuhn</u>stenaar/arshee<u>tekt</u>*
What style/period is that?	**Welke stijl/periode is dat?** *velker stayl/peryoder is dat*

Romance   11th–12th century

Churches in the north were modeled on contemporary architecture in the Rhineland, especially blind arcading and towers (St. Servatius and St. Mary's, Maastricht; St. Peter's and St. Mary's, Utrecht).

Gothic   12th–end 16th century

A famous example is the Cathedral at Utrecht. The Gothic style, with its characteristic simplicity, was spread by the master builders of Brabant (St. John's, 's Hertogenbosch; St. Bavo, Haarlem; Grote Kerk, Dordrecht).

Renaissance   16th–17th century

The 17th century is known as the Golden Age: art, science, trade, colonization, and wealth all flourished. Italian architects introduced new ideas. Famous examples are Hendrik de Keyser's Zuyderkerk (Amsterdam), the Delft Town Hall, Jacob van Campen's Mauritshuis (the Hague), the Amsterdam Town Hall, and the Nieuwe Kerk (Haarlem).

Classicism   mid 18th–mid 19th century

The influence of Louis XIV style (for example the engravings of architect Daniel Marot) is characteristic. Houses were built in a more decorative style. Famous for Neo-Classicism is the Town Hall in Weesp.

Gothic Revival   19th century

English-inspired country houses and churches are characteristic. The Rijksmuseum in Amsterdam, by the architect Cuypers, is from this era.

Art nouveau   1880's–1920's

Renewal was introduced through the De Stijl group. Typical for this period is Rietveld, the house in Prins Hendriklaan, Utrecht, built in 1924.

Modern architecture

The post-war reconstruction of Rotterdam city center shows some exciting examples of new Dutch architecture.

History Geschiedenis

Early history   51 B.C.

Julius Caesar ruled the Celts and Germanic people in the
land south of the Rhine. The Frisians and Saxons north of the
Rhine were converted to Christianity by the Franks (King
Charlemagne, crowned 800).

Middle Ages   500–1568

Trade flourished and the bourgeoisie was created. The Low Countries fell
into the hands of the Duke of Burgundy (15th century), but in 1504 were
conquered by the Spanish Hapsburgs. William the Silent, Prince of Orange,
led a rebellion against the Catholic Philip II of Spain in 1568.

Eighty-year war against Spain   1568–1648

After a long struggle the Dutch Republic was proclaimed in 1648. The
southern part of the Netherlands remained in Spanish hands, however,
which led eventually to Belgian independence.

Golden Age   17th century

Enormous wealth was generated by worldwide trade, colonization (Dutch
East Indies, Surinam, Netherlands Antilles), and the settlements in North
America (New York, Brooklyn). Art and science flourished.

French invasion/Belgian independence   18th/19th century

The French occupied the Netherlands and influenced the language and
culture considerably. In 1795 the Batavian Republic was proclaimed. In
1806 Napoleon's brother Louis annexed Holland to France (1810–13).
The south of the Netherlands broke away in 1830 to become Belgium.

World War II

The Dutch were occupied by the Nazis from 1940–45.

Post-war period

The Dutch relinquished their most treasured colony, Indonesia, in 1949.
West New Guinea followed in 1963, and Surinam in 1975. The Netherlands
Antilles (Caribbean) are still Dutch, but have full internal autonomy.

Places of worship Bedehuizen

The Netherlands is predominantly Protestant with the only Catholic
provinces in the south. Denominations include Dutch Reformed and
Calvinist. There are also mosques and synagogues.

Catholic/Protestant church	**de katholieke/protestantse kerk**
	der kahtoleeker/protestanter kehrk
What time is mass/the service?	**Hoe laat is de mis/de kerkdienst?**
	hoo laht is de mis/kehrkdeenst

In the countryside
Op het platteland

I'd like a map of …	**Ik wil graag een kaart van …** *ik vil khraakh ayn kaart fan*
this region	**deze regio** *dayzer raykhee-oa*
walking routes	**de wandelroutes** *der vanderlrooters*
cycle routes	**de fietsroutes** *der feetsrooters*
How far is it to …?	**Hoe ver is het naar …?** *hoo fehr is het naar*
Is there a right of way?	**Is er een recht van doorgang?** *is ehr ayn rehkht fan doarkhang*
Is there a trail/scenic route to …?	**Is er een natuurpad/schilderachtige route naar …?** *is ehr ayn natuwrpat/ skilderakhtikher rooter naar*
Can you show me on the map?	**Kunt u me dat op de kaart laten zien?** *kuhnt uw mer dat op der kaart laatern zeen*
I'm lost.	**Ik ben verdwaald.** *ik ben ferdwaalt*

Organized walks Georganiseerde wandelingen

When does the guided walk start?	**Wanneer begint de begeleide wandeling?** *vannayr berkhint der berkherlayder vanderling*
When will we return?	**Wanneer komen we terug?** *vannayr koamern vay trukh*
Is it a hard course?	**Is het een zware tocht?** *is het ayn zwaarer tokht*
gentle/medium/tough	**makkelijk/vrij moeilijk/zwaar** *maklik/fray mooilerk/zwaar*
I'm exhausted.	**Ik ben uitgeput.** *ik ben oaitkherpuht*
How long are we resting here?	**Hoe lang rusten we hier uit?** *hoo lang ruhstern vay heer oait*
What kind of … is that?	**Wat voor … is dat?** *vat foar … is dat*
animal/bird	**dier/vogel** *deer/foakherl*
flower/tree	**bloem/boom** *bloom/boam*

HIKING GEAR ➤ 145

Geographic features
Geografische kenmerken

beach	**het strand** _het strant_
bridge	**de brug** _der bruhkh_
canal (in countryside)	**het kanaal** _het kanaal_
canal (in town)	**de gracht** _der ghraght_
cave	**de grot** _der khrot_
cliff	**de klif** _der klif_
farm	**de boerderij** _der boorderay_
field	**het weiland** _het vaylant_
footpath	**het voetpad** _het footpat_
forest	**het woud** _het vowt_
hill	**de heuvel** _der huverl_
lake	**het meer** _het mayr_
mountain	**de berg** _der behrkh_
mountain pass	**de bergpas** _der behrkhpas_
mountain range	**de bergketen** _der behrkhkaytern_
nature reserve	**het natuurreservaat** _het natuwrrayzerfaat_
panorama	**het panorama** _het panoraama_
park	**het park** _het park_
peak	**de bergtop** _der behrkhtop_
picnic area	**het picknickgebied** _het piknik-kherbeet_
pond	**de vijver** _der fayfer_
rapids	**de stroomversnelling** _der stroamfersnelling_
river	**de rivier** _der reefeer_
sea	**de zee** _der zay_
stream	**het beekje** _het baykyer_
valley	**de vallei** _der fallay_
viewpoint	**het uitkijkpunt** _het oaitkaykpuhnt_
village	**het dorp** _het dorp_
waterfall	**de waterval** _der vaaterfal_
winery [vineyard]	**de wijngaard** _der vaynkhaart_
wood	**het bos** _het bos_

Leisure

The VVV is always a good source of information on events, as are the local papers and listings magazines such as *Culture in Amsterdam*, *What's on in Amsterdam*, and *Usit*.

Events Evenementen

Do you have a program of events?	**Heeft u een evenementenprogramma?** *hayft uw ayn evennementernproakhramma*
Can you recommend a ...?	**Kunt u een ... aanbevelen?** *kuhnt uw ayn ... aanberfaylern*
ballet	**ballet** *ballet*
concert	**concert** *konsehrt*
movie [film]	**film** *film*
opera	**opera** *oapera*
play	**toneelstuk** *toanaylstuhk*

Availability Verkrijgbaarheid

When does it start?	**Wanneer begint het?** *vannayr berkhint het*
When does it end?	**Wanneer is het afgelopen?** *vannayr is het afkherloapern*
Are there any seats for tonight?	**Zijn er plaatsen voor vanavond?** *zayn ehr plaatsern foar fanaafont*
Where can I get tickets?	**Waar kan ik kaartjes krijgen?** *vaar kan ik kaarkyers kraykhern*
There are ... of us.	**We zijn met z'n ...** *ver zayn met zern ...*
two/three/four/five	**tweeën/drieën/vieren/vijven** *tvayern/dree-ern/feerern/fayfern*

Tickets Kaartjes

How much are the seats?	**Hoeveel kosten de plaatsen?** _hoofayl kostern der plaatsern_
Do you have anything cheaper?	**Heeft u iets goedkopers?** _hayft uw eets khootkoopers_
I'd like to reserve …	**Ik wil graag … reserveren.** _ik vil khraakh … rayzervayrern_
three tickets for Sunday evening	**drie kaartjes voor zondagavond** _dree kaarkyers foar zondakhaafont_
one ticket for Friday matinée	**één kaartje voor de matinee van vrijdag** _ayn kaarkyer foar der matinay fan fraydakh_

Wat is het nummer van uw creditcard?	What's your credit card number?
Wat voor soort creditcard heeft u?	What type of credit card do you have?
Wat is de afloopdatum?	What's the expiration [expiry] date?
Kunt u hier even tekenen?	Can you sign here, please?
U mag de kaartjes … ophalen.	Please pick up the tickets …
niet later dan …	by p m.
bij de reserveringsbalie	at the reservations desk

May I have a program, please?	**Mag ik een programma, alstublieft?** _makh ik ayn prokhramma, alstuwbleeft_
Where's the coatcheck [cloakroom]?	**Waar is de garderobe?** _vaar is der kharderober_

– Kan ik u helpen? (Can I help you?)
– _Ik wil graag twee kaartjes voor het concert van vanavond, alstublieft._ (I'd like two tickets for tonight's concert, please.)
– Dat kan. (Certainly.)
– _Mag ik met een creditcard betalen?_ (Can I pay by credit card?)
– Jazeker. (Yes.)
– _Dan betaal ik met Visa._ (In that case I'll pay by Visa)
– Dank u wel. Kunt u hier even tekenen? (Thank you. Can you sign here, please?)

UITVERKOCHT	sold out
KAARTJES VOOR VANDAAG	tickets for today
RESERVERINGEN (VOORAF)	advance reservations

NUMBERS ➤ 216

Movies [Cinema] Bioscoop

The Dutch believe in subtitling, so you can enjoy the original
language version. There are commercial movie theaters
(**bioscoop**), and art-house movie theaters (**filmhuis**) with a good
choice of continental films. Festivals include the Dutch Film Days
(September), the Rotterdam Film Festival (February), and the Amsterdam
Documentary Film Festival.

Is there a movie theater [cinema] near here?	**Is er een bioscoop in de buurt?** *is ehr ayn biyoskoap in der buwrt*
What's playing at the movies [on at the cinema] tonight?	**Welke films draaien er vanavond?** *velker films draayern ehr fanaafont*
Is the film dubbed?	**Is de film nagesynchroniseerd?** *is der film naakhersinkroanizayrt*
Is the film subtitled?	**Is de film ondertiteld?** *is der film onderteeterlt*
Is the film in the original English?	**Is de film in het originele Engels?** *is der film in het oareezheenayler engils*
A …, please.	**Een …, alstublieft.** *Ayn …, alstuwbleeft*
box [carton] of popcorn	**zak popcorn** *zak popkorn*
chocolate ice cream [choc-ice]	**chocolade ijs** *shokolaader ays*
hot dog	**warme worst** *warmer worst*
soft drink	**frisdrank** *frisdrank*
small/regular/large	**klein/normaal/groot** *klayn/normaal/khroat*

Theater Theater

What's playing at the Carré Theater?	**Wat wordt er in Theater Carré vertoond?** *vat vort ehr in tayaater Karray fertoant*
Who's the playwright?	**Wie is de toneelschrijver?** *vee is der toanaylskrayver*
Do you think I'd enjoy it?	**Denkt u dat ik het leuk zal vinden?** *denkt uw dat ik het luk zal findern*
I don't know much Dutch.	**Ik ken niet veel Nederlands.** *ik ken neet fayl nayderlands*

Opera/Ballet/Dance
Opera/Ballet/Dans

The Netherlands Opera is based at the Stopera Muziektheater.
Also in Amsterdam is the renowned Royal Concertgebouw
Orchestra in the Concertgebouw. The Dutch National Ballet
has a worldwide reputation (classical), as has the Netherlands
Dance Theatre (modern). There is also an English-language theater in
Amsterdam, the Theater Boom Chicago. The Holland Festival of theater,
music, dance, and art takes place in June (mostly in Amsterdam). For jazz,
there is the North Sea Jazz Festival in the Hague.

Where's the theater?	**Waar is het theater?** _vaar is het tayaater_
Who is the composer/soloist?	**Wie is de componist/solist?** _vee is der kompoanist/solist_
Is formal dress required?	**Is nette kleding vereist?** _is netter klayding ferayst_
Who's dancing?	**Wie danst er?** _vee danst ehr_
I'm interested in contemporary dance.	**Ik ben geïnteresseerd in moderne dans.** _ik ben kher-interesayrt in moadehrner dans_

Music/Concerts Muziek/Concerten

Where's the concert hall?	**Waar is het concertgebouw?** _vaar is het konsehrtkherbow_
Which orchestra/band is playing?	**Welk orkest/Welke band speelt er?** _velk orkest/velker behnd spaylt ehr_
What are they playing?	**Wat spelen ze?** _vat spaylern zer_
Who is the conductor/soloist?	**Wie is de dirigent/solist?** _vee is der deereekhent/solist_
Who is the support band?	**Wie speelt er in het voorprogramma?** _vee spaylt ehr in het foarproakhrammaa_
I really like …	**Ik hou erg van …** _ik how ehrkh fan_
folk/country music	**volks/country muziek** _folks/kowntree muwzeek_
jazz/soul music	**jazz/soul** _jehz/soal_
music of the sixties	**muziek uit de jaren zestig** _muwzeek ouit der jahrern sestigh_
pop/rock music	**popmuziek/rock** _popmuwzeek/rok_
Are they popular?	**Zijn ze populair?** _zayn zer poapuhlehr_

111

Nightlife Nachtleven

What is there to do at night?	**Wat is er 's avonds te doen?**	*vat is ehr saafonts ter doon*
Can you recommend a …?	**Kunt u een … aanbevelen?**	*kuhnt uw ayn … aanberfaylern*
Is there a …?	**Is er een …?**	*is ehr ayn*
bar/restaurant	**bar/restaurant**	*baar/restoarant*
cabaret/casino	**cabaret/casino**	*kabaret/kazeenoa*
discotheque	**discotheek**	*diskoatayk*
gay club	**gay club**	*gay kluhb*
nightclub	**nachtclub**	*nakhtkluhb*
What type of music do they play?	**Wat voor soort muziek spelen ze?**	*vat foar soart muwzeek spaylern zer*
How do I get there?	**Hoe kom ik er?**	*hoo kom ik ehr*
Is there an admission charge?	**Moet ik entree betalen?**	*moot ik antray bertaalern*

Admission Toegang

What time does the show start?	**Hoe laat begint de show?**	*hoo laat berkhint der show*
Is there a cover charge?	**Moet ik couvert betalen?**	*moot ik koovehr bertaalern*
Is a reservation necessary?	**Moet ik reserveren?**	*moot ik rayzervayrern*
Do we need to be members?	**Moeten we lid zijn?**	*mootern vay lit zayn*
Can you have dinner there?	**Kun je er dineren?**	*kuhn yer ehr dinayrern*
How long will we have to stand in line [queue]?	**Hoe lang moeten we in de rij staan?**	*hoo lang mootern vay in der ray staan*
I'd like a good table.	**Ik wil graag een goede tafel.**	*ik vil khraakh ayn khooder taaferl*

EEN GRATIS DRANKJE INBEGREPEN	includes one complimentary drink

Children Kinderen

Can you recommend something for the children?
Kunt u iets aanbevelen voor de kinderen? *kuhnt uw eets aanberfaylern foar der kinderern*

Are there changing facilities here for babies?
Kan ik mijn baby hier verschonen? *kan ik mayn baybee heer ferskoanern*

Where are the bathrooms [toilets]?
Waar is het toilet? *vaar is het toilet*

amusement arcade
de speelhal *der spaylhal*

fairground
de kermis *der kermis*

kiddie [paddling] pool
het kinderbadje *het kinderbatyer*

playground
de speeltuin *der spayltoain*

play group
de peuterspeelzaal *der puterspaylzaal*

zoo
de dierentuin *der deerentoain*

Babysitting Babysitters

Can you recommend a reliable babysitter?
Kunt u een betrouwbare babysitter aanbevelen? *kuhnt uw ayn bertrowbaarer baybeesitter aanberfaylern*

Is there constant supervision?
Wordt er constant toezicht gehouden? *vort ehr konstant toozikht kherhowdern*

Is the staff properly trained?
Is het personeel goed opgeleid? *is het pehrsoanayl khoot opkherlayt*

When can I bring them?
Wanneer kan ik ze brengen? *vannayr kan ik zer brengern*

I'll pick them up at …
Ik haal ze om … op. *ik haal zer om … op*

We'll be back by …
We zijn niet later dan … terug. *vay zayn neet laater dan … trukh*

She's three and he's 18 months.
Zij is drie en hij is achttien maanden. *zay is dree en hay is akhteen maandern*

113

Sports Sport

Cycling is probably the number one sport, both the leisure variety (**fietsen**) and the competitive variety (**wielrennen**). Cycling is learned from an early age and practiced well into old age. In the morning huge crowds of cyclists, on their way to school or work, dominate the roads. The Dutch also use the bicycle for shopping and leisure purposes. There are good cycle paths everywhere.

Soccer, tennis, and volleyball are popular sports, both to watch and to play. The Dutch also like swimming (**zwemmen**), fishing (**vissen**), and horseback riding (**paardrijden**). Sailing (**zeilen**) is especially attractive on the Frisian lakes (**Friese meren**).

The national passion for skating (**schaatsen**) is evident when the ditches and lakes freeze over at the beginning of the year and everyone goes on the ice, including dogs, and push chairs. If it is cold for long enough, the **Elfstedentocht**, a long-distance skating race around eleven towns in the province of Friesland, becomes a huge event for both participants, spectators, and the media.

Spectator Kijken

Is there a soccer [football] game [match] this Saturday?	**Is er zaterdag een voetbalwedstrijd?** _is ehr <u>zaater</u>dakh ayn <u>footbal</u>-vetstrayt_
Which teams are playing?	**Welke teams spelen er?** _<u>vel</u>ker teems <u>spay</u>lern ehr_
Can you get me a ticket?	**Kunt u een kaartje voor me krijgen?** _kuhnt uw ayn <u>kaar</u>kyer foar mer <u>kray</u>khern_
What's the admission charge?	**Wat is de toegangsprijs?** _vat is der <u>took</u>hangsprays_
Where's the racetrack [race course]?	**Waar is de renbaan?** _vaar is der <u>ren</u>baan_
Where can I place a bet?	**Waar kan ik wedden?** _vaar kan ik <u>ved</u>dern_
What are the odds on ...?	**Hoe liggen de kansen van ...?** _hoo <u>lik</u>hern der <u>kan</u>sern fan_

rappeling [abseiling]	**abseiling** _ab_sayling
aerobics	**aerobics** e_roa_biks
American football	**Amerikaans voetbal** _aa_me_reekaans football_
angling	**vissen** _fis_sern
archery	**boogschieten** _boakh_skeetern
athletics	**atletiek** atler_teek_
badminton	**badminton** _bad_mintern
baseball	**baseball** _bays_bol
basketball	**basketbal** _basket_bal
boxing	**boxen** _bok_sern
canoeing	**kanovaren** kaa_noa_faarern
cycling	**wielrennen** _veel_rennern
field hockey	**hockey** _hok_kee
gliding	**zweefvliegen** _zvayf_fleekhern
golf	**golf** golf
greyhound racing	**windhondenrennen** _vind_hondernrennern
horse-racing	**paardenrennen** _paar_der-rennern
ice hockey	**ijshockey** _ays_hokkee
judo	**judo** _joo_doa
rowing	**roeien** _rooi_yern
rugby	**rugby** _ruhg_bee
billiards [snooker]	**biljarten** bil_yar_tern
soccer [football]	**voetbal** _foot_bal
squash	**squash** skwash
swimming	**zwemmen** _zvem_mern
table tennis	**tafeltennis** _taa_ferltennis
tennis	**tennis** _ten_nis
volleyball	**volleybal** _vol_leebal

Participating Spelen

	Is there a ... nearby?	**Is er een ... in de buurt?**
		is ehr ayn ... in der buwrt
	golf course	**golfbaan** *golfbaan*
	sports club	**sportvereniging**
		sportferaynerkhing
	Are there any tennis courts?	**Zijn er ook tennisbanen?**
		zayn ehr oak tennisbaanern
	What's the charge per ...?	**Wat zijn de kosten per ...?**
		vat zayn der kostern pehr
	day	**dag** *daakh*
	round	**ronde** *ronder*
	hour	**uur** *uwr*
	Do I need to be a member?	**Moet ik lid zijn?** *moot ik lit zayn*
	Where can I rent ...?	**Waar kan ik ... huren?**
		vaar kan ik ... huwrern
	boots	**laarzen** *laarzern*
	clubs	**golfclubs** *golfkluhbs*
	equipment	**een uitrusting** *ayn oaitruhsting*
	a racket	**een racket** *ayn rakket*
	Can I get lessons?	**Kan ik les krijgen?** *kan ik les kraykhern*
	Do you have a fitness room?	**Heeft u een fitnessruimte?**
		hayft uw ayn fitnersroaimter
	Can I join in?	**Mag ik meedoen?** *makh ik maydoon*

Het spijt me, we zijn volgeboekt.	I'm sorry, we're booked up.
Er is een aanbetaling van ...	There is a deposit of ...
Welke maat heeft u?	What size are you?
U heeft een paspoortfoto nodig.	You need a passport-size photo.

KLEEDKAMERS	changing rooms

At the beach Op het strand

The beaches along the North Sea coast are all sandy and very popular, even with daytrippers from Germany. Many beaches (**strand**) are supervised by lifeguards (**strandmeester**). Topless bathing is accepted on most Dutch beaches and there are also naturist resorts.

Is the beach pebbly/sandy?	**Is het een kiezelstrand/zandstrand ?** *is het ayn <u>kee</u>zerlstrant/<u>zant</u>strant*
Is there a … here?	**Is er hier een …?** *is ehr heer ayn*
children's pool	**kinderzwembad** *<u>kin</u>derzwembat*
swimming pool	**zwembad** *<u>zwem</u>bat*
indoor	**overdekt** *<u>oa</u>ferdekt*
open-air	**openlucht** *<u>oa</u>pernlukht*
Is it safe to swim/dive here?	**Is het veilig om hier te zwemmen/duiken?** *is het <u>fay</u>likh om heer ter <u>zvem</u>mern/ <u>doai</u>kern*
Is it safe for children?	**Is het veilig voor kinderen?** *is het <u>fay</u>likh foar <u>kin</u>derern*
Is there a lifeguard?	**Is er een strandmeester?** *is ehr ayn <u>strant</u>mayster*
I want to rent a/some …	**Ik wil een/wat … huren.** *ik vil ayn/vat … <u>huw</u>rern*
deck chair	**ligstoel** *<u>likh</u>stool*
jet-ski	**jet-ski** *<u>jet</u>skee*
motorboat	**speedboot** *<u>speed</u>boat*
diving equipment	**duikapparatuur** *<u>doai</u>kapparaatuwr*
umbrella [sunshade]	**parasol** *<u>par</u>rasol*
surfboard	**surfplank** *<u>surf</u>plangk*
water skis	**waterski's** *<u>vaa</u>terskees*
For … hours.	**Voor … uur.** *foar … uwr*

Making friends Kennismaken

Introductions Voorstellen

It is polite to shake hands when you meet someone.

Use the formal form of you (**u**) to address someone you don't know well. **Tutoyeren** (to address someone with the familiar **jij** and **je**, plural form **jullie**) is best left until the other person says you can.

Meneer (sir) and **mevrouw** (ma'am) are used more commonly than in English, especially for strangers, older people, acquaintances, and teachers (although this has been relaxed recently).

Hello, we haven't met.	**Dag, we kennen elkaar niet.** *daakh, vay <u>kennern</u> el<u>kaar</u> neet*
My name is …	**Ik ben …** *ik ben*
May I introduce …?	**Mag ik u voorstellen aan …?** *makh ik uw <u>foar</u>stellern aan*
Pleased to meet you.	**Aangenaam.** *anghenahm*
What's your name?	**Wat is uw naam?** *vat is uhw naam*
How are you?	**Hoe gaat het met u?** *hoo khaat het met uw*
Fine, thanks. And you?	**Prima, dank u. En met u?** *preema, dangk uw. en met uw*

– *Dag, hoe gaat het met u?*
(Hello, how are you?)
– *Prima, dank u. En met u?*
(Fine, thanks. And you?)
– *Prima, dank u.*
(Fine, thanks.)

Where are you from?
Waar komt u vandaan?

Where are you from?	**Waar komt u vandaan?** *vaar komt uw fandaan*
Where were you born?	**Waar bent u geboren?** *vaar bent uw kherboarern*
I'm from …	**Ik kom uit …** *ik kom oait*
Australia	**Australië** *owstraalceyer*
Britain	**Groot-Brittannië** *khroatbritanyer*
Canada	**Canada** *kannada*
England	**Engeland** *engerlant*
Ireland	**Ierland** *eerlant*
Scotland	**Schotland** *skhotlant*
the US	**de Verenigde Staten** *der feraynikhder staatern*
Wales	**Wales** *vayls*
Where do you live?	**Waar woont u?** *vaar voant uw*
What part of the Netherlands are you from?	**Uit welk deel van Nederland komt u?** *oalt velk dayl fan nayderlant komt uw*
Belgium / Germany	**België/Duitsland** *belkheeyer/doaitslant*
Luxembourg	**Luxemburg** *luhksermbuhrkh*
We come here every year.	**We komen hier elk jaar.** *vay koamern heer elk yaar*
It's my/our first visit.	**Dit is mijn/ons eerste bezoek.** *dit is mayn/ons ayrster berzook*
Have you ever been to …?	**Bent u wel eens in … geweest?** *bent uw vel ayns in … khervayst*
the U.K. / U.S.	**Groot-Brittannië/de Verenigde Staten** *khroatbritanyer/der feraynikhder staatern*
Do you like it here?	**Vindt u het hier fijn?** *fint uw het heer fayn*
What do you think of …?	**Wat vindt u van …?** *vat fint uw fan*
I love … here.	**Ik ben dol op … hier.** *ik ben dol op … heer*
I don't really like … here.	**Ik hou niet erg van … hier.** *ik how neet ehrkh fan … heer*
the food/people	**het eten/de mensen** *het aytern/der mensern*

Who are you with? Met wie bent u?

Who are you with?	**Met wie bent u?** *met vee bent uw*
I'm on my own.	**Ik ben op mijn eentje.** *ik ben op mayn <u>ayn</u>tyer*
I'm with a (male/female) friend.	**Ik ben met een vriend/vriendin.** *ik ben met ayn freent/freen<u>din</u>*
I'm with my …	**Ik ben met mijn …** *ik ben met mayn*
husband/wife	**man/vrouw** *man/frow*
family	**gezin** *kher<u>zin</u>*
children/parents	**kinderen/ouders** *<u>kin</u>derern/<u>ow</u>ders*
boyfriend/girlfriend	**vriend/vriendin** *freent/freen<u>din</u>*
father/son	**vader/zoon** *<u>faa</u>der/zoan*
mother/daughter	**moeder/dochter** *<u>moo</u>der/<u>dokh</u>ter*
brother/uncle	**broer/oom** *broor/oam*
sister/aunt	**zus/tante** *zuhs/tanter*
What's your son's/wife's name?	**Hoe heet uw zoon/vrouw?** *hoo hayt uhw zoan/frow*
Are you married?	**Bent u getrouwd?** *bent uw kher<u>trowt</u>*
I'm …	**Ik ben …** *ik ben*
engaged	**verloofd** *fer<u>loaft</u>*
married/single/divorced	**getrouwd/ongetrouwd/gescheiden** *kher<u>trowt</u>/<u>on</u>khertrowt/gheskhaydern*
We are separated.	**We zijn uit elkaar.** *vay zayn oait el<u>kaar</u>*
We live together.	**We wonen samen.** *vay <u>voa</u>nern <u>saa</u>mern*
Do you have any children?	**Heeft u kinderen?** *hayft uw <u>kin</u>derern*
We have two boys and a girl.	**We hebben twee jongens en een meisje.** *vay <u>hep</u>bern tvay <u>yon</u>gerns en ayn <u>mays</u>yer*
How old are they?	**Hoe oud zijn ze?** *hoo owt zayn zer*
They're ten and twelve.	**Ze zijn tien en twaalf.** *zer zayn teen en tvaalf*

What do you do? Wat doet u?

What do you do?	**Wat doet u?** *vat doot uw*
What are you studying?	**Wat studeert u?** *vat stuhdayrt uw*
I'm studying …	**Ik studeer …** *ik stuhdayr*
I'm in …	**Ik werk in …** *ik verk in*
business	**de zakenwereld** *der zaakernvayrerlt*
engineering	**de techniek** *der tekhneek*
sales	**de verkoop** *der ferkoap*
Who do you work for …?	**Voor wie werkt u …?** *foar vee verkt uw*
I work for …	**Ik werk voor …** *ik verk foar*
I'm (a/an) …	**Ik ben …** *ik ben*
accountant	**accountant** *akkownternt*
housewife	**huisvrouw** *hoaisfrow*
student	**student** *stuhdent*
retired	**gepensioneerd** *kherpenshonayrt*
between jobs	**tussen twee banen in** *tuhssern tvay baanern in*
I'm self-employed.	**Ik werk voor mezelf.** *ik wehrk fohr merself*
What are your interests?	**Wat zijn uw interesses?** *vat zayn uhw interessers*
I like …	**Ik hou van …** *ik how fan*
music	**muziek** *muhzeek*
reading	**lezen** *layzern*
sports	**sport** *sport*
I play …	**Ik speel …** *ik spayl*
Would you like to play …?	**Wilt u …?** *vilt uw*
cards	**kaarten** *kaartern*
chess	**schaken** *skhaakern*

What weather! Wat een weer!

What a lovely day!	**Wat een prachtige dag!** *vat ayn prachtikher dakh*
What terrible weather!	**Wat een vreselijk weer!** *vat ayn frayserlik vayr*
It's hot/cold today!	**Het is warm/koud vandaag!** *het is varm/kowt fandaakh*
Is it usually this warm?	**Is het normaal ook zo warm?** *is het normaal oak zoa varm*
Do you think it's going to … tomorrow?	**Denkt u dat het morgen …?** *denkt uw dat het morkhern*
be a nice day	**een mooie dag wordt** *ayn mooiyer daakh vort*
rain	**gaat regenen** *khaat raykhernern*
snow	**gaat sneeuwen** *khaat snaywern*
What is the weather forecast for tomorrow?	**Wat is het weerbericht voor morgen?** *vat is het vayrberikht foar morghern*
It's …	**Het is …** *het is*
cloudy	**bewolkt** *bervolkt*
foggy	**mistig** *misterkh*
icy	**glad** *khlat*
It's stormy.	**Het stormt.** *het stormt*
It's windy.	**Het waait.** *het vaait*
It's raining.	**Het regent.** *het raykhernt*
It's snowing.	**Het sneeuwt.** *het snaywt*
It's sunny.	**Het is zonnig.** *het is zonnerkh*
Has the weather been like this for long?	**Is het weer al lang zo?** *is het vayr al lang zoa*
What's the pollen count?	**Wat is de pollentelling?** *vat is der pollerntelling*
high/medium/low	**hoog/gemiddeld/laag** *hoakh/khermidderlt/laakh*

WEERBERICHT	weather forecast

Enjoying your trip?
Heeft u een leuke reis?

Bent u op vakantie?	Are you on vacation?
Hoe bent u hier gekomen?	How did you travel here?
Waar logeert u?	Where are you staying?
Hoe lang bent u hier al?	How long have you been here?
Hoe lang blijft u?	How long are you staying?
Wat heeft u tot dusver gedaan?	What have you done so far?
Waar gaat u straks naar toe?	Where are you going next?
Heeft u een leuke vakantie?	Are you enjoying your vacation?

I'm here on …	**Ik ben hier met …** _ik ben heer met_
business	**zaken** _zaakern_
vacation [holiday]	**vakantie** _fakansee_
We came by …	**We zijn met … gekomen.** _vay zayn met … kherkoamern_
train/bus/plane	**de trein/de bus/het vliegtuig** _der trayn/der buhs/hot fleekhtoaikh_
car/ferry	**de auto/de veerboot** _der owto/der fayrboat_
I have a rental [hire] car.	**Ik heb een huurauto.** _ik hep ayn huwrowto_
We're staying …	**We logeren …** _vay loazhayrern (in/op)_
in a campsite	**op een kampeerplaats** _op ayn kampayrplaats_
at a guesthouse/hotel	**in een pension/hotel** _in ayn penshon/hoatel_
in a youth hostel	**in een jeugdherberg** _in ayn yukhtherberkh_
with friends	**bij vrienden** _bay freendern_
Can you suggest …?	**Kunt u … voorstellen?** _kuhnt uw … foarstellern_
places to eat/visit	**plaatsen om te eten/bezoeken** _plaatsern om ter ayternberzookern_
We're having a great/terrible time.	**We hebben het erg/helemaal niet naar onze zin.** _vay hepbern het ergh/haylermaal neet naar onzer zin_

Invitations Uitnodigingen

Would you like to have dinner with us on …? **Wilt u op … met ons dineren?** *vilt uw op … met ons dinayrern*

May I invite you to lunch? **Mag ik u op de lunch uitnodigen?** *makh ik uw op der luhnsh oaitnoadikhern*

Can you come for a drink this evening? **Komt u vanavond langs voor een borrel?** *komt uw fanaafont langs foar ayn borrerl*

We are having a party. Can you come? **We houden een feestje. Kunt u komen?** *vay howdern ayn faystyer. kuhnt uw koamern*

May we join you? **Mogen we bij u komen zitten?** *moakhern vay bay uw koamern zittern*

Would you like to join us? **Wilt u bij ons komen zitten?** *vilt uw bay ons koamern zittern*

Going out Uit gaan

What are your plans for …? **Wat zijn uw plannen voor …?** *vat zayn uhw plannern foar*

today / tonight **vandaag/vanavond** *fandaakh/fanaafont*

tomorrow **morgen** *morkhern*

Are you free this evening? **Bent u vanavond vrij?** *bent uw fanaafont fray*

Would you like to …? **Wilt u …?** *vilt uw*

go dancing **gaan dansen** *khaan dansern*

go for a drink **iets gaan drinken** *eets khaan dringkern*

go out for a meal **uit eten gaan** *oait aytern khaan*

go for a walk **gaan wandelen** *khaan vanderlern*

go shopping **gaan winkelen** *khaan vingkerlern*

I'd like to go to … **Ik wil graag naar …** *ik vil khraakh naar*

I'd like to see … **Ik wil graag … zien.** *ik vil khraakh … zeen*

Do you enjoy …? **Houdt u van …?** *howt uw fan*

124

Accepting/Declining
Accepteren/Afslaan

Thank you. I'd love to.	**Dank u. Dat zou erg leuk zijn.** *dangk uw. dat zow ehrkh luk zayn*
Thank you, but I'm busy.	**Dank u, maar ik heb het te druk.** *dangk uw, maar ik hep het ter druhk*
May I bring a (male/female) friend?	**Mag ik een vriend/vriendin meenemen?** *makh ik ayn freent/freendin maynaymern*
Where shall we meet?	**Waar zullen we elkaar ontmoeten?** *vaar zuhllern vay elkaar ontmootern*
I'll meet you …	**Ik ontmoet u …** *ik ontmoot uw*
in front of your hotel	**voor uw hotel** *foar uhw hoatel*
I'll pick you up at 8.	**Ik haal u om acht uur op.** *ik haal uw om akht uwr op*
Could we make it a bit later/earlier?	**Kan het iets later/vroeger?** *kan het eets laater/frookher*
How about another day?	**Kan het ook op een andere dag?** *kan het oak op ayn anderer daakh*
That will be fine.	**Dat is prima.** *dat is preema*

Dining out/in Uit eten/Thuis dineren.

When you are invited to someone's home, remember to shake hands on arrival and departure, and to bring a gift, such as flowers, chocolates, or wine.

Let me buy you a drink.	**Wilt u iets drinken?** *vilt uw eets dringkern*
Do you like …?	**Houdt u van …?** *howt uw fan*
What are you going to have?	**Wat neemt u?** *vat naymt uw*
That was a lovely meal.	**Dat was een heerlijke maaltijd.** *dat vas ayn hayrlerker maaltayt*

TIME ➤ 220

Encounters Ontmoetingen

Do you mind if …?	**Vindt u het goed als …?**	*fint uw het khoot als*
I sit here/I smoke	**ik hier zit/ik rook**	*ik heer zit/ik roak*
Can I get you a drink?	**Mag ik u een drankje aanbieden?**	*makh ik uw ayn drangkyer aanbeedern*
I'd love to have some company.	**Ik zou graag wat gezelschap hebben.**	*ik zow khraakh vat gerzelskhap hepbern*
What's so funny?	**Wat is er zo grappig?**	*vat is ehr zoa khrapperkh*
Is my Dutch that bad?	**Is mijn Nederlands zo slecht?**	*is mayn nayderlands zoa slehkht*
Shall we go somewhere quieter?	**Zullen we een rustig plekje opzoeken?**	*zuhllern vay ayn ruhstikh plehkyer opzookern*
Leave me alone, please!	**Laat me met rust, alstublieft!**	*laat mer met ruhst, alstuwbleeft*
You look great!	**U ziet er fantastisch uit!**	*uw zeet ehr fantastees oait*
Would you like to come home with me?	**Wilt u met me mee naar huis?**	*vilt uw met mer may naar hoais*
I'm not ready for that.	**Dat gaat me een beetje te snel.**	*dat khaat mer ayn baytyer ter snel*
I'm afraid we've got to leave now.	**Ik vrees dat we nu weg moeten.**	*ik frays dat vay nuw vekh mootern*
Thanks for the evening.	**Bedankt voor de avond.**	*berdangkt foar der aafont*
It was great.	**Het was erg gezellig.**	*het vas ehrkh gerzellerkh*
Can I see you again tomorrow?	**Kan ik u morgen weer zien?**	*kan ik uw morkhern vayr zeen*
See you soon.	**Tot gauw.** *tot khow*	
Can I have your address?	**Mag ik uw adres hebben?**	*makh ik uhw adres hepbern*

Telephoning Telefoneren

Dutch telephone booths (**telefooncel**) are green and you can use coins or a phonecard (**telefoonkaart**) available from stores and post offices. Lift the receiver, wait for the dial tone, insert card, and dial. For a call to the operator you need to insert a coin, which will be returned; in card phones you insert a card which will not be charged.

To call direct from the Netherlands, dial 00, wait for the tone, then dial the country code and area code, omitting the initial 0.

Can I have your telephone number?	**Mag ik uw telefoonnummer?** *makh ik uhw taylerfoannuhmmer*
Here's my number.	**Dit is mijn nummer.** *dit is mayn nuhmmer*
Please call me.	**Kunt u mij bellen?** *kuhnt uw may bellern*
I'll give you a call.	**Ik zal u bellen.** *ik zal uw bellern*
Where's the nearest telephone booth?	**Waar is de dichtstbijzijnde telefooncel?** *vaar is der dikhtstbayzaynder taylerfoansel*
May I use your phone?	**Mag ik uw telefoon gebruiken?** *makh ik uhw taylerfoan kherbroaikern*
It's an emergency.	**Het is een noodgeval.** *het is ayn noatkherfal*
I'd like to call someone in England.	**Ik wil graag iemand in England bellen.** *ik vil khraakh eemant in engerlant bellern*
What's the area [dialling] code for …?	**Wat is het kengetal voor …?** *vat is het kenkhertal foar*
I'd like a phone card, please.	**Ik wil graag een telefoonkaart, alstublieft.** *ik vil khraakh ayn taylerfoankaart, alstuwbleeft*
What's the number for Information [Directory Enquiries]?	**Wat is het nummer voor Inlichtingen?** *vat is het nuhmmer foar inlikhtingern*
I'd like to call collect [reverse the charges].	**Ik wil graag voor rekening van de opgeroepene bellen.** *ik vil khraakh foar raykerning fan der opkherooperner bellern*

Speaking Spreken

Hello. This is …	**Dag. U spreekt met …** *daakh. uw spraykt met*
I'd like to speak to …	**Ik wil graag met … spreken.** *ik vil khraakh met … spraykern*
Extension …	**Toestel …** *toostel*
Speak louder, please.	**Kunt u iets harder spreken?** *kuhnt uw eets harder spraykern*
Speak more slowly, please.	**Kunt u iets langzamer spreken?** *kuhnt uw eets langzaamer spraykern*
Could you repeat that, please.	**Kunt u dat herhalen?** *kuhnt uw dat hayrhaalern*
I'm afraid he/she's not in.	**Ik vrees dat hij/ze er niet is.** *ik frays dat hay/zer ehr neet is*
You have the wrong number.	**U bent verkeerd verbonden.** *uh bent ferkayrt ferbondern*
Just a moment, please.	**Een ogenblikje, alstublieft.** *ayn oakhernblikyer, alstuwbleeft*
Hold on, please.	**Blijft u aan de lijn?** *blayft uw aan der layn*
When will he/she be back?	**Wanneer komt hij/ze terug?** *vannayr komt hay/zer trukh*
Will you tell him/her that I called?	**Kunt u zeggen dat ik heb gebeld?** *kuhnt uw zehkhern dat ik hep kherbelt*
My name is …	**Mijn naam is …** *mayn naam is*
Would you ask him/her to call me?	**Wilt u hem/haar vragen me te bellen?** *vilt uw hem/haar fraakhern mer ter bellern*
I have to go now.	**Ik moet nu ophangen.** *ik moot nuw ophangern*
Thank you for calling.	**Dank u voor het bellen.** *dangk uw foar het bellern*
I'll be in touch.	**Ik neem nog contact op.** *ik naym nokh kontakt op*
Bye.	**Dag.** *dakh*

Stores & Services

Well-known stores include De Bijenkorf, Vroom & Dreesmann (V&D), HEMA and C&A. There is a Marks & Spencer in Amsterdam. The **Kalverstraat** in Amsterdam is a famous shopping street. Outdoor markets are popular and some cities have a flea market (**vlooienmarkt**). Gouda and Edam have a cheese market (**kaasmarkt**) on certain days of the week.

ESSENTIAL

I'd like …	**Ik wil graag …** *ik vil khraakh*
Do you have …?	**Heeft u …?** *hayft uw*
How much is that?	**Hoeveel kost dat?** *hoofayl kost dat*
Thank you.	**Dank u.** *dangk uw*

GEOPEND	open
GESLOTEN	closed
VERKOOP	sale

129

Stores and services
Winkels en diensten

Where is …? Waar is …?

Where's the nearest …? **Waar is de dichtstbijzijnde …?**
vaar is der dikhstbayzaynder

Is there a good …? **Is er een goed(e) …?**
is ehr ayn khoot (khooder)

Where's the main shopping mall [centre]? **Waar is het grootste winkelcentrum?**
vaar is het khroatster vinkerlsentrerm

Is it far from here? **Is het ver hiervandaan?**
is het fehr heerfandaan

How do I get there? **Hoe kom ik er?** *hoo kom ik ehr*

Stores Winkels

bakery	**de bakker(swinkel)** *der bakker(svinkerl)*
bank	**de bank** *der bank*
bookstore	**de boekwinkel** *der bookvinkerl*
butcher	**de slager** *de slakher*
camera store	**de fotowinkel** *der foatoavinkerl*
cigarette kiosk [tobacconist]	**de sigarenwinkel** *der sikhaarernvinkerl*
clothing store [clothes shop]	**de klerenwinkel** *der klayrernvinkerl*
convenience store	**de avondwinkel** *der aafontvinkerl*
department store	**het warenhuis** *het vaarernhoais*
drugstore	**de drogisterij** *der droakhisteray*
fish store [fishmonger]	**de visboer** *der fisboor*
florist	**de bloemenwinkel** *der bloomernvinkerl*
gift store	**de cadeauwinkel** *der kadoavinkerl*
greengrocer	**de groenteboer** *der khroonterboor*

health food store	**de reformwinkel** *der rayformvinkerl*
jeweler	**de juwelier** *der yuwverleer*
liquor store [off-licence]	**de slijter** *der slayter*
music store	**de platenwinkel** *der plaaternvinkerl*
newsstand [newsagent]	**de kiosk** *der keeosk*
pastry shop	**de banketbakker** *der bangketbakker*
pharmacy [chemist]	**de apotheek** *der apoatayk*
produce store	**de groenteboer** *der khroonterboor*
shoe store	**de schoenenwinkel** *der skhoonernvinkerl*
souvenir store	**de souvenirwinkel** *der sooverneervinkerl*
sporting goods store	**de sportwinkel** *der sportvinkerl*
supermarket	**de supermarkt** *der suwpermarkt*
toy store	**de speelgoedwinkel** *der spaylkhootvinkerl*

Services Diensten

clinic	**de kliniek** *der klineek*
dentist	**de tandarts** *der tantarts*
doctor	**de dokter** *der dokter*
dry cleaner	**de stomerij** *der stoameray*
hairdresser/barber	**de kapper** *der kapper*
hospital	**het ziekenhuis** *het zeekernhoais*
laundromat	**de wasserette** *der vasseretter*
optician	**de opticiën** *der optishyen*
police station	**het politiebureau** *het poaleetseebuwroa*
post office	**het postkantoor** *het postkantoar*
travel agency	**het reisbureau** *het raysbuwroa*

Opening hours Openingstijden

Stores are open Monday through Friday 8.30 or 9 a.m. to 5.30 or 6 p.m., and Saturday 8.30 or 9 a.m. to 4 or 5 p.m. Most stores close for a day or half a day (often on Monday) and/or at lunchtime (see store window).

Late-night shopping is available on Thursday or Friday. Shopping laws are being relaxed, so **avondwinkels** (convenience stores which are open late) and Sunday openings are becoming more common. In Amsterdam stores can stay open seven days a week until 10 p.m.

When does the … open/shut?	**Wanneer gaat de/het … open/dicht?** van_nayr_ khaat der/het … oapern/dikht
Are you open in the evening?	**Bent u 's avonds geopend?** bent uw saafonts kheroapernt
Where is the …?	**Waar is de …?** vaar is der
cashier [cash desk]	**kassa** kassa
escalator	**roltrap** roltrap
elevator [lift]	**lift** lift
store directory	**winkelplattegrond** vinkerlplatterkhront
first [ground] floor	**begane grond** berkhaaner khront
second [first] floor	**eerste verdieping** ayrster ferdeeping
Where's the … department?	**Waar is de afdeling …?** vaar is der afdayling

OPENINGSTIJDEN	opening hours
INGANG	entrance
ROLTRAP	escalator
UITGANG	exit
NOODUITGANG/BRANDTRAP	emergency/fire exit
LIFT	elevator [lift]
TRAP	stairs
TOILET	restroom

Service Dienstverlening

Can you help me?	**Kunt u me helpen?** *kuhnt uw mer helpern*
I'm looking for …	**Ik zoek naar …** *ik zook naar*
I'm just browsing.	**Ik kijk alleen.** *ik kayk allayn*
It's my turn.	**Ik ben aan de beurt.** *ik ben aan der burt*
Do you have any …?	**Heeft u ook …?** *hayft uw oak*
I'd like to buy …	**Ik wil graag … kopen.** *ik vil khraakh … koapern*
Could you show me …?	**Kunt u me … laten zien?** *kuhnt uw mer … laatern zeen*
How much is this/that?	**Hoeveel kost dit/dat?** *hoofayl kost dit/dat*
That's all, thanks.	**Dat is het, dank u.** *dat is het, dangk uw*

Goedemorgen/goedemiddag mevrouw/meneer.	Good morning/afternoon, ma'am/sir.
Kan ik u helpen?	Can I help you?
Is dat alles?	Is that everything?
Anders nog iets?	Anything else?

– *Kan ik u helpen?* (Can I help you?)
– Nee, dank u. Ik kijk alleen.
(No, thanks. I'm just browsing.)
– *Prima.* (Fine.)

– Pardon. (Excuse me.)
– *Ja, kan ik u helpen?* (Yes, can I help you?)
– Hoeveel kost dat? (How much is that?)
– *Eh, even kijken … Het kost zeventien euro's vijfennegentig.*
(Hm, I'll just check … That's seventeen euros ninety-five.)

ZELFBEDIENING	self-service
UITVERKOOP	clearance

Preferences Voorkeur

It must be …	**Het moet … zijn.** *het moot … zayn*
big/small	**groot/klein** *khroat/klayn*
cheap/expensive	**goedkoop/duur** *khoo<u>koop</u>/duwr*
dark/light (color)	**donker/licht** *dongker/likht*
light/heavy	**licht/zwaar** *likht/zwaar*
oval/round/square	**ovaal/rond/vierkant** *ofaal/ront/<u>feer</u>kant*
genuine/imitation	**echt/imitatie** *ehkht/imi<u>taat</u>see*
I don't want anything too expensive.	**Het mag niet te duur zijn.** *het makh neet ter dur zayn*
Around … euros.	**Ongeveer … euro's.** *onger<u>fayr</u> … uros*

Wat voor … wilde u?	What … would you like?
kleur/vorm	color/shape
kwaliteit/hoeveelheid	quality/quantity
Hoeveel wilt u er?	How many would you like?
Wat voor soort wilt u?	What kind would you like?
Hoeveel mag het kosten?	What price range are you thinking of?

Do you have anything …?	**Heeft u iets …?** *hayft uw eets*
larger/smaller	**groters/kleiners** *<u>khroa</u>ters/<u>klay</u>ners*
better quality	**van betere kwaliteit** *fan <u>bay</u>terer kwalee<u>tayt</u>*
cheaper	**goedkopers** *<u>khoot</u>koapers*
Can you show me …?	**Kunt u me … laten zien?** *kuhnt uw mer … <u>laa</u>tern zeen*
this one/these	**deze/deze** *<u>day</u>zer/<u>day</u>zer*
that one/those	**die/die** *dee/dee*
the one in the window/ display case	**die in de etalage/vitrine** *die in der ayta<u>laa</u>zher/vi<u>tree</u>ner*
some others	**wat andere** *vat <u>an</u>derer*

COLOR ➤ 143

Conditions of purchase Koopvoorwaarden

Is there a guarantee? | **Zit er garantie op?**
zit ehr kharantsee op

Are there any instructions with it? | **Zit er een gebruiks-aanwijzing bij?** *zit ehr ayn kherbroaiksaanvayzing bay*

Out of stock Niet meer in voorraad

Het spijt, die hebben we niet.	I'm sorry, we don't have any.
We hebben ze niet meer in voorraad.	We're out of stock.
Kan ik u iets anders/een andere soort laten zien?	Can I show you something else/a different type?
Zullen we het voor u bestellen?	Shall we order it for you?

Can you order it for me? | **Kunt u het voor me bestellen?**
kuhnt uw het foar mer berstellern

How long will it take? | **Hoe lang duurt het?** *hoo lang durt het*

Is there another store that sells ...? | **Is er een andere winkel die ... verkoopt?**
is ehr ayn anderer vinkerl dee ... ferkoapt

Decisions Beslissing

That's not quite what I want. | **Dat is niet helemaal wat ik zoek.**
dat is neet haylermaal vat ik zook

No, I don't like it. | **Nee, ik vind het niet mooi.**
nay, ik fint het neet moay

That's too expensive. | **Dat is te duur.** *dat is te duwr*

I'll take it. | **Ik neem hem.** *ik naym hem*

– Goedemorgen. Ik zoek naar een sweatshirt.
(Good morning. I'm looking for a sweatshirt.)

– Jazeker. Wat voor kleur wilde u?
(Certainly. What color would you like?)

– Oranje, alstublieft. En het moet groot zijn.
(Orange, please. And I want something big.)

– Alstublieft. Deze kost twintig euro's vijfennegentig.
(Here you are. That's twenty euros ninety-five.)

– Hmm, dat is niet helemaal wat ik zoek. Dank u.
(Hmm, that's not quite what I want. Thank you.)

Paying Betalen

BTW is the Dutch sales tax [VAT]. It is levied at 17.5 percent and is always included in store and restaurant prices and in most other retail prices. Refunds are available through the "Tax-free for Tourists" plan.

Where do I pay?	**Waar moet ik betalen?** *vaar moot ik bertaalern*
How much is that?	**Hoeveel kost dat?** *hoofayl kost dat*
Could you write it down, please?	**Kunt u het opschrijven, alstublieft?** *kuhnt uw het opskhrayfern, alstuwbleeft*
Do you accept traveler's checks [cheques]?	**Accepteert u reischeques?** *akseptayrt uw rayssheks*
I'll pay by ...	**Ik wil graag met ... betalen.** *ik vil khraakh met ... bertaalern*
cash	**contanten** *kontantern*
credit card	**een creditcard** *ayn kredeetkaart*
I don't have any smaller change.	**Ik heb niets kleiners.** *ik hep neets klayners*
Sorry, I don't have enough money.	**Sorry, ik heb niet genoeg geld.** *sorree, ik hep neet khernookh khelt*

Hoe betaalt u?	How are you paying?
Deze transactie is niet goedgekeurd/geaccepteerd.	This transaction hasn't been approved/accepted.
Deze kaart is niet geldig.	This card isn't valid.
Heeft u nog andere identificatie?	May I have some more identification?
Heeft u iets kleiners?	Do you have any smaller change?

Could I have a receipt please?	**Mag ik een bonnetje, alstublieft?** *makh ik ayn bonnetyer, alstuwbleeft*
I think you gave me the wrong change.	**U heeft me, geloof ik, het verkeerde wisselgeld gegeven.** *uw hayft mer, kherloof ik, het ferkayrder visserlkhelt kherkhayfern*

HIER BETALEN A.U.B.	please pay here

136

Complaints Klachten

This doesn't work.	**Deze doet het niet.** *dayzer doot het neet*
Can you exchange this, please?	**Kunt u dit ruilen, alstublieft?** *kuhnt uw dit roailern, alstuwbleeft*
I'd like a refund.	**Ik wil graag mijn geld terug.** *ik vil khraakh mayn khelt trukh*
Here's the receipt.	**Hier is het bonnetje.** *heer is het bonnetyer*
I don't have the receipt.	**Ik heb het bonnetje niet.** *ik hep het bonnetyer neet*
I'd like to see the manager.	**Ik wil graag de manager zien.** *ik vil khraakh der manadzher zeen*

Repairs/Cleaning Reparaties/Stomen

This is broken. Can you repair it?	**Dit is gebroken. Kunt u het repareren?** *dit is kherbroakern. kuhnt uw het rayparayrern*
Do you have … for this?	**Heeft u hier … voor?** *hayft uw heer … foar*
a battery	**een batterij** *ayn batteray*
replacement parts	**vervangingsonderdelen** *ferfangingsonderdaylern*
There's something wrong with …	**Er is iets mis met …** *ehr is eets mis met*
Can you … this?	**Kunt u dit …?** *kuhnt uw dit*
dry clean	**stomen** *stoamern*
press	**persen** *pehrsern*
mend	**verstellen** *ferstellern*
Could you alter this?	**Kunt u dit vermaken?** *kuhnt uw dit fermaakern*
When will it be ready?	**Wanneer is het klaar?** *vannayr is het klaar*
This isn't mine.	**Dit is niet van mij.** *dit is neet fan may*
There's … missing.	**Er ontbreekt een …** *er ontbraykt ayn*

TIME ➤ 220; DATE ➤ 218

Bank / Currency exchange
Bank/Geldwisselkantoor

Cash can be obtained from ATMs [cash machines] (**geldautomaat**), banks (open Monday through Friday, 9 a.m. to 4 or 5 p.m.) and GWK offices. Most credit cards are accepted. Remember to take your passport. Money can also be changed at post offices. GWK services include foreign currency, cash, traveler's checks [cheques] and Western Union Money transfers. Offices can be found at train stations, border crossing points, and Schiphol Airport. They are open 7 days a week, some 24 hours a day.

Where's the nearest …?	**Waar is de dichtstbijzijnde …?** *vaar is der dikhtstbayzaynder*
bank	**bank** *bangk*
currency exchange office [bureau de change]	**geldwisselkantoor** *kheltvisserlkantoar*

GELDWISSELKANTOOR	currency exchange office
GEOPEND/GESLOTEN	open / closed
KASSA'S	cashiers

Changing money Geld wisselen

Can I exchange foreign currency here?	**Kan ik hier buitenlands geld wisselen?** *kan ik heer boaiternlans khelt visserlern*
I'd like to change some dollars/pounds into euros.	**Ik wil graag wat dollars/ponden in euro's omwisselen.** *ik vil khraakh vat dollaars/pondern in uros omvisserlern*
I want to cash some traveler's checks [cheques].	**Ik wil wat reischeques verzilveren.** *ik vil vat rayssheks ferzilverern*
What's the exchange rate?	**Wat is de wisselkoers?** *vat is der visserlkoors*
How much commission do you charge?	**Hoeveel commissie berekent u?** *hoofayl kommissee beraykernt uw*
Could I have some small change, please?	**Mag ik wat kleingeld, alstublieft?** *makh ik vat klaynkhelt, alstuwbleeft*
I've lost my traveler's checks. These are the numbers.	**Ik heb mijn reischeques verloren. Dit zijn de nummers.** *ik hep mayn rayssheks ferloarern. dit zayn der nuhmmers*

138

Security Beveiliging

Mag ik ... zien?	Could I see ...?
uw paspoort	your passport
wat identificatie	some identification
uw bankpasje	your bank card
Wat is uw adres?	What's your address?
Waar logeert u?	Where are you staying?
Kunt u dit formulier even invullen?	Fill out this form, please.
Kunt u hier even tekenen?	Can you sign here?

ATMs [Cash machines] Geldautomaten

Can I withdraw money on my credit card here?	**Kan ik hier geld opnemen met mijn creditcard?** *kan ik heer khelt <u>op</u>naymern met mayn kre<u>deet</u>kaart*
Where are the ATMs [cash machines]?	**Waar zijn de geldautomaten?** *vaar zayn der <u>khelt</u>oatoamaatern*
Can I use my ... card in the ATM [cash machine]?	**Kan ik mijn ... kaart in de geldautomaat gebruiken?** *kan ik mayn ... kaart in der <u>khelt</u>oatoamaat kher<u>broai</u>kern*
The machine has eaten my card.	**De geldautomaat heeft mijn kaart opgegeten.** *der <u>khelt</u>oatoamaat hayft mayn kaart <u>op</u>kherkhaytern*

GELDAUTOMAAT	automated teller machine (ATM) [cash machine]

In 2002 the currency in most EU countries, including the Netherlands, changed to the euro (€), divided into 100 cents. The plural of euro is written in Dutch with 's (**euro's**).

> *Coins:* 1, 2, 5, 10, 20, 50 c.; €1, 2
>
> *Notes:* €5, 10, 20, 50, 100, 200, 500

Pharmacy Apotheek

The **apotheek** (pharmacy) is for prescriptions and the **drogisterij** (drug store) for non-prescription items such as toiletries and cosmetics. There are pharmacies open at night and at weekends (you'll find them listed in the store window).

Where's the nearest (all-night) pharmacy?	**Waar is de dichtstbijzijnde apotheek (met nachtdienst)?** *vaar is der dikhtstbayzaynder apoatayk (met nakhtdeenst)*
What time does the pharmacy open/close?	**Hoe laat gaat de apotheek open/dicht?** *hoo laat khaat der apoatayk opern/dikht*
Can you make up this prescription for me?	**Kunt u dit recept voor me klaarmaken?** *kuhnt uw dit rersept foar mer klaarmaakern*
Shall I wait?	**Kan ik erop wachten?** *kan ik ehrop vakhtern*
I'll come back for it.	**Ik haal het straks op.** *ik haal het straks op*

Dosage instructions Doseringsinstructies

How much should I take?	**Hoeveel moet ik er innemen?** *hoofayl moot ik ehr innaymern*
How many times a day should I take it?	**Hoeveel keer per dag moet ik het innemen?** *hoofayl kayr pehr dakh moot ik het innaymern*
Is it suitable for children?	**Is het geschikt voor kinderen?** *is het kherskhhikt foar kinderern*

Neem ...	Take ...
... tabletten/... theelepels	... tablets/... teaspoons
voor/na de maaltijd	before/after meals
met water	with water
heel	whole
's morgens/'s avonds	in the morning/at night
voor ... dagen	for ... days

UITSLUITEND VOOR UITWENDIG GEBRUIK	for external use only
NIET INWENDIG TE GEBRUIKEN.	not to be taken internally
NIET AUTORIJDEN NA HET INNEMEN VAN HET GENEESMIDDEL	do not drive after taking the medication

Asking advice Advies vragen

I'd like some medicine for …	**Ik wil graag medicijnen voor …** *ik vil khraakh medisaynern foar*
a cold	**verkoudheid** *ferkowthayt*
a cough	**hoesten** *hoostern*
diarrhea	**diarreee** *diaray*
a hangover	**een kater** *ayn kaater*
hay fever	**hooikoorts** *hooykoarts*
insect bites	**een insectenbeet** *ayn insekternbayt*
a sore throat	**keelpijn** *kaylpayn*
sunburn	**zonnebrand** *zonnerbrant*
motion [travel] sickness	**reisziekte** *raiszeekter*
an upset stomach	**maagpijn** *maakhpayn*
Can I get it without a prescription?	**Kan ik het zonder recept krijgen?** *kan ik het zonder rersept kraykhern*
Can I have some …?	**Mag ik wat … hebben?** *makh ik vat … hepbern*
antiseptic cream	**antiseptische crème** *antiseptisser kraym*
aspirin	**aspirine** *aspireener*
condoms	**condooms** *kondoams*
cotton [cotton wool]	**watten** *vattern*
gauze [bandages]	**gaasverband** *khaasferbant*
insect repellent	**insektenwerend middel** *insekternvayrent midderl*
medicated dressing [plasters]	**pleisters** *playsters*
painkillers	**pijnstillers** *paynstillers*
vitamins	**vitaminetabletten** *vitameenertablettern*

Toiletries Toiletartikelen

I'd like some …	**Ik wil graag wat …**	ik vil khraakh vat
after-shave	**aftershave**	_aaf_tershayv
after-sun lotion	**after-sun lotion**	aaftersan loas_hon_
deodorant	**deodorant**	day-oadoa_rant_
razor blades	**scheermesjes**	_skhayr_mesyers
sanitary napkins [towels]	**maandverband**	_maant_ferbant
soap	**zeep**	zayp
sun block	**sun block**	_san_blok
suntan lotion	**zonnebrandcrème**	_zon_nerbrantkraym
factor …	**factor…**	_fak_tor
tampons	**tampons**	tam_pons_
tissues	**tissues**	_ti_shoos
toilet paper	**toiletpapier**	toi_let_papeer
toothpaste	**tandpasta**	_tant_pasta

Haircare Haarverzorging

comb	**de kam**	der kam
conditioner	**de conditioner**	der kon_dish_erner
hair mousse/gel	**de haarmousse/gel**	der _haar_moos/zhel
hair spray	**de haarspray**	der _haar_spray
shampoo	**de shampoo**	der _sham_poa

For the baby Voor de baby

baby food	**de babyvoeding**	der _bay_beefooding
baby wipes	**de babydoekjes**	der _bay_beedookyers
diapers [nappies]	**de luiers**	der _loai_yers
sterilizing solution	**steriliseringoplossing**	sterili_zay_ringoplossing

Clothing Kleding

There is a good choice of clothing. Look for the signs
dameskleding, herenkleding, and **kinderkleding** (ladies',
men's, children's clothing) or **damesmode, herenmode,** and
kindermode (ladies', men's, children's fashion).

General Algemeen

I'd like ...	**Ik wil graag ...** *ik vil khraakh*
Do you have any ...?	**Heeft u ook ...?** *hayft uw oak*

DAMESKLEDING	ladieswear
HERENKLEDING	menswear
KINDERKLEDING	childrenswear

Color Kleur

I'm looking for something in ...	**Ik zoek naar iets in ...** *ik zook naar eets in*
beige	**beige** *bayzh*
black	**zwart** *zvart*
blue	**blauw** *blow*
brown	**bruin** *broain*
green	**groen** *khroon*
gray	**grijs** *khrays*
orange	**oranje** *oranyer*
pink	**roze** *rozer*
purple	**paars** *paars*
red	**rood** *roat*
white	**wit** *vit*
yellow	**geel** *khayl*
light ...	**licht ...** *likht*
dark ...	**donker ...** *dongker*
I want a darker / lighter shade.	**Ik wil een donkerder/lichtere tint.** *ik vil ayn dongkerder/likhterer tint*
Do you have the same in ...?	**Heeft u hetzelfde in ...?** *hayft uw hetzelfder in*

143

Clothes and accessories
Kleding en accessoires

belt	**de riem** *der reem*
bikini	**de bikini** *der bikini*
blouse	**de bloes** *der bloos*
bra	**de beha** *der bayhaa*
briefs	**de onderbroek** *der onderbrook*
cap	**de pet** *der pet*
coat	**de jas** *der yas*
dress	**de jurk** *der yuhrk*
handbag	**de handtas** *der hantas*
hat	**de hoed** *der hoot*
jacket	**het jasje** *het yashyer*
jeans	**de spijkerbroek** *der spaykerbrook*
leggings	**de leggings** *der leggings*
pants (U.S.)	**de lange broek** *der langer brook*
pantyhose [tights]	**de panty** *der pantee*
raincoat	**de regenjas** *der raykhernyas*
scarf	**de sjaal** *der shaal*
shirt (men's)	**het overhemd** *het oaferhemt*
with long/short sleeves	**met lange/korte mouwen** *met langer/korter mowern*
shorts	**de korte broek** *der korter brook*
skirt	**de rok** *der rok*
socks	**de sokken** *der sokkern*
stockings	**de kousen** *der kowsern*
suit	**het pak** *het pak*
sweater	**de trui** *der troai*
with V-/round neck	**met V-/ronde nek** *met fay/ronder nek*
sweatshirt	**het sweatshirt** *het swetshirt*
swimming trunks	**de zwembroek** *der zwembrook*
swimsuit	**het zwempak** *het zwempak*
T-shirt	**het T-shirt** *het teeshirt*
tie	**de das** *der das*
trousers	**de lange broek** *der langer brook*
underpants	**de onderbroek** *der onderbrook*

Shoes Schoenen

boots	**de laarzen** der _laars_ern
flip-flops	**de teenslippers** der _tayn_slippers
running [training] shoes	**de sportschoenen** der _sport_skhoonern
sandals	**de sandalen** der san_daa_lern
shoes	**de schoenen** der _skhoon_ern
slippers	**de sloffen** der _slof_fern

Walking/Hiking gear Wandelkleding

knapsack	**de knapzak** der _knap_zak
walking boots	**de wandelschoenen** der _vanderls_khoonern
waterproof jacket [anorak]	**het regenjek** het _rayk_hernyek
windbreaker [cagoule]	**het windjek** het _wint_yek

Fabric Stof

I want something in …	**Ik wil iets in …** ik vil eets in
cotton	**katoen** ka_toon_
denim	**spijkerstof** _spay_kerstof
lace	**kant** kant
leather	**leer** layr
linen	**linnen** _lin_nern
wool	**wol** vol
Is this …?	**Is dit …?** is dit
pure cotton	**zuiver katoen** _zoai_ver ka_toon_
synthetic	**synthetisch** sin_tay_tees
Is it hand/machine washable?	**Moet het met de hand/in de machine worden gewassen?** moot het met der hant/in der ma_shee_ner _vor_dern kher_vas_sern

ALLEEN STOMEN	dry clean only
ALLEEN MET DE HAND WASSEN	handwash only
NIET STRIJKEN	do not iron
NIET STOMEN	do not dry clean

Does it fit? Past het?

Can I try this on?	**Mag ik dit aanpassen?** *makh ik dit <u>aan</u>passern*
Where's the fitting room?	**Waar is de paskamer?** *vaar is der <u>pas</u>kaamer*
It fits well. I'll take it.	**Het past goed. Ik neem het.** *het past khoot. ik naym het*
It doesn't fit.	**Het past niet.** *het past neet*
It's too …	**Het is te …** *het is ter*
short / long	**kort/lang** *kort/lang*
tight / loose	**krap/los** *krap/los*
Do you have this in size …?	**Heeft u dit in maat …?** *hayft uw dit in maat*
What size is this?	**Welke maat is dit?** *velker maat is dit*
Could you measure me, please?	**Kunt u mijn maat nemen, alstublieft?** *kuhnt uw mayn maat <u>nay</u>mern, alstuw<u>bleeft</u>*
I don't know Dutch sizes.	**Ik ken de Nederlandse maten niet.** *ik ken der <u>nay</u>derlantser <u>maa</u>tern neet*

Size Maat

English conventions are used for sizes: XL (extra large), L (large), M (medium), and S (small).

	Dresses/Suits						Women's shoes			
American	8	10	12	14	16	18	6	7	8	9
British	10	12	14	16	18	20	$4^{1/2}$	$5^{1/2}$	$6^{1/2}$	$7^{1/2}$
Continental	36	38	40	42	44	46	37	38	40	41

	Shirts				Men's shoes								
American } British	15	16	17	18	5	6	7	8	$8^{1/2}$	9	$9^{1/2}$	10	11
Continental	38	41	43	45	38	39	41	42	43	43	44	44	45

1 centimeter (cm.) = 0.39 in.	1 inch = 2.54 cm.
1 meter (m.) = 39.37 in.	1 foot = 30.5 cm.
10 meters = 32.81 ft.	1 yard = 0.91 m.

Health and beauty
Gezondheid en schoonheid

I'd like a …	**Ik wil graag een …** *ik vil khraakh ayn*
facial	**gezichtsbehandeling** *kherzikhtsberhanderling*
manicure	**manicure** *maaneekuwrer*
massage	**massage** *massaazher*
waxing	**harsen** *haarsern*

Hairdresser Kapper

It isn't necessary to tip a hairdresser or barber.

I'd like to make an appointment for …	**Ik wil graag een afspraak maken voor …** *ik vil khraakh ayn afspraak maakern foar*
Can you make it a bit earlier/later?	**Mag het iets vroeger/later?** *makh het eets frookher/laater*
I'd like a …	**Ik wil graag …** *ik vil khraakh*
cut and blow-dry	**knippen en föhnen** *knippern en fuwnern*
shampoo and set	**shampoo en versteviger** *shampoa en ferstayverkher*
trim	**bijknippen** *bayknippern*
I'd like my hair …	**Ik wil … in mijn haar.** *ik vil … in mayn haar*
highlighted	**coupe soleil** *koop solayl*
permed	**een permanent** *ayn pehrmaanent*
Don't cut it too short.	**Niet te kort, alstublieft.** *neet ter kort, alstuwbleeft*
A little more off the …	**Een beetje meer weg aan de …** *ern beytyer mayr vehkh aan der*
back/front	**achterkant/voorkant** *akhterkant/foarkant*
neck/sides	**nek/zijkanten** *nek/zaykantern*
top	**bovenkant** *boafernkant*
That's fine, thanks.	**Dat is prima, dank u.** *dat is preema, dangk uw*

Household articles
Huishoudelijke artikelen

I'd like a(n)/some … **Ik wil graag een/wat …**
ik vil khraakh ayn/vat

adapter	**adaptor** *aadaptor*
alumin(i)um foil	**aluminiumfolie** *aaloominiuhmfoalee*
bottle opener	**flesopener** *flesoaperner*
can [tin] opener	**blikopener** *blikoaperner*
clothes pins [pegs]	**wasknijpers** *vasknaypers*
corkscrew	**kurketrekker** *kuhrkertrekker*
light bulb	**lichtpeer** *likhtpayr*
matches	**lucifers** *luwsifers*
paper napkins	**papieren servetten** *papeerern serfettern*
plastic wrap [cling film]	**huishoudfolie** *hoaishoutfoalee*
plug	**plug** *plukh*
scissors	**schaar** *skhaar*
screwdriver	**schroevendraaier** *skhrooferndraaiyer*

Cleaning items Schoonmaakmiddelen

bleach	**het bleekmiddel** *het blaykmidderl*
dishcloth [tea towel]	**de theedoek** *der taydook*
dishwashing [washing-up] liquid	**het afwasmiddel** *het afvasmidderl*
garbage [refuse] bags	**de vuilniszakken** *der foailniszakkern*
detergent [washing powder]	**het waspoeder** *het vaspooder*
sponge	**de spons** *der spons*

Dishes/Utensils [Crockery/Cutlery] Serviesgoed/Bestek

bowls	**de kommen** *der kommern*
cups	**de kopjes** *der kopyers*
forks	**de vorken** *der forkern*
glasses	**de glazen** *der khlaazern*
knives	**de messen** *der messern*
mugs	**de mokken** *der mokkern*
plates	**de borden** *der bordern*
spoons	**de lepels** *der layperls*
teaspoons	**de theelepels** *der taylayperls*

Jeweler Juwelier

Could I see …? **Mag ik … zien?**
makh ik … zeen

this/that **dit/dat** *dit/dat*

It's in the window/ **Het is in de etalage/vitrine.**
display cabinet. *het is in der aytaalaazher/feetreener*

alarm clock **de alarmklok** *der alarmklok*

battery **de batterij** *der batteray*

bracelet **de armband** *der armbant*

brooch **de broche** *der brosher*

chain **het kettinkje** *het kettingkyer*

clock **de klok** *der klok*

earrings **de oorbellen** *der oarbellern*

necklace **de halsketting** *der halsketting*

ring **de ring** *der ring*

watch **het horloge** *het horloazher*

Materials Materialen

Is this real silver/gold? **Is dit echt zilver/goud?**
is dit ehkht zilver/khowt

Is there a certificate for it? **Zit er een certificaat bij?**
zit ehr ayn sertifikaat bay

Do you have anything in …? **Heeft u iets in …?** *hayft uw eets in*

copper **koper** *koaper*

crystal (quartz) **kristal** *kristal*

cut glass **geslepen glas** *kherslaypern khlas*

diamond **diamant** *deeamant*

enamel **email** *ehmayer*

gold **goud** *khowt*

gold plate **doublé** *dooblay*

pearl **paarlemoer/parel** *paarlermoor/paarerl*

pewter **tin** *tin*

platinum **platinum** *plattinuhm*

silver **zilver** *zilver*

silver plate **zilverdoublé** *zilverdooblay*

stainless steel **roestvrij staal** *roostfray staal*

Newsstand [Newsagent]/
Tobacconist Kiosk/Sigarenwinkel

Newspapers and magazines (**kranten, tijdschriften**) are usually available in newsstands (**kiosk**), bookstores, train stations, and airports, including many foreign publications on the day of issue.

Do you sell English-language books/newspapers?	**Verkoopt u Engelse boeken/kranten?** *ferkoopt uw engilser book*ern/*krant*ern
I'd like a(n)/some ...	**Ik wil graag een/wat ...** *ik vil khraakh ayn/vat*
book	**boek** *book*
candy [sweets]	**snoep** *snoop*
chewing gum	**kauwgom** *kowkhom*
chocolate bar	**chocoladereep** *shoakoalaaderrayp*
cigarettes (pack of)	**sigaretten (pakje)** *seekhar*ettern (pak*yer*)
cigars	**sigaren** *sikhaarern*
dictionary	**woordenboek** *voardernbook*
English–Dutch	**Engels-Nederlands** *engils-nay*derlants
envelopes	**enveloppen** *enverloppern*
guidebook of ...	**gids van ...** *khits fan*
lighter	**aansteker** *aanstayker*
magazine	**tijdschrift** *tayt*skhrift
map	**kaart** *kaart*
map of the town	**kaart van de stad** *kaart fan der stat*
matches	**lucifers** *luwsifers*
newspaper	**krant** *krant*
American/English	**Amerikaanse/Engelse** *amayrikaan*ser/*engil*ser
pen	**pen** *pen*
road map of ...	**wegenkaart van ...** *vaykhern*kaart fan
stamps	**postzegels** *postzaykherls*
tobacco	**tabak** *tabak*
writing paper	**schrijfpapier** *skhrayf*papeer

Photography Fotografie

I'm looking for a … camera.	**Ik zoek naar een … fototoestel.** *ik zook naar ayn … foatoatoostel*
automatic	**automatisch** *oatoamaatees*
compact	**compact** *kompakt*
disposable	**wegwerpbaar** *vekhverpbaar*
SLR (single lens reflex)	**spiegelreflexcamera** *speekherlreeflekskaamera*
I'd like a/an …	**Ik wil graag een …** *ik vil khraakh ayn*
battery	**batterij** *batteray*
camera case	**cameratasje** *kameratashyer*
electronic flash	**elektronische flits** *aylektroaneeser flits*
filter	**filter** *filter*
lens	**lens** *lens*
lens cap	**lensdop** *lensdop*

Film/Processing Fotorolletje/Ontwikkelen

I'd like a … film.	**Ik wil graag een … film.** *ik vil khraakh ayn … film*
black and white	**zwart-wit** *zwart-vit*
color	**kleuren** *klurern*
24/36 exposures	**vierentwintig/zesendertig opnames** *feerentwinterkh/zesendehrterkh opnaamers*
I'd like this film developed.	**Ik wil dit fotorolletje laten ontwikkelen.** *ik vil dit foatoarollertyer laatern ontvikkerlern*
Would you enlarge this, please?	**Kunt u dit vergroten, alstublieft?** *kuhnt uw dit ferkhroatern alstuwbleeft*
How much does it cost for … exposures?	**Hoeveel kost het voor … opnames?** *hoofayl kost het foar … opnaamers*
When will the photos be ready?	**Wanneer zijn de foto's klaar?** *vannayr zayn der foatoas klaar*
I've come to pick up my photos.	**Ik kom mijn foto's ophalen.** *ik kom mayn foatoas ophaalern*
Here's the receipt.	**Hier is de bon.** *heer is der bon*

Post office Postkantoor

Post offices (**postkantoor**) can be recognized by the **PTT** sign.
They also sell phone cards. Mailboxes are red and have two
slots: local and other destinations (**overige bestemmingen**).

General inqueries Algemene inlichtingen

Where's the post office?	**Waar is het postkantoor?** *vaar is het postkantoar*
What time does the post office open/close?	**Hoe laat gaat het postkantoor open/dicht?** *hoo laat khaat het postkantoar oapern/dikht*
Does it close for lunch?	**Gaat het tussen de middag dicht?** *khaat het tuhssern der middakh dikht*
Where's the mailbox [postbox]?	**Waar is de brievenbus?** *vaar is der breefernbuhs*
Is there any mail for me?	**Is er ook post voor me?** *is ehr oak post foar mer*

Buying stamps Postzegels kopen

I'd like to send these postcards to …	**Ik wil deze kaarten graag naar … sturen.** *ik vil dayzer kaartern khraakh naar … stuwrern*
A stamp for this postcard/letter, please.	**Een postzegel voor deze kaart/brief, alstublieft.** *ayn postzaykherl foar dayzer kaart/breef, alstuwbleeft*
A … cent stamp, please.	**Een postzegel van … cent, alstublieft.** *ayn postzaykherl fan … sent, alstuwbleeft*
What's the postage for a letter to …?	**Hoeveel moet er op een brief naar …?** *hoofayl moot ehr op ayn breef naar*

– Dag, ik wil deze kaarten naar de Verenigde Staten sturen.
(Hello, I'd like to send these postcards to the U.S.)

– Hoeveel heeft u er? *(How many?)*

– Negen. *(Nine.)*

– *Dat is negen keer tachtig cent:*
zeven euro's twintig, alstublieft.
(That's nine times eighty cents:
seven euros twenty, please.)

152

Sending a parcel Een pakje versturen

I want to send this package [parcel] by …	**Ik wil dit pakje (per) … versturen** *ik vil dit pakyer (pehr) … ferstuwrern bay*
airmail	**per luchtpost** *pehr lukhtpost*
special delivery [express]	**per expres** *pehr ekspres*
registered mail	**aangetekend** *aankhertaykernt*
It contains …	**Er zit(ten) … in.** *er zit(tern) … in*

Kunt u even de douaneverklaring invullen?	Please fill out the customs declaration.
Wat is de waarde?	What's the value?
Wat zit erin?	What's inside?

Telecommunications Telecommunicatie

I'd like a phone card, please.	**Ik wil graag een telefoonkaart.** *ik vil khraakh ayn taylerfoankaart*
10/25/50/100 units.	**Tien/Vijfentwintig/Vijftig/Honderd eenheden.** *teen/fayfentvinterkh/fayfterkh/hondert aynhaydern*
Do you have a photocopier?	**Heeft u een fotokopieerapparaat?** *hayft uw ayn foatoakopyayrapparaat*
I'd like to send a/an …	**Ik wil graag een … versturen.** *ik vil khraakh ayn … ferstuwrern*
e-mail/fax	**e-mail/fax** *eemayl/faks*
What's your e-mail address?	**Wat is uw e-mail adres?** *vat is uhw eemayl adres*
Can I access the Internet here?	**Kan ik hier toegang verkrijgen tot het Internet?** *kan ik heer tookhang ferkraykhern tot het internet*
What are the charges per hour?	**Wat zijn de kosten per uur?** *vat zayn der kostern pehr uwr*
How do I log on?	**Hoe moet ik inloggen?** *hoo moot ik inlokhern*

PAKJES	parcels
VOLGENDE LICHTING …	next collection …
POSTE RESTANTE	general delivery [poste restante]
POSTZEGELS	stamps
TELEGRAMMEN	telegrams

Souvenirs Souvenirs

The Dutch are especially famous for their flowers, bulbs and plants, as wells as cigars, pewter, antiques – especially around the Nieuwe Spiegelstraat in Amsterdam – diamonds (Amsterdam), Delft blue pottery, Makkum pottery, tiles, clogs, candles (Gouda), and edibles such as cheese (Gouda, Edam), chocolate (Droste), biscuits (Verkade) and syrup waffles (Gouda). Souvenir shops tend to be expensive, but there are many specialty stores, as well as airport tax-free shopping.

cheese	**de kaas** *der kaas*
Delft blue pottery	**Delfts blauw** *delfts blow*
(Gouda) candles	**(Goudse) kaarsen** (*khowtser*) *kaarsern*
porcelain	**het porselein** *het porserlayn*
pottery	**het aardewerk** *het aardervehrk*
dolls in local costume	**poppen in klederdracht** *poppern in klayderdrakht*
clogs	**klompen** *klompern*
(decorative) tiles	**tegels** *taykherls*
miniature windmill	**miniatuur molen** *miniatuwr moalern*
chocolate	**chocolade** *shoakoalaader*
biscuits	**biscuits** *biskvees*
liquorice	**drop** *drop*
Dutch gin	**jenever** *yernayfer*
Dutch egg liqueur	**advocaat** *adfoakaat*
diamonds	**diamanten** *diamantern*

Gifts Cadeaux

bottle of wine	**een fles wijn** *ayn fles vayn*
box of chocolates	**een doos bonbons** *ayn doas bonbons*
calendar	**een kalender** *ayn kalender*
key ring	**een sleutelring** *ayn sloaiterlring*
postcards	**de prentkaarten** *der prentkaartern*
scarf	**de sjaal** *der shaal*
souvenir guide	**de souvenirgids** *der sooverneerkhits*
tea towel	**de theedoek** *der taydook*
T-shirt	**het T-shirt** *het teeshirt*

Music Muziek

I'd like a …	**Ik wil graag een …** *ik vil khraakh ayn*
cassette	**cassette** *kass<u>e</u>tter*
compact disc	**CD** *s<u>ay</u>day*
record	**grammofoonplaat** *khrammoa<u>foan</u>plaat*
video cassette	**videocassette** *<u>vee</u>dayoakassetter*
Who are the popular Dutch singers/bands?	**Wie zijn de populaire Nederlandse zangers/bands?** *vee zayn der poapuw<u>leh</u>rer <u>nay</u>derlantser <u>zang</u>ers/behnds*

Toys and games Speelgoed en spelletjes

I'd like a toy/game …	**Ik wil graag een speelgoedje/spelletje …** *ik vil khraakh ayn <u>spayl</u>khtootyer/ <u>spell</u>ertyer*
for a boy	**voor een jongen** *foar ayn <u>yong</u>ern*
for a 5-year-old girl	**voor een meisje van vijf jaar** *foar ayn <u>may</u>syer fan fayf yaar*
ball	**de bal** *der bal*
chess set	**het schaakspel** *het <u>skhaak</u>spel*
doll	**de pop** *der pop*
electronic game	**het elektronische spelletje** *het aylek<u>troa</u>neeser spellertyer*
teddy bear	**de teddybeer** *der <u>tedd</u>eebayr*
pail and shovel [bucket and spade]	**het emmertje en schepje** *het <u>emm</u>ertyer en <u>skhep</u>yer*

Antiques Antiek

How old is this?	**Hoe oud is dit?** *hoo owt is dit*
Do you have anything of the … era?	**Heeft u iets uit het … tijdperk?** *hayft uw eets oait het … <u>tayt</u>perk*
Can you send it to me?	**Kunt u het aan mij verzenden?** *kuhnt uw het aan may fer<u>zen</u>dern*
Will I have problems with customs?	**Krijg ik problemen met de douane?** *kraykh ik proa<u>blay</u>mern met der <u>doo</u>aaner*
Is there a certificate of authenticity?	**Is er een certificaat van echtheid?** *is ehr ayn sertifi<u>kaat</u> fan <u>ehkht</u>hayt*

WHO/WHAT/WHEN? ➤ 104

Supermarket/Minimart
Supermarkt/Kruidenier

Albert Heijn is the best-known supermarket chain. There are also the smaller Spar supermarkets, grocery shops (**kruidenier**), local markets, and discount-stores. Shopping laws have been strict, but **avondwinkels** (convenience stores which are open late) are becoming more widespread.

At the supermarket In de supermarkt

Excuse me. Where can I find …?	**Pardon. Waar vind ik …?** *pardon. vaar fint ik*
Do I pay for this here?	**Moet ik dit hier betalen?** *moot ik dit heer bertaalern*
Where are the carts [trolleys]/ baskets?	**Waar zijn de wagentjes/mandjes?** *vaar zayn der <u>vaak</u>herntyers/mantyers*
Is there a … here?	**Is er hier een …?** *is ehr heer ayn*
pharmacy	**apotheek** *apo<u>tayk</u>*
deli	**delicatessen** *dellika<u>tess</u>ern*

LEVENSMIDDELEN IN BLIK	canned foods
ZUIVELPRODUCTEN	dairy products
VERSE VIS	fresh fish
VERS VLEES	fresh meat
VERSE GROENTEN EN FRUIT	fresh produce
DIEPVRIESPRODUCTEN	frozen foods
HUISHOUDELIJKE ARTIKELEN	household goods
KIP	poultry
WIJN EN STERKE DRANK	wines and spirits
BROOD EN CAKE	bread and cakes

Weights and measures
- **1 kilogram** or **kilo (kg.)** = **1000 grams (g.)**; **100 g.** = 3.5 oz.; **1 kg.** = 2.2 lb 1 oz. = **28.35 g.**; 1 lb. = **453.60 g.**
- **1 liter (l.)** = 0.88 imp. quart or 1.06 US quart 1 imp. quart = **1.14 l.** 1 US quart = **0.951 l.** 1 imp. gallon = **4.55 l.** 1 US gallon = **3.8 l.**

Food hygiene Voedselhygiëne

BINNEN ... DAGEN NA OPENMAKEN GEBRUIKEN	eat within ... days of opening
IN DE KOELKAST BEWAREN	keep refrigerated
GESCHIKT VOOR DE MAGNETRON	microwaveable
GESCHIKT VOOR VEGETARIERS	suitable for vegetarians
HOUDBAAR TOT ...	use by ...

At the minimart Bij de kruidenier

I'd like some of that/those.	**Ik wil graag wat van dat/die.** *ik vil khraakh vat fan dat/dee*
this one/that one	**deze/die** *dayzer/dee*
these/those	**deze/die** *dayzer/dee*
to the left/right	**naar links/rechts** *naar links/rekhts*
over there/here	**daarzo/hierzo** *daarzoa/heerzoa*
Where is/are the ...?	**Waar is/zijn de ...?** *vaar is/zayn der*
I'd like some ...?	**Ik wil graag wat ...?** *ik vil khraakh vat*
a kilo (of)/half a kilo (of)	**een kilo/halve kilo** *ayn keeloa/halver keeloa*
a liter (of)/half a liter (of)	**een liter/halve liter** *ayn leeter/halver leeter*
apples	**appels** *apperls*
beer	**bier** *beer*
bread	**brood** *broat*
coffee	**koffie** *koffee*
cheese	**kaas** *kaas*
soft drinks	**frisdrank** *frisdrangk*
cookies [biscuits]	**koekjes** *kookyers*
eggs	**eieren** *ayyerern*
ham	**ham** *ham*
jam	**jam** *zham*
milk	**melk** *melk*
potato chips [crisps]	**chips** *chips*
tomatoes	**tomaten** *toamaatern*
That's all, thanks.	**Dat is het, dank u.** *dat is het, dangk uw*

Provisions/Picnic Proviand/Picknick

beer	**het bier** *het beer*
butter	**de boter** *der boater*
cakes	**de cakes** *der kayks*
cheese	**de kaas** *der kaas*
cooked meats	**vleeswaren** *flaysvaarern*
cookies [biscuits]	**de koekjes** *der kookyers*
grapes	**de druiven** *der droaifern*
instant coffee	**de oploskoffie** *der oploskoffee*
lemonade	**de limonade** *der leemoanaader*
margarine	**de margarine** *der markhariner*
oranges	**de sinaasappels** *der sinaasapperls*
yogurt	**de yoghurt** *der yokhuhrt*
rolls (bread)	**de broodjes** *der broatyers*
sausage	**de worst** *der vorst*
tea bags	**theezakjes** *tayzakyers*
wine	**de wijn** *der vayn*

Dutch bakeries (**bakker**) have first-class bread and pastries. If you ask for
één gesneden bruin, a brown loaf will be sliced for you on the spot. Try the
delicious **krentenbollen** (currant buns), **roggebrood** (pumpernickel) or any
of the **gebak** (pastries).

Police Politie

The emergency telephone number is 06-11. For other problems contact the police station (**politiebureau**).

Where's the nearest police station?	**Waar is het dichtstbijzijnde politiebureau?** _vaar is het <u>dikhtst</u>bayzaynder poa<u>lit</u>seebuwroa_
Does anyone here speak English?	**Spreekt er iemand Engels hier?** _spraykt ehr <u>ee</u>mant <u>eng</u>ils heer_
I want to report a/an ...	**Ik wil een ... melden.** _ik vil ayn ... <u>mel</u>dern_
accident	**ongeluk** _<u>ong</u>kherluhk_
attack/mugging	**aanval/beroving** _<u>aan</u>fal/ber<u>roa</u>fing_
rape	**verkrachting** _fer<u>krakh</u>ting_
My child is missing.	**Ik ben mijn kind kwijt.** _ik ben mayn kint kwayt_
Here's a photo of him/her.	**Hier is een foto van hem/haar.** _heer is ayn <u>foa</u>toa fan hem/haar_
Someone's following me.	**Ik word door iemand gevolgd.** _ik vort door <u>ee</u>mant kher<u>folkht</u>_
I need an English-speaking lawyer.	**Ik heb een Engels sprekende advocaat nodig.** _ik hep ayn engils-<u>spray</u>kernder adfoa<u>kaat</u> <u>noa</u>dikh_
I need to call someone.	**Ik moet iemand bellen.** _ik moot <u>ee</u>mant <u>bel</u>lern_
I need to contact the ... Consulate.	**Ik moet contact opnemen met het ... consulaat.** _ik moot kon<u>takt</u> <u>op</u>naymern met het ... konsuh<u>laat</u>_
American/British	**Amerikaanse/Britse** _amayri<u>kaan</u>ser/<u>brit</u>ser_

Kunt u hem/haar beschrijven?	Can you describe him/her?
mannelijk/vrouwelijk	male/female
blond haar/bruin haar	blonde/brunette
rood haar/grijs haar	red-headed/gray
lang/kort haar	long/short hair
kaal	balding
ongeveer ... lang	approximate height ...
(ongeveer) ... jaar oud	aged (approximately) ...
Hij/Zij droeg ...	He/She was wearing ...

CLOTHES ➤ 144; COLOR ➤ 143

Lost property/Theft
Gevonden voorwerpen/Diefstal

I want to report a theft.	**Ik wil een diefstal melden.** *ik vil ayn <u>deef</u>stal <u>mel</u>dern*
My ... has been stolen from my car.	**Mijn ... is uit mijn auto gestolen.** *mayn ... is oait mayn <u>oa</u>toa kher<u>stoa</u>lern*
I've been robbed/mugged.	**Ik ben beroofd.** *ik ben be<u>roaft</u>*
I've lost my ...	**Ik heb mijn ... verloren.** *ik hep mayn ... fer<u>loa</u>rern*
My ... has been stolen.	**Mijn ... is gestolen.** *mayn ... is kher<u>stoa</u>lern*
bicycle	**fiets** *feets*
camera	**fototoestel** *<u>foa</u>toatoostel*
car/rental car	**auto/huurauto** *<u>oa</u>toa/<u>huwr</u>oatoa*
credit card	**creditcard** *kre<u>deet</u>kaart*
handbag/money	**handtas/geld** *<u>han</u>tas/khelt*
passport	**paspoort** *<u>pas</u>poart*
purse/wallet	**portemonnaie/beurs** *portermon<u>nay</u>/burs*
ticket	**kaartje** *<u>kaar</u>tyer*
watch	**horloge** *hor<u>loa</u>zher*
What shall I do?	**Wat zal ik doen?** *vat zal ik doon*
I need a police report for my insurance claim.	**Ik heb een politierapport voor mijn verzekeringsclaim nodig.** *ik hep ayn poa<u>leet</u>seerapport foar mayn fer<u>zay</u>keringsklaim*

Wat bent u kwijt?	What's missing?
Wat is er gestolen?	What's been taken?
Wanneer is het gestolen?	When was it stolen?
Wanneer is het gebeurd?	When did it happen?
Waar logeert u?	Where are you staying?
Waar werd het uit gestolen?	Where was it taken from?
Waar was u op dat moment?	Where were you at the time?
We halen een tolk voor u.	We're getting an interpreter for you.
We zullen de zaak onderzoeken.	We'll look into the matter.
Kunt u dit formulier even invullen?	Please fill out this form.

Health

EU citizens with a Form E111 usually receive free treatment if they consult a doctor practicing within the **ziekenfonds** (health insurance plan), but will have to pay 10 percent of the cost of the prescribed medication. Provide a photocopy of Form E111. Information may be obtained from ANOZ Verzekeringen (030 233 066) or the local health insurance fund office (**zorgverzekeraar**).

Doctor (general) Dokter (algemeen)

Is there a hospital/dentist [surgery] nearby?	**Is er een ziekenhuis/tandarts in de buurt?** *is ehr ayn zeekernhoois/tandarts in der burt*
Is there a doctor/dentist who speaks English?	**Is er een dokter/tandarts die Engels spreekt?** *is ehr ayn dokter/tantaarts dee engils spraykt*
When is the office open?	**Wanneer is de praktijk open?** *vannayr is der praktayk oapern*
Could the doctor come to see me here?	**Kan de dokter naar mij toekomen?** *kan der dokter naar may tookoamern*
Can I make an appointment for …?	**Kan ik een afspraak maken voor …?** *kan ik ayn afspraak maakern foar*
today/tomorrow	**vandaag/morgen** *fandaakh/morkhern*
as soon as possible	**zo snel mogelijk** *zoa snel moakherlerk*
It's urgent.	**Het is dringend.** *het is dringernt*
I've got an appointment with Doctor …	**Ik heb een afspraak met dokter …** *ik hep ayn afspraak met dokter*

– Ik wil graag zo snel mogelijk een afspraak.
(I'd like an appointment as soon as possible.)
– We zitten vandaag helemaal vol. Is het dringend?
(We're fully booked today. Is it urgent?)
– Ja. (Yes.)
– Zou tien uur vijftien u schikken met dokter …?
(Would 10:15 with doctor … be okay?)
– Tien uur vijftien. Hartelijk bedankt.
(10:15. Thank you very much.)

Accident and injury   Ongelukken en verwondingen

My … is injured.	**Mijn … is gewond.**	mayn … is kher<u>von</u>t
husband/wife	**man/vrouw**	man/frow
son/daughter	**zoon/dochter**	zoan/<u>dokh</u>ter
child/friend	**kind/vriend**	kint/freent
He/She is …	**Hij/Zij is …**	hay/zay is
unconscious	**bewusteloos**	ber<u>vuh</u>sterloas
(seriously) injured	**(zwaar) gewond**	(zvaar) kher<u>von</u>t
He's/She's bleeding (heavily).	**Hij/Zij bloedt (erg).**	hay/zay bloot (ehr<u>k</u>)
I have a/an …	**Ik heb een …**	ik hep ayn
blister	**blaar**	blaar
boil	**steenpuist**	<u>stayn</u>poaist
bruise	**blauwe plek**	<u>blow</u>er plek
burn	**brandwond**	<u>brant</u>vont
cut	**snijwond**	<u>snay</u>vont
insect bite/sting	**insectenbeet/steek**	in<u>sek</u>ternbayt/stayk
lump	**gezwel**	kher<u>zwel</u>
strained muscle	**spier verrekt**	speer fer<u>rehkt</u>
scratch [graze]	**schaafwond**	<u>skhaaf</u>vont
swelling	**zwelling**	<u>zwelling</u>
I have a rash.	**Ik heb uitslag.**	ik hep <u>oait</u>slakh
My … hurts.	**Mijn … doet pijn.**	mayn … doot payn

Symptoms Symptomen

I've been feeling sick [ill] for … days.	**Ik voel me al … dagen niet lekker.** *ik fool mer al … daakhern neet lekker*
I feel faint.	**Ik voel me duizelig.** *ik fool mer doaiserlikh*
I have a fever.	**Ik heb koorts.** *ik hep koarts*
I've been vomiting.	**Ik heb overgegeven.** *ik hep oaferkherkhayfern*
I have diarrhea.	**Ik heb diarree.** *ik hep deearray*
It hurts here.	**Het doet hier pijn.** *het doot heer payn*
I have (a/an) …	**Ik heb (een) …** *ik hep (ayn)*
backache	**rugpijn** *ruhkhpayn*
cramps	**kramp** *kramp*
earache	**oorpijn** *oarpayn*
headache	**hoofdpijn** *hoaftpayn*
sore throat	**keelpijn** *kaylpayn*
stomachache	**maagpijn** *maakhpayn*
I have a cold.	**Ik ben verkouden.** *ik ben ferkowdern*
I have sunstroke.	**Ik ben verbrand.** *ik ben ferbrant*

Conditions Gezondheidstoestand

I have arthritis.	**Ik heb jicht.** *ik hep yikht*
I have asthma.	**Ik heb astma.** *ik hep asmaa*
I am …	**Ik ben …** *ik ben*
deaf	**doof** *doaf*
diabetic	**suikerpatiënt** *soaikerpasheeyent*
epileptic	**epileptisch** *aypeeleptees*
handicapped	**gehandicapt** *kherhandikapt*
(… months) pregnant	**(… maanden) zwanger** *(… maandern) zvanger*
I have a heart condition.	**Ik heb een hartconditie.** *ik hep ayn hartkondeetsee*
I have high/low blood pressure.	**Ik heb hoge/lage bloeddruk.** *ik hep hoakher/laakher blootdruhk*
I had a heart attack … years ago.	**Ik heb … jaar geleden een hartaanval gehad.** *ik hep … yaar kherlaydern ayn hartaanfal kherhat*

163

Doctor's inquiries Vragen van de dokter

Hoe lang voelt u zich al zo?	How long have you been feeling like this?
Is dit de eerste keer dat u dit heeft?	Is this the first time you've had this?
Neemt u nog andere medicijnen in?	Are you taking any other medication?
Bent u ergens allergisch voor?	Are you allergic to anything?
Bent u ingeënt tegen tetanus?	Have you been vaccinated against tetanus?
Heeft u een gezonde eetlust?	Is your appetite OK?

Examination Medisch onderzoek

Ik zal uw temperatuur/bloeddruk opnemen.	I'll take your temperature/ blood pressure.
Kunt u uw mouw even opstropen?	Please roll up your sleeve.
Kleed u zich even tot aan uw taille uit.	Please undress to the waist.
Gaat u even liggen.	Please lie down.
Kunt u uw mond opendoen?	Open your mouth.
Even diep ademhalen.	Breathe deeply.
Hoest u eens.	Please cough.
Waar doet het pijn?	Where does it hurt?
Doet het hier pijn?	Does it hurt here?

Diagnosis Diagnose

Ik wil een röntgenfoto laten maken.	I want to have an X-ray taken.
Ik neem een monster van uw bloed/ontlasting/urine.	I'm taking a specimen of your blood/stool/urine.
Ik verwijs u door naar een specialist.	I want you to see a specialist.
Ik verwijs u door naar het ziekenhuis.	I want you to go to the hospital.
Hij is gebroken/verstuikt.	It's broken/sprained.
Hij is ontwricht/gescheurd.	It's dislocated/torn.

U heeft	You have (a/an) ...
blindedarmontsteking	appendicitis
blaasontsteking	cystitis
griep	flu
voedselvergiftiging	food poisoning
een breuk	fracture
maagontsteking	gastritis
aambeien	hemorrhoids
een hernia	hernia
inflammatie van ...	inflammation of ...
de mazelen	measles
longontsteking	pneumonia
ischias	sciatica
amandelontsteking	tonsilitis
een tumor	tumor
geslachtsziekte	venereal disease
Het is ontstoken.	It's infected.
Het is besmettelijk.	It's contagious.

Treatment Behandeling

Ik geef u een ...	I'll give you a/an ...
antiseptisch middel	antiseptic
pijnstiller	painkiller
Ik geef u een recept voor ...	I'm going to prescribe ...
een antibioticakuur	a course of antibiotics
zetpillen	some suppositories
Bent u allergisch voor bepaalde medicijnen?	Are you allergic to any medication?
Neem ... één pil in	Take one pill ...
om de ... uur	every ... hours
... keer per dag	... times a day
voor/na elke maaltijd	before/after each meal
als u pijn heeft	if you are in pain
... dagen lang	for ... days
Raadpleeg bij thuiskomst een dokter.	Consult a doctor when you get home.

Parts of the body Lichaamsdelen

appendix	**de blindedarm** *der blinderdarm*
back	**de rug** *der ruhkh*
bladder	**de blaas** *der blaas*
bone	**het bot** *het bot*
breast	**de borst** *der borst*
chest	**de borst(kas)** *der borst(kas)*
ear	**het oor** *het oar*
eye	**het oog** *het oakh*
face	**het gezicht** *het kherzikht*
finger	**de vinger** *der finger*
foot	**de voet** *der foot*
gland	**de klier** *der kleer*
hand	**de hand** *der hant*
head	**het hoofd** *het hoaft*
heart	**het hart** *het hart*
jaw	**de kaak** *der kaak*
joint	**het gewricht** *het khervrikht*
kidney	**de nier** *der neer*
knee	**de knie** *der knee*
leg	**het been** *het bayn*
liver	**de lever** *der layver*
mouth	**de mond** *der mont*
muscle	**de spier** *der speer*
neck	**de nek** *der nek*
nose	**de neus** *der nus*
shoulder	**de schouder** *der skhowder*
skin	**de huid** *der hoait*
stomach	**de maag** *der maakh*
thigh	**de dij** *der day*
throat	**de keel** *der kayl*
thumb	**de duim** *der doaim*
toe	**de teen** *der tayn*
tongue	**de tong** *der tong*
tonsils	**de amandelen** *der aamanderlern*
vein	**de ader** *der aader*

Gynecologist Gynaecoloog

I have ...	**Ik heb ...** *ik hep*
abdominal pains	**pijn in mijn buik** *payn in mayn boaik*
period pains	**menstruatiepijn** *menstruwaatseepayn*
a vaginal infection	**een vaginale infectie** *ayn vakhinaaler infektsee*
I haven't had my period for ... months.	**Ik ben al ... maanden niet ongesteld geweest.** *ik ben al ... maandern neet onkherstelt khervayst*
I'm on the Pill.	**Ik ben aan de pil.** *ik ben aan der pil*

Hospital Ziekenhuis

Please notify my family.	**Kunt u mijn familie op de hoogte brengen?** *kuhnt uw mayn faameelee op der hoakhter brengern*
I'm in pain.	**Ik heb pijn.** *ik hep payn*
I can't eat/sleep.	**Ik kan niet eten/slapen.** *ik kan neet aytern/slaapern*
When will the doctor come?	**Wanneer komt de dokter?** *vannayr komt der dokter*
Which room is ... in?	**Op welke afdeling ligt ...?** *op velker afdayling likht*
I'm visiting ...	**Ik kom op bezoek bij ...** *ik kom op berzook bay*

Optician Opticiën

I'm near [short-] sighted/ far [long-] sighted.	**Ik ben bijziend/verziend.** *ik ben bayzeent/fehrzeent*
I've lost ...	**Ik heb ... verloren.** *ik hep ... ferloarern*
one of my contact lenses	**een van mijn contactlenzen** *ayn fan mayn kontaktlenzern*
my glasses/a lens	**mijn bril/een lens** *mayn bril/ayn lens*
Can you replace it?	**Kunt u hem vervangen?** *kuhnt uw hem ferfangern*

Dentist Tandarts

I have toothache.	**Ik heb kiespijn.** *ik hep <u>kees</u>payn*
This tooth hurts.	**Deze kies doet pijn.** *<u>day</u>zer kees doot payn*
I've lost a filling/tooth.	**Ik heb een vulling/kies verloren.** *ik hep ayn <u>fuhl</u>ling/kees fer<u>loa</u>rern*
Can you repair this denture?	**Kunt u dit kunstgebit repareren?** *kuhnt uw dit <u>kuhnst</u>kherbit raypa<u>ray</u>rern*
I don't want it extracted.	**Ik wil hem niet laten uittrekken.** *ik vil hem neet <u>laa</u>tern <u>oa</u>ittrekkern*

Ik ga u een injectie/ verdovingsmiddel geven.	I'm going to give you an injection/an anesthetic.
U heeft een vulling/kroon nodig.	You need a filling/cap [crown].
Hij moet eruit.	It has to come out.
Ik kan er alleen tijdelijk iets aan doen.	I can only fix it temporarily.
U mag … uur niets eten.	Don't eat anything for … hours.

Payment and insurance
Betaling en verzekering

How much do I owe you?	**Hoeveel ben ik u verschuldigd?** *<u>hoo</u>fayl ben ik uw fer<u>skhuhl</u>dikht*
I have insurance.	**Ik ben verzekerd.** *ik ben fer<u>zay</u>kert*
Can I have a receipt for my insurance?	**Mag ik een kwitantie voor mijn verzekering hebben?** *makh ik ayn kvi<u>tant</u>see foar mayn fer<u>zay</u>kering <u>hep</u>bern*
Would you fill out this insurance form, please?	**Kunt u dit verzekeringsformulier even invullen?** *kuhnt uw dit fer<u>zay</u>kerings-formuhleer <u>ay</u>fern <u>in</u>fuhllern*

Dictionary (A-Z)
English – Dutch

To enable correct usage, most terms in this dictionary are either
followed by an expression or cross-referenced to pages where the word
appears in a phrase. The notes below provide some basic grammar guidelines.

Nouns

Nouns are either masculine (m), feminine (f), or neuter (n).
Masculine/feminine nouns take the definite article **de**, neuter nouns take
het. All nouns take the indefinite article **een** (a/an). The plural is generally
formed by adding **en**, most nouns ending with **je**, **el**, **em**, **en**, and **aar** take **s**
(➤ 15). A few words make their plural by adding **'s**: **café/café's**.

de deur	**de deuren** (m/f)	the door	the doors
het raam	**de ramen** (n)	the window	the windows
het huisje	**de huisjes** (n)	the house	the houses

Adjectives

Adjectives usually end with an **e**. The main exception is before a neuter
indefinite (singular) noun.

de kleine jongen/een kleine jongen/de kleine jongens (m/f)
the small boy/a small boy/the small boys
het kleine kind/een klein kind/de kleine kinderen (n)
the small child/a small child/the small children

However, no **e** is added when the adjective *follows* the noun, or when the
noun is preceded by **elk/ieder** (each), **veel** (much), **zulk** (such), and **geen** (no).

de jongen is klein	the boy is small
geen warm water	no warm water

Verbs

In this dictionary, verbs are generally shown in the infinitive (to say, to
eat, etc.). Here are the indispensable verbs *to have* and *to be*, and an
example of a regular verb, in the present tense:

	hebben (to have)	**zijn** (to be)	**lachen** (to laugh)
ik (I)	heb	ben	lach
u/jij (you sing. form./inf.)	heeft/hebt	bent	lacht
hij/zij (he/she)	heeft	is	lacht
wij (we)	hebben	zijn	lachen
u/jullie (you pl. form./inf.)	heeft/hebben	bent/zijn	lacht/lachen
zij (they)	hebben	zijn	lachen

To put the verb into the negative, place **niet** (not) after the verb, or after
the direct object.

Ik rook niet.	I don't smoke.
Ik heb de kaartjes niet.	I don't have the tickets.

A a few of ... een paar ... 15
a little een beetje 15
a lot veel 15
a quarter past *(after)* kwart over 220
a quarter to *(before)* kwart voor 220
a.m. 's morgens
about *(approximately)* ongeveer 15
abroad in het buitenland
abseiling abseiling n 115
accept, to accepteren 136; **do you accept ...?** accepteert u ...? 42, 136
accident *(road)* ongeluk n 92, 159
accidentally per ongeluk 28
accompany, to meegaan 65
accountant accountant m/f 121
acne acné
across naar de overkant 12
acrylic acryl
actor/actress acteur/actrice m/f
adapter adaptor m/f 26, 148
address adres n 23, 84, 93, 126
adjoining room kamer ernaast m/f 22
admission charge toegangsprijs m/f 114
adult *(noun)* volwassene m/f 81, 100
advocaat advocaat m/f 154
aerobics aerobics m/f 115
afraid; I'm ~ *(I'm sorry)* Ik vrees 126
after na 13, 95, 165
after shave aftershave m/f 142
after-sun lotion after-sun lotion m/f 142
afternoon middag m/f; **in the ~** 's middags 221; **good ~** goedemiddag 224
aged ...; to be ~ ...jaar oud zijn 159
ago geleden 221; **... years ago** ... jaar geleden 163
agree; I don't ~ ik ben het er niet mee eens

air lucht m/f : **~ conditioning** airconditioning m/f 22, 25; **~ mattress** luchtbed n 31; **~ pump** luchtpomp m/f 87; **~ sickness bag** papieren zak m/f 70
airmail luchtpost m/f 153
airport luchthaven m/f, vliegveld n 84, 96
aisle seat plaats bij het gangpad m/f 69, 74
alarm clock alarmklok m/f 149
alcoholic *(drink)* alcoholisch
all alle
allergic; to be ~ allergisch zijn 164, 165
allergy allergie
allowance toegestane hoeveelheid m/f 67
almost bijna
alone alleen: **leave me ~!** laat me met rust! 126
already al 28
also ook 19
alter; to ~ vermaken 137
alumin(i)um foil aluminumfolie m/f 148
always altijd 13
am; I ~ ik ben 7
amazing verbazingwekkend 101
ambassador ambassadeur m/f
ambulance ziekenwagen m/f 92
American *(adj.)* Amerikaans 150, 159: **~ football** Amerikaans voetbal n 115; **~ Plan [A.P.]** vol pension 24
amount *(money)* bedrag n 42
amusement arcade speelhal m/f 113
anaesthetic verdovingsmiddel n 168
and en 19
angling vissen n 115
animal dier n 106
anorak regenjack n 145; anorak m/f
another een ander(e) 21, 25, 125
antacid antacidum

antibiotics antibiotica m/fpl 165

antifreeze antivries m/f

antique *(noun)* antiek n 155

antiseptic *(noun)* antiseptisch middel n 165; *(adj.)* ~ **cream** antiseptische crème m/f 141

any wat

anyone iemand 67; **does ~ speak English?** spreekt er iemand hier Engels?

anything else? verder nog iets?

apartment appartement n 28

apologize; I ~ ik verontschuldig mij

appendicitis blindedarmontsteking m/f 165

appendix blindedarm m/f 166

appetite eetlust m/f 164

apples appels m/fpl 157

appointment afspraak m/f 161; **to make an ~** een afspraak maken 147

approximately ongeveer 159

April april 218

archery boogschieten n 115

architect architect m/f 104

are there ...? zijn er ...? 17

area code kengetal n 127

arm arm m/f

around *(time)* rond 13

arrive; to ~ aankomen in 13, 68, 70, 71, 76

art gallery kunstgalerie m/f 99

arthritis, to have jicht hebben 163

artificial sweetener zoetjes npl 38

artist kunstenaar m/f 104

ashtray asbak m/f 39

ask; I asked for ... ik heb om ... gevraagd 41

aspirin aspirine m/f 141

asthma; to have ~ astma hebben 163

at *(time)* om 13, 84, 221; *(place)* op 12

At last! Eindelijk! 19

at least minstens 23

athletics atletiek m/f 115

attack aanval m/f 159

attractive aantrekkelijk

audio-guide audiorondleiding m/f

August augustus 218

aunt tante m/f 120

Australia Australië 119

authentic; is it authentic? is het authentiek?

authenticity echtheid m/f 155

automated teller (ATM) geldautomaat m/f 139

automatic *(car)* auto met automatische versnelling m/f 86; *(camera)* automatisch fototoestel n 151

automobile auto m/f

autumn herfst m/f 219

available *(free)* vrij 77

avalanche lawine

awful afschuwelijk 101

B **baby** baby m/f 39, 113; ~ **food** babyvoeding m/f 142; ~ **wipes** babydoekjes npl 142; **~sitter** babysitter m/f 113

back rug m/f 166; **~ache** rugpijn m/f 163

back *(not front)* achterkant m/f 147

back; to be ~ terug zijn 98

backpacking rondtrekken

bad slecht 14

badminton badminton m/f 115

bag tas m/f 160

baggage bagage m/f 32, 71; ~ **check** bagage-reclaim m/f 71; bagagedepot n 73

bakery bakkerswinkel m/f 130

balcony balkon n 29

ball bal m/f 155

ballet ballet n 108, 111

band *(musical group)* band m/f 111, 155

bandage verband n 141
bank bank m/f 96, 130, 138
bar bar m/f 26, 112
barber herenkapper m/f 131
baseball baseball m/f 115
basement kelder m/f
basket mandje n 156
basketball basketbal m/f 115
bath bad 21; **~ towel** badhanddoek m/f 27; **~room** badkamer m/f 26, 29, 98, 113
battery accu m/f 88; batterij m/f 137, 149, 151
battle site slagveld n 99
be; to ~ zijn 17, 121
beach strand n 107, 117
beam *(headlights)* volle lichten m/fpl 86
beard baard m/f
beautiful mooi 14; prachtig 101
because omdat 15; **~ of** door 15
bed bed n 21; **~ and breakfast** logies-ontbijt 24
bedding beddegoed n 29
bedroom slaapkamer m/f 29
beer biertje n 40; bier n 157, 158
before voor 165; *(time)* voor 13, 221
begin; to ~ beginnen
behind achter 95
beige beige 143
Belgium België 119
belong; this ~s to me dit is van mij
belt riem m/f 144
berth couchette m/f 74, 77
best best
better beter 14
between tussen 221; **~ jobs** tussen banen in 121
bib slabbetje n
bicycle fiets m/f 75, 83, 160

bidet bidet n
big groot 14, 134; **bigger** groter 24
bikini bikini m/f 144
bill rekening m/f 32
bill *(restaurant, etc.)* rekening m/f 42
bin liner vuilniszak m/f
binoculars verrekijker m/f
bird vogel m/f 106
birthday verjaardag m/f 219
biscuit koekje n 154, 157, 158
bite *(insect)* steek m/f
bitten: I've been bitten by a dog ik ben door een hond gebeten
bitter bitter 41
bizarre bizar
black zwart 143; **~** *(coffee)* zonder melk 40
black and white film *(camera)* zwart-wit film n 151
bladder blaas m/f 166
blanket deken m/f 27
bleach bleekmiddel n 148
bleeding; he's bleeding hij bloedt 162
blind jaloezie m/f 25
blister blaar m/f 162
blocked; to be ~ verstopt zijn 25
blood bloed n 164; **~ group** bloedgroep m/f; **~ pressure** bloeddruk m/f 163, 164
blouse blouse m/f 144
blow-dry föhnen 147
blue blauw 143
blush rosé 50
board; on ~ aan boord
boarding card boarding-kaart m/f 70
boat trip boottocht m/f 81; rondvaart m/f 97
boil steenpuist m/f 162
boiled gekookt
boiler boiler m/f 29
bone bot n 166

book boek n 150; **~store** boekwinkel m/f 130

book of tickets strippenkaart m/f 79

booted; to be ~ een wielklem op de auto krijgen 87

boots laarzen m/fpl 116, 145

boring saai 101

born; to be ~ geboren zijn 119; **I was ~ in** ik ben geboren in …

borrow; may I ~ your ...? mag ik uw … lenen?

botanical garden botanische tuin m/f 99

bottle fles m/f 37; **~ of wine** fles wijn m/f 154; **~-opener** flessenopener m/f 148

bowel darm m/f

bowls kommen m/fpl 148

box zak m/f 110; **~ of chocolates** doos bonbons m/f 154

boxing boxen 115

boy jongen m/f 120, 155

boyfriend vriend m/f 120

bra beha m/f 144

bracelet armband m/f 149

brakes remmen 83

bread brood n 38, 157

break down; to ~ *(go wrong)* pech hebben 88; **the cooker has broken down** het fornuis doet het niet 28

break; to ~ breken 28

breakdown truck takelwagen m/f 88

breakfast ontbijt n 27

breast borst m/f 166

breathe; to ~ ademhalen 92, 164

breathtaking adembenemend 101

bridge brug m/f 95, 107

briefs onderbroek m/f 144

bring; to ~ meenemen 125; brengen 113

Britain Groot-Brittannië 119

British *(adj.)* Brits 159

brochure brochure m/f

broken gebroken 137

broken; to be ~ gebroken zijn 25, 164

bronchitis bronchitis

brooch broche m/f 149

brother broer m/f 120

brown bruin 143

browse; to ~ *(in shop)* kijken 133

bruise blauwe plek m/f 162

bucket emmertje n 155

building gebouw n

built; to be ~ gebouwd zijn 104

bulletin board mededelingenbord n 26

bureau de change geldwisselkantoor n 138

burger burger m/f 40

burger stand patatkraam m/f 35

burn brandwond m/f 162

bus bus m/f 70, 71, 79, 123; **~ route** busroute m/f 96; **~ station** busstation n 78; **~ stop** bushalte m/f 65, 78, 96

business zaken m/fpl 123; **~ class** business class 68; **~ world** zakenwereld m/f 121; **on ~** voor zaken 66

busy; to be ~ *(occupied)* het druk hebben 36, 125

but maar 19

butane gas butagas npl 30, 31

butcher slager m/f 130; **~ shop** slagerij m/f

butter boter m/f 38, 158

button knoop m/f

buy; to ~ kopen 79, 80, 81, 98, 125, 133

by *(near)* bij 36; *(time)* niet later dan 13, 221; **~ bus** met de bus 17; **~ car** met de auto 17, 94; **~ train** met de trein 17; **~ cash** met contanten 17; **~ credit card** met een creditcard 17

bye! dag!

C **cabaret** cabaret n 112

cabin hut m/f 81

café eethuisje n 35

cagoule windjek n 145

cake cake m/f 40

cakes cakes m/fpl 158

calendar kalender m/f 154

call; to ~ *(telephone)* bellen 87, 92, 127, 128, 159; **to ~ collect** voor rekening van de opgeroepene bellen 127; **to ~ for s.o.,** iemand ophalen 125; **~ the police!** bel de politie! 92

called: to be called heten 94

camera fototoestel n 151, 160; **~ case** cameratasje n 151; **~ store** fotowinkel m/f 130

camp; to ~ camperen; **~site** kampeerplaats m/f 30, 123; **~bed** kampeerbed n 31

can I have? mag ik … hebben? 18

can opener blikopener m/f 148

can: I can/I can't Ik kan/Ik kan niet 18

Canada Canada 119

canal kanaal n 107, gracht m/f 107

cancel, to cancellen 68

cancer *(disease)* kanker

candle kaars m/f 154

candy snoep n 150

canoeing kanovaren 115

cap pet m/f 144; *(dental)* kroon m/f 168

car auto m/f 30, 73, 81, 86, 88, 93, 123, 160; **~ ferry** autoveerboot m/f 81; **~ park** parkeerplaats m/f 26, 96; **~ rental** autoverhuurbedrijf n 70; **by ~** met de auto 95; *(train compartment)* wagon m/f 75

carafe karaf m/f 37

caravan caravan m/f 30

cards: to play cards kaarten 121

careful: be careful! voorzichtig!

carpet *(rug)* tapijt n

carrier bag boodschappentas m/f

carry-cot reiswiegje n

cart wagentje n 156

carton zak m/f 110

case *(suitcase)* koffer m/f 69

cash contanten n/fpl 42, 136; **~ desk** kassa m/f 132; **~ machine** geldautomaat m/f 139; **~ register receipt** betalingsbewijs m/f; **to ~** verzilveren 138

cashier kassa m/f 132

casino casino n 112

cassette cassette m/f 155

castle kasteel n 99

catch, to *(bus)* halen

cathedral kathedraal m/f 99

Catholic katholiek 105

cave grot m/f 107

CD CD m/f ; **~player** CD-speler m/f

cemetery begraafplaats m/f 99

center of town stadscentrum n 21

central heating centrale verwarming m/f

ceramics ceramiek m/f

certificate certificaat n 149, 155

chain kettinkje n 149

change *(noun)* wisselgeld n 84, 87, 136

change; to ~ *(buses, trains)* overstappen 75, 79, 80; *(money)* wisselen 138; *(reservation)* veranderen 68; *(baby)* verschonen 39, 113; **changing facilities** verschoningsfaciliteiten voor baby's

charcoal houtskool m/f 31

charge kosten m/fpl 30, 116, 153

charter flight chartervlucht m/f

cheap goedkoop 14, 134

cheaper goedkoper 21, 24, 109, 134

check book chequeboekje n

check; please ~ the ... controleer de ..., alstublieft; **to ~ in** inchecken 68; **~-in desk** check-in desk m/f 69; **to ~ out** (hotel) uitchecken 32

cheers! proost!

cheese kaas m/f 154, 157, 158

chemist drogisterij m/f 131

cheque book chequeboekje n

chess; to play ~ schaken 121; **~ set** schaakspel n 155

chest borst(kas) m/f 166

chewing gum kauwgom m/f 150

child kind n 159, 162; **~'s cot** ledikant 22; **~'s seat** kinderstoeltje n 39; **~minder** kinderoppas m/f ; **children** kinderen m/fpl 22, 24, 39, 66, 81, 100, 113, 117, 120, 140

Chinese (cuisine) Chinees 35

choc-ice chocolade ijs n 110

chocolate chocolade m/f 40; **~ bar** chocoladereep m/f 150; **~ ice cream** chocolade ijs n 110

Christmas Kerst n 219

church kerk m/f 96, 99, 105

cigarette kiosk sigarenwinkel m/f 130

cigarettes sigaretten m/fpl 150

cigars sigaren m/fpl 150

cinema bioscoop m/f 110

claim check reclaim-kaartje n 71

clamped; to be ~ een wielklem op de auto krijgen 87

clean schoon 14, 39

cliff klif m/f 107

cling film huishoudfolie m/f 148

clinic kliniek m/f 131

cloakroom garderobe m/f 109

clock klok m/f 149

clog klomp m/f 154

close dichtbij 93, 95

close; to ~ (store) dichtgaan 140, 152

clothes pins wasknijpers m/fpl 148

clothing store [shop] klerenwinkel m/f 130

cloudy, to be bewolkt zijn 122

clubs (golf) golfstokken m/fpl 116

coach reisbus m/f 78; **~ station** busstation n 78; (train compartment) wagon m/f 75

coast kust m/f

coat jas m/f 144; **~check** garderobe m/f 109; **~hanger** kleerhanger m/f

cockroach kakkerlak m/f

code (area, dialling) code m/f

coffee koffie m/f 40, 157

coin munt m/f

cold koud 14, 41, 122; ('flu) verkoudheid m/f 141; **I have a ~** ik ben verkouden 163

collapse; he's ~d hij is ingestort

collect; to ~ ophalen 113, 151

color kleur m/f 143; **~ film** kleurenfilm m/f 151

comb kam m/f 142

come; to ~ komen 36, 124, 126; **to ~ back** (for collection) ophalen 140

commission commissie m/f 138

compact; ~ camera compact fototoestel m/f 151; **~disc** CD m/f 155

company (business) bedrijf n 93 ; (companionship) gezelschap n 126

compartment (train) compartiment m/f

composer componist m/f 111

computer computer

concert concert n 108, 111; **~ hall** concertgebouw n 111

concession concessie m/f

concussion; he has a ~ hij heeft een hersenschudding

conditioner conditioner m/f 142

condom condoom n 141

conductor dirigent m/f 111

confirm; to ~ bevestigen 22, 68

congratulations! gefeliciteerd!

A-Z

connection *(train)* verbinding m/f 76
conscious; he's ~ hij is bij bewustzijn
constant constant 113
constipation constipatie m/f
Consulate consulaat n 159
consult; to ~ raadplegen 165
contact lens contactlens m/f 167
contact; to ~ bereiken 28
contagious; to be ~ besmettelijk zijn 165
contain; to ~ bevatten 39, 69; erin zitten 153
contemporary dance moderne dans m/f 111
contraceptive voorbehoedsmiddel n
cook kok; to ~ koken; ~ed meats vleeswaren pl 158; ~er fornuis n 28, 29;
cookies koekjes m/fpl 157, 158
cooking *(cuisine)* keuken m/f; ~ facilities kookfaciliteiten m/fpl 30
coolbox coolbox m/f
copper koper n 149
copy copie m/f
corkscrew schroevendraaier m/f 148
correct correct
cosmetic cosmetisch
cost; to ~ kosten 84, 89
cottage vakantiehuisje n 28
cotton katoen n 145; ~ wool watten m/fpl 141
cough; to ~ hoesten 141, 164
could I have ...? mag ik …? 18
country *(nation)* land; ~ music country muziek m/f 111
courier *(guide)* koerier m/f
course *(meal)* gang m/f; *(track, path)* pad n 106; ~ of *(medication)* kuur m/f 165; of ~ natuurlijk
cousin neef (m)/nicht (f)
cover charge couvert n 112

craft shop handwerkwinkel m/f
cramps kramp m/f 163
crèche crèche m/f
credit card creditcard m/f 42, 109, 136, 139, 160; ~ number creditcard nummer n 109
crib wieg m/f 22
crisps chips m/fpl 157
crockery serviesgoed n 29
cross *(crucifix)* kruis n
cross; to ~ oversteken 95
crowded vol 31
crown *(dental)* kroon m/f 168
cruise *(noun)* cruise
crutches krukken m/f
crystal *(quartz)* kristal n 149
cup kopje n 39 148
cupboard kast m/f
currency valuta m/f 67, 138; ~ exchange geldwisselkantoor n 70, 73, 138
curtain gordijn n
customs douane m/f 67, 155
cut snijwond m/f 162; to ~ *(hair)* knippen 147; ~ glass geslepen glas n 149; to ~ grass gras maaien
cutlery bestek n 29
cycle route fietsroute m/f 106
cycling wielrennen m 115
cystitis blaasontsteking m/f 165

D daily dagelijks
damaged; to be ~ beschadigd zijn 28, 71
damp *(noun/adj.)* vochtig
dance dans m/f 111; to ~ dansen 111; to go dancing gaan dansen 124
dangerous gevaarlijk
dark donker 14, 24, 134, 143; ~er donkerder 143
daughter dochter m/f 120, 162
dawn dageraad m/f 221

day dag m/f 23, 97, 122, 221; **~ ticket** dagkaartje n; **~ trip** dagtocht m/f

dead (battery) leeg 88

deaf; to be ~ doof zijn 163

December december 218

deck chair ligstoel m/f 117

declare, to aangeven 67

deduct; to ~ (money) aftrekken

deep diep; **~ freeze** diepvriezen

defrost; to ~ ontdooien

degrees (temperature) graden m/f

delay vertraging m/f 70

delicatessen delicatessen m/f 156

delicious heerlijk 14

deliver; to (give birth) bevallen; (bring) afleveren

denim spijkerstof m/f 145

dental; ~ floss tanddraad m/f; **~ office** tandarts m/f 161; **~ surgery** tandarts m/f 161

dentist tandarts m/f 131, 168

denture kunstgebit n 168

deodorant deodorant m/f 142

depart; to ~ (train, bus) vertrekken

department store warenhuis m/f 96, 130

departure lounge vertrekhal m/f

deposit vooruitbetalen 24; **pay a ~** vooruitbetalen 83

describe; to ~ beschrijven 159

destination bestemming m/f

detail detail n

detergent reinigingsmiddel n 148; wasmiddel n

develop; to ~ (photos) ontwikkelen 151

diabetes suikerziekte m/f

diabetic (noun) diabeticus m/f 39; **to be ~** suikerpatiënt zijn 163

dialling code kengetal n 127

diamond diamant m/f 149, 154

diapers luiers m/fpl 142

diarrhea diarree m/f 141; **to have ~** diarree hebben 163; **I have ~** ik heb diarree

dice dobbelsteen m/f

dictionary woordenboek n 150

diesel diesel m/f 87

diet; I'm on a ~ ik volg een diëet

difficult moeilijk 14

dining; ~ car restauratiewagen m/f 75, 77; **~ room** eetkamer m/f 26, 29

dinner; ~ jacket smoking(jasje) m/f; **to have ~** dineren 124

direct (train, journey, etc.) rechtstreeks 75

direct; to ~ (to a place) de weg wijzen naar 18

direction; in the ~ of ... in de richting van ... 95

director (company) directeur/manager m/f

directory (telephone) telefoonboek n

dirty vuil 14, 28

disabled (noun) gehandicapten m/fpl 22, 100

discotheque discotheek m/f 112

discount korting m/f 24

dish (meal) gerecht n 37, 39; **~cloth** theedoek m/f 148; **~washing liquid** afwasmiddel n 148

dislocated; to be ~ ontwricht zijn 164

display; ~ cabinet vitrine m/f 149; **~ case** vitrine m/f 134

disposable camera wegwerpbaar fototoestel n 151

distilled water gedistilleerd water n

disturb; don't ~ niet storen

dive; to ~ duiken 117

diving equipment duikapparatuur m/f 117

divorced; to be ~ gescheiden zijn 120

dizzy; I feel ~ ik voel me draaierig

do; what ~ you ~? wat doet u? 121

A-Z

A-Z

doctor dokter m/f 92, 131, 167

doll pop m/f 154, 155

dollar dollar m/f 67, 138

door deur m/f 25, 29

double; ~ room tweepersoonskamer m/f 21; **~ cabin** tweepersoonshut m/f 81

downtown stadscentrum n 83, 99

dozen; a ~ dozijn n 217

draft [draught] getapt bier n 40

dress jurk m/f 144

drink; to ~ drinken 70; *(noun)* drankje n 37, 125, 126; **~ing water** drinkwater n 30

drip; to ~ druppelen; **the faucet [tap] ~s** de kraan druppelt

drive; to ~ rijden 93

driver chauffeur m/f; **~'s license** rijbewijs n 93

drop someone off; to ~ iemand afzetten 83

drown; someone's ~ing iemand verdrinkt

drugstore drogisterij m/f 130

drunk dronken

dry droog 50; **to ~ clean** stomen 137; **~ cleaner** stomerij m/f 131

dubbed; to be ~ nagesynchroniseerd zijn 110

dummy *(pacifier)* fopspeen

during tijdens; **~ the day** overdag 221

dustbins vuilnisbakken m/fpl 30

Dutch (language) Nederlands 11, 110, 126

duvet dekbed n

E **e-mail** e-mail m/f 153; **~ address** e-mail adres n 153

ear oor n 166; **~ drops** oordruppels m/f; **~ache** oorpijn m/f 163; **~rings** oorbellen m/fpl 149

earlier vroeger 125, 147

early vroeg 14; *(too soon)* te vroeg 221

east; to the ~ ten oosten 95

Easter Pasen m/f 219

easy makkelijk 14

eat; to ~ eten 123, 167; *(chew up/damage)* opeten 139

economy class economy class m/f 68

eggs eieren npl 157

elastic *(adj.)* elastisch

electric shaver scheerapparaat n

electrical outlets stopcontacten npl 30

electric meter electriciteitsmeter m/f 28

electronic electronisch 69; **~ flash** elektronische flits m/f 151; **~ game** elektronisch spelletje 155

elevator lift m/f 26, 132

else; something ~ iets anders

embassy ambassade m/f

emerald smaragd m/f

emergency noodgeval n 127; **~ exit** nooduitgang m/f 132

empty leeg 14

enamel email n 149

end; to ~ afgelopen zijn 108; **at the ~** aan het eind 95

engaged; to be ~ verloofd zijn 120

engine motor m/f

engineering techniek m/f 121

England Engeland 119

English Engels 11, 67, 110, 150, 159

English-speaking Engelstalig 98, 100, 159

enjoy; to ~ leuk vinden 110; houden van 124

enjoyable prettig 32

enlarge; to ~ *(photos)* vergroten 151

enough genoeg 15, 42, 136

ensuite bathroom ensuite badkamer m/f

entertainment guide uitgaansgids m/f

entrance fee entreeprijs m/f 100

entry visa inreisvisum m/f

envelope envelop m/f 150

epileptic; to be ~ epileptisch zijn 163

equipment *(sports)* uitrusting m/f 116

era tijdperk n 155

error vergissing m/f

escalator roltrap m/f 132

essential essentieel 89

euro euro m/f 139

Eurocheque Eurocheque m/f

evening avond m/f 109, 124, 132;
in the ~ 's avonds 221; **good ~**
goedenavond 224

every elk 119; **~ day** elke dag; **~ hour**
om het uur 76; **~ week** elke
week 13

examination *(medical)* onderzoek n

example voorbeeld n; **for ~**
bijvoorbeeld (bv.)

except uitgezonderd

excess baggage overvracht m/f 69

exchange rate wisselkoers m/f 138

exchange, to ruilen 137; wisselen 138

excursion excursie m/f 97

excuse me pardon 10, 11, 94; *(to a
man/woman) (getting attention)*
Meneer/Mevrouw 10

exhausted; I'm ~ ik ben uitgeput 106

exit uitgang m/f 70, 83, 132

expensive duur 14, 134

expiration [expiry] date afloopdatum
m/f 109

exposure *(photos)* opname m/f 151

express expres 153

extension *(telephone)* toestel n 128

extra *(additional)* extra 23, 27

extract; to ~ *(tooth)* uittrekken 168

eye oog n 166

F **fabric** stof m/f 145
face gezicht n 166

facial
gezichtsbehandeling
m/f 147

facilities faciliteiten
m/fpl 22, 30

factor ... factor ... m/f

faint; to feel ~ zich duizelig voelen
163

fairground kermis m/f 113

fall herfst m/f 219

family gezin n 66, 74, 120;
familie m/f 167

famous beroemd

fan ventilator m/f 25

far ver 12, 95, 130; **~sighted**
verziend 167; **how ~ is it?** hoe ver is
het? 73, 94, 106

farm boerderij m/f 107

fast snel 17, 93

fast *(clock)* voor 221; **~-food restaurant**
fast-food restaurant n 35

father vader m/f 120

faucet kraan m/f 25

faulty; this is ~ dit werkt niet

favorite [favourite] favoriet

fax fax m/f 22, 153; **~ machine**
faxapparaat n 153

February februari 218

feed; to ~ voeden 39

feeding bottle babyflesje n

feel ill; to ~ zich ziek voelen 163

female vrouwelijk m/f 159

ferry veerboot m/f 81, 123

fever koorts m/f 163

few weinig 15

fiancé(e) verloofde m/f

field weiland n 107; **~ hockey**
hockey 115

fifth vijfde 217

fight *(brawl)* gevecht

fill out; to ~ *(a form)* invullen 168

fill up; to ~ *(with gas)* volgooien 87

A-Z

filling *(dental)* vulling m/f 168

film *(movie)* film m/f 110; *(camera)* fotorolletje n 151

filter filter m/f 151

find; to ~ vinden 18

fine *(good)* goed 19; *(well)* prima 118; *(police)* boete m/f 93

finger vinger m/f 166

fire vuur n; brand m/f; **there's a ~!** er is een brand!; **~ alarm** brandalarm n; **~ department [brigade]** brandweer m/f 92; **~ escape** branduitgang m/f; **~ exit** brandtrap m/f 132; **~ extinguisher** brandblusser m/f; **~wood** brandhout n

first eerste 68, 75, 81, 132, 217; **~ floor** begane grond m/f 132; **~ class** eerste klas m/f 68, 74

fish vis; **~ restaurant** visrestaurant n 35; **~ store [~monger]** visboer m/f 130

fit; to ~ *(clothes)* passen 146; **fitting room** paskamer m/f 146

fix; to ~ *(do something about)* iets doen aan 168

flashlight [torch] zaklantaarn m/f 31

flat plat 83, 88

flavor [flavour]; what ~s do you have? wat voor smaken heeft u?

flea vlo m/f

flight vlucht m/f 68, 70; **~ number** vluchtnummer n 68

flip-flops teenslippers m/fpl 145

floor *(level)* verdieping m/f 132

florist bloemenwinkel m/f 130

flower bloem m/f 106

flu griep m/f 165

flush; the toilet won't ~ het toilet trekt niet door

fly *(insect)* vlieg m/f

foggy; to be ~ mistig zijn 122

folk art volkskunst m/f

folk music volksmuziek m/f 111

follow; to ~ volgen 95, 159

food voedsel n 39, 119; **~ poisoning** voedselvergiftiging m/f 165

foot voet m/f 166; **~ path** voetpad n 107; **~ball** voetbal m/f 115

for voor 13, 94, 117; **~ a day** voor een dag 86; **~ a week** voor een week 86

foreign currency buitenlandse valuta m/f 138

forest bos n 107

forget; to ~ vergeten 42

fork vork m/f 39, 41, 148

form formulier n 23, 160, 168

formal dress nette kleding m/f 111

fortnight twee weken m/f

fortunately gelukkig 19

fountain fontein m/f 99

four-door car vierdeurs auto m/f 86

four-wheel drive *(car)* vierwielaandrijving m/f 86

fourth vierde 217

foyer *(hotel, theater)* foyer m/f

fracture breuk m/f 165

frame *(glasses)* montuur m/f

free *(available)* vrij 36, 124; **~ of charge** gratis 69

freezer vrieskast m/f 29

French *(cuisine)* Frans 35; **~ dressing** slasaus m/f 38; **~ fries** Franse frietjes npl 38

frequent; how ~? hoe vaak? 76

frequently vaak

fresh vers 41

Friday vrijdag m/f 218

fried gebakken

friend vriend m/f 123, 162; *(male/female)* vriend/vriendin m/f 125; **~ly** vriendelijk

fries Franse frietjes m/fpl 40

frightened: to be ~ bang zijn

from uit 12, 70; van 73;
~ ... **to** *(time)* van … tot 13, 221;
where are you ~? waar komt u vandaan? 119

front voor 83; voorkant m/f 147

frosty; to be ~ vriezen 122

frying pan koekepan m/f 29

fuel *(gasoline/petrol)* brandstof m/f 86

full vol 14; **to be ~** vol zitten 21, 36

full board vol pension 24

fun; to have ~ pret hebben

funny grappig 126

furniture meubels m/fpl

fuse zekering m/f 28; ~ **box** zekeringkast m/f 28

G **gallon (U.S.=3.78 liters; U.K. = 4.55 litres)** gallon

game *(race)* wedstrijd m/f 114; *(toy)* spelletje n 155

garage garage m/f 26, 88

garbage bags vuilniszakken m/fpl 148

garden tuin m/f 35

gas; I smell ~! ik ruik gas!; ~ **bottle** gasfles m/f 28; ~ **station** benzinestation n 87; ~/**gasoline** benzine m/f 88

gastritis maagontsteking m/f 165

gate *(airport)* gate m/f 70

gauze gaas n 141

gay club gay club m/f 112

gear versnelling m/f

genuine echt 134

Germany Duitsland 119

get; to ~ *(receive)* krijgen 30, 84; **to ~ back** *(return)* terugkomen 98; **to ~ off** *(bus, etc.)* uitstappen 79; **to ~ to** komen bij/in 70, 77; **how do I ~ …?** hoe kom ik bij/in …? 73, 94

gift cadeau n 67, 154; ~ **store [shop]** cadeauwinkel m/f 131

gin gin 154

girl meisje n 120, 155; ~ **riend** vriendin m/f 120

give; to ~ geven 136

gland klier m/f 166

glass glas n 37, 39; ~**es** glazen npl 148; ~**es** *(optical)* bril m/f 167

gliding zweefvliegen n 115

glossy finish *(photos)* glans afwerking

glove handschoen m/f

go; to ~ gaan 18; ~ **away!** ga weg!;
to ~ for a walk gaan wandelen 124; **Go on.** Gaat u verder. 19;
to ~ out *(in evening)* uitgaan;
to ~ out for a meal uit eten gaan 124; **to ~ shopping** gaan winkelen 124; **to ~** gaan naar 66, 124;
to ~ *(move)* rijden 93; **it's to ~ [take away]** het is om mee te nemen 40; **let's ~!** we gaan!;
where does this bus ~? waar gaat deze bus heen?

goggles beschermende bril m/f

gold goud n 149; ~ **plate** doublé m/f 149

golf golf m/f 115; ~ **course** golfbaan m/f 116

good goed 14, 35, 42; ~ **afternoon** goedemiddag 10; ~ **evening** goedenavond 10; ~ **morning** goedemorgen 10; ~ **night** goedenacht 10; **to be ~ value** waar voor je geld zijn 101

good-bye dag 10, 224

gramme [gram] gram m/f 157

grandparents grootouders m/fpl

grapes druiven m/fpl 158

grass gras n

gray grijs 143

graze schaafwond m/f 162

great prima 19

green groen 143

greengrocer groenteboer m/f 131

greyhound racing windhonden-rennen 115

grilled gegrild

grocer kruidenier m/f; **grocery store** kruidenier m/f

A-Z

ground (*earth*) grond m/f 31; **~ floor** (= *U.S. first floor*) begane grond; **~cloth** [~**sheet**] grondzeil n 31

group groep m/f 66, 100

guarantee garantie m/f 135

guesthouse pension n 123

guide (*tour*) gids m/f 98; **~book** gids m/f 100, 150

guided; ~ tour rondleiding m/f 100; **~ walk** begeleide wandeling m/f 106

guitar gitaar m/f

gum tandvlees n

guy rope stormlijn m/f 31

gynecologist gynaecoloog m/f 167

H **hair** haar n 147; **~ mousse** haarmousse m/f 142; **~ spray** haarspray m/f 142; **~cut** kapsel n; **~dresser** kapper m/f 131, 147

half; a ~ helft m/f 217; **~ board** half pension 24; **~ past** half 220

ham ham m/f 157

hammer hamer m/f 31

hand hand m/f 166; **~ luggage** handbagage m/f 69; **~ washable** met de hand wassen 145; **~bag** handtas m/f 144, 160

handicapped; to be ~ gehandicapt zijn 163; **handicap** (*golf*) handicap

handicrafts ambachten m/fpl

handkerchief zakdoek m/f

hanger klerenhanger m/f 27

hangover kater m/f 141

happen; to gebeuren 93

happy blij; **I'm not ~ with the service** ik ben ontevreden met de service

harbor haven m/f

hard hard 31; (*difficult*) zwaar 106

hat hoed m/f 144

have; to ~ hebben 18, 42, 70, 120, 133; **could I ~ ...?** mag ik ...? 38; **does the hotel ~ (a/an) ...?** Heeft het hotel (een) ...? 22; **I'll ~ ...** ik neem ... 37

hay fever hooikoorts m/f 141

head hoofd n 166; **~ waiter** manager m/f 41; **~ache** hoofdpijn m/f 163

heading; to be ~ (*in a direction*) gaan naar 83

health gezondheid m/f; **~ food store** reformwinkel m/f 131; **~ insurance** ziekteverzekering n 168

hear; to ~ horen

hearing aid gehoorapparaat n

heart hart n 166; **~ attack** hartaanval m/f 163; **~ condition** hartconditie 163

hearts (*cards*) harten

heater verwarming m/f

heating verwarming m/f 25

heavy zwaar 14, 69, 134

height (*person*) lang 159

hello dag 10, 118

help; can you ~ me? Kunt u mij helpen? 18, 92, 133

hemorrhoids aambeien m/fpl 165

her haar 16

here hier 17, 31, 35, 77, 106, 119

hernia hernia m/f 165

hers van haar 16; **it's ~** het is de hare

hi! hallo! 10

high hoog 122, 163

highlight (*hair*) highlight m/f 147

highway snelweg m/f 88, 92, 94

hiking wandelen; **~/walking gear** wandeluitrusting m/f

hill heuvel m/f 107

him hem 16

hire huur m/f 83

his van hem/zijn 16; **it's ~** het is de zijne

historic site historische plaats m/f 99

HIV-positive HIV-positief
hobby hobby m/f 121
hold on; to ~ volhouden; *(wait on the phone)* aan de lijn blijven 128; **to ~ to** vasthouden aan
hole gat
holiday vakantie m/f 123; **~ resort** vakantieoord; **on ~** op vakantie 66
home naar huis 126; **we're going ~** wij gaan naar huis
homosexual *(adj.)* homosexueel
honeymoon; we're on our ~ wij zijn op huwelijksreis
hopefully hopelijk 19
horse paard n; **~racing** paardenrennen n 115
hospital ziekenwagen m/f 96, 131, 161, 164, 167
hot heet 14, 122; **~ dog** warme worst m/f 110; **~ spring** warme bron m/f; **~ water** warm water 25
hotel hotel n 21, 123
hour uur n 97, 117; **in an ~** over een uur 84
house huis n; **~ wine** huiswijn 50; **~wife** huisvrouw m/f 121
hovercraft hovercraft n 81
how hoe 17; **~ long?** hoe lang? 23, 68, 75, 76, 78, 88, 94, 98, 106, 135; **~ many times?** hoeveel keer? 140; **~ many?** hoeveel? 15, 21, 65, 68, 79, 80, 89, 100, 109, 136, 140; **~ old?** hoe oud? 120, 155; **How are things?** Hoe gaat het ermee? 19; **~ are you?** hoe gaat het met u? 118
hundred honderd m/f 217
hungry; I'm ~ ik heb honger
hurry; I'm in a ~ ik heb haast
hurt; to ~ pijn doen 164; **to be ~** gewond zijn 92, 162; **my ... ~s** mijn ... doet pijn 162
husband man m/f 120, 162

I ice ijs n 38; **~cream** ijs n 40; **~-cream parlor** ijssalon m/f 35; **~hockey** ijshockey m/f 115
icy; to be ~ glad zijn 122
identification identificatie m/f
ill; I'm ~ ik ben ziek
illegal; is it ~? is het illegaal?
imitation imitatie m/f 134
in 12, 88; **~ front of** voor 125
include inbegrepen 24
included; to be ~ inbegrepen zijn 42; **is ... included?** is ... inbegrepen? 86, 98
incredible ongelooflijk 101
indicate; to ~ aanwijzen
indigestion indigestie m/f
Indonesian *(cuisine)* Indonesisch 35
indoor pool overdekt zwembad n 117; binnenzwembad n
inexpensive redelijk geprijsd 35
infected; to be ~ ontstoken zijn 165
infection infectie m/f 167
inflammation inflammatie m/f 165
informal informeel
information informatie m/f 97; **~ desk** informatiebalie m/f 73; **~ office** informatiebureau n 96
injection injectie m/f 168
injured, to be gewond zijn 92, 162
innocent onschuldig
insect insect n 25; **~ bite** insectenbeet m/f 141, 162; **~ repellent** insektenwerend middel n 141; **~ sting** insectenbeet m/f 162
inside binnen 12
insist; I insist ik insisteer
insomnia slapeloosheid
instant coffee oploskoffie m/f 158
instead of ... in plaats van 38

instructions gebruiksaanwijzing m/f 135

instructor instructeur m/f

insulin insuline m/f

insurance verzekering m/f 86, 89, 93, 160, 168; **~ card [certificate]** verzekeringskaart m/f 93; **~ claim** verzekeringsclaim m/f 160

interest (*hobby*) interesse/hobby m/f 121; **to be ~ed in** geïnteresseerd zijn in 111

interesting interessant 101

International Student Card Internationale Studentenkaart m/f 29

Internet Internet n 153

interpreter tolk m/f 160

intersection kruispunt n 95

into naar 70; **~ town** de stad in 12

introduce oneself; to ~ zich voorstellen 118

invite; to ~ uitnodigen 124

iodine jodium m/f

Ireland Ierland 119

is is; **~ it ...?** is het ...? 17; **~ there ...?** is er ...? 17; **it ~ ...** het is ... 17

Italian (*cuisine*) Italiaans 35

itch; it ~es het jeukt

item ding n 69

itemized bill gedetailleerde rekening m/f 32

J **jacket** jasje n 144

jam jam m/f 157

jammed; to be ~ vast zitten 25

January januari 218

jaw kaak m/f 166

jazz jazz m/f 111

jeans spijkerbroek m/f 144; jeans m/f

jellyfish kwal m/f

jet lag; I'm jet lagged ik ben jet lagged

jet-ski jet-ski m/f 117

jeweler juwelier m/f 131, 149

job baan m/f; **what's your ~?** wat voor werk doet u?

join; to ~ in meedoen 116; (*sit with*) **can we ~ you** mogen we erbij komen zitten? 124

joint gewricht n 166

joint passport gezamenlijk paspoort n 66

joke grap m/f

journalist journalist m/f

journey reis m/f 76, 78

judo judo m/f 115

jug (*water*) kan m/f

July juli 218

jump leads startkabel m/f

jumper trui m/f

junction kruispunt n 95; (*intersection*) afslag m/f

June juni 218

K **keep; to ~** houden 84; **~ the change!** laat maar zitten!

kerosene stove primus m/f 31

ketchup ketchup m/f

kettle ketel m/f 29

key sleutel m/f 27, 28, 88; **~ ring** sleutelring m/f 154

kiddie pool kinderbadje n 113

kidney nier m/f 166

kilometer kilometer m/f 88

kind (*pleasant*) aardig; (*type*) **what ~ of ...** wat voor ...

kiss; to ~ kussen

kitchen keuken m/f 29

knapsack rugzak m/f 31; knapzak m/f 145

knee knie m/f 166

knickers slipje n

knife mes n 39, 41; **knives** messen npl 148

know; to ~ kennen 146

kosher kosher

L **label** label n
lace kant n 145

ladder ladder m / f

lake meer n 107

lamp lamp m / f 25, 29

land; to ~ *(airplane)* landen 70

language course taalcursus m / f

large groot 40, 69, 110; **larger** groter 134

last laatst 14, 68, 75, 80, 81; *(previous)* vorig / vorige 218

last; to ~ meegaan

late laat 14; **(too) ~** te laat 221; *(delayed)* vertraagd 70; **later** later 125, 147

laundromat wasserette m / f 131

laundry; ~ facilities wasfaciliteiten m / fpl 30; **~ service** wasservice 22

lavatory urinoir n

lawyer advocaat m / f 159

laxative laxerend middel n

lead; to ~ *(in a direction)* gaan naar 94

lead-free [unleaded] loodvrij 87

leader *(group)* groepsleider m / f

leak; to ~ lekken

learn; to ~ *(language)* leren

leather leer n 145

leave, to vertrekken 32, 41, 68, 70, 76, 81, 98; *(deposit)* achterlaten 73; *(place)* weggaan 126; **I've left my bag** ik heb mijn tas vergeten

left; on the ~ aan de inkerkant 76, 95

left-luggage office gevonden voorwerpen m / fpl 71; bagagedepot n 73

leg been n 166

legal; is it ~? is het legaal?

leggings leggings m / f 144

lemon citroen m / f 38

lemonade limonade m / f 158

lend; could you ~ me ...? zou u me … kunnen lenen?

length lengte m / f

lens lens m / f 151, 167; **~ cap** lensdop m / f 151

lesbian club lesbische club m / f

less minder 15

lesson les m / f 116

let; to ~ laten; **~ me know!** laat het me maar weten!

letter brief m / f 152; **~box** brievenbus

level *(adj.)* gelijk 31

library bibliotheek m / f

licorice drop m / f 154

lie down; to ~ gaan liggen 164

life leven n; **~belt** reddingsgordel; **~boat** reddingsboot; **~guard** strandmeester m / f 117; **~jacket** reddingsvest

lift lift m / f 26, 132

lift; to ~ *(hitchhiking)* liften 83

light licht 14, 25, 83, 134; **~ bulb** lichtpeer m / f 148; **lighter** lichter 143

lighter *(noun)* aansteker m / f 150

like this zo

like; to ~ mooi vinden 101; *(find pleasant)* fijn vinden 119; *(love)* houden van 121, 125, 135; **I don't ~ it** ik houd daar niet van; **I ~ it** ik vind dat leuk ; **I'd ~ ...** Ik wil graag … 18, 37, 40, 43, 141, 157

limousine limousine m / f

line *(subway)* lijn m / f 80

linen linnen n 145

lip lip m / f

lipstick lippenstift m / f

liqueur likeur m / f

liquor store slijter m / f 131

A-Z

liter liter m/f 87
little (small) klein
live; to ~ wonen 119;
to ~ together
samenwonen 120
liver lever m/f 166

living room huiskamer m/f 29
lobby *(theater, hotel)* hal m/f
local plaatselijk 37; **~ dishes**
plaatselijke gerechten m/fpl 35
lock; to ~ sluiten 88; *(noun)* slot n 25;
to ~ oneself out zichzelf
buitensluiten 27
log on; to ~ inloggen 153
long lang 144, 146; **~-distance bus**
reisbus m/f 78; **~-sighted**
verziend 167
look kijken; **to ~ for** zoeken naar 18,
133; **I'm ~ing for ...** ik zoek naar ...
143; **to ~ like** eruit zien als 71; **I'm
just ~ing** ik kijk alleen even
loose los 146
lorry *(UK)* vrachtauto m/f
lose, to verliezen 28, 138, 160; **I've lost**
ik heb verloren 100, 160; ik ben ...
kwijtgeraakt 71; **I'm lost** ik ben
verdwaald 106
lost-and-found [lost property office]
gevonden voorwerpen m/fpl 73
lots of fun erg leuk 101
louder harder 128
love; to ~ houden van; dol zijn op
119; **I ~ you** ik hou van jou
lovely *(beautiful)* prachtig 122;
(delicious) heerlijk 125
low laag 122, 163
low-fat mager
lower *(berth)* onder 74
luck; good ~ succes n 219
luggage bagage m/f 32, 69, 71;
~ carts [trolleys] bagagewagentjes
npl 71
lump gezwel n 162
lunch lunch m/f 98; **at ~time** tussen
de middag 152

lung long
Luxembourg Luxemburg 119

M **machine washable** in de
machine wassen 145
madam mevrouw
magazine tijdschrift n 150
magnificent magnifiek 101
maid kamermeisje n 27; werkster
m/f 28
mail post m/f 27, 152; **by ~** met de
post 22; **to ~** posten 27; opsturen;
~box brievenbus m/f 152
main grootst 130; **~ street**
hoofdstraat m/f 95
make up; to ~ klaarmaken 140
make-up make-up m/f
male mannelijk m/f 159
mallet houten hamer m/f 31
man man m/f
manager manager m/f 25, 41, 137
manicure manicure m/f 147
manual *(car)* met handversnelling
many veel 15
map kaart m/f 94, 106, 150
March maart 218
margarine margarine m/f 158
market markt m/f 99
married; to be ~ getrouwd zijn 120
mascara mascara m/f
mask *(diving)* masker n
mass mis m/f 105
massage massage m/f 147
match wedstrijd m/f 114
matches lucifers m/fpl 31, 148, 150
matinée matinee m/f 109
matte finish *(photos)* mat afwerking
matter; it doesn't ~ het maakt niet uit;
what's the ~? wat is er aan de
hand?
mattress matras n
May mei 218
may I? mag ik? 18

maybe misschien

me mij 16

meal maaltijd m/f 38, 42, 70, 125, 165

mean; what does this ~? Wat betekent dit? 11

measles mazelen m/fpl 165

measure; to ~ de maat nemen 146

measurement afmeting m/f

meat vlees n 41

mechanic monteur m/f 88

medication medicijnen npl 164, 165

medicine geneesmiddel n 141

medium normaal 40; (average) gemiddeld 122

meet, to ontmoeten 125

meet; pleased to ~ you leuk u te ontmoeten 118

meeting place [point] ontmoetingsplaats 12

member lid n 88, 112, 116

memorial gedenkteken n 99

men (toilets) herentoilet n

mention; don't ~ it geen dank 10

menu menu n

message boodschap m/f 27

metal metaal n

metro station metrostation n 80, 96

microwave (oven) magnetronoven m/f

midday middag m/f

midnight middernacht 13, 220

migraine migraine m/f

milk melk m/f 157; with ~ met melk 40

million miljoen n 217

mind; do you ~? is het goed? 77; vindt u het goed? 126

mine van mij 16; it's ~! dat is van mij!

mineral water mineraalwater n

mini-bar minibar m/f 32

minimart kruidenier m/f 156

minute minuut m/f

mirror spiegel m/f

missing; to be ~ ontbreken 137; kwijt zijn 159

mistake fout m/f 32, 41, 42

misunderstanding; there's been a ~ dat was een misverstand

mobile home camper m/f

Modified American Plan [M.A.P.] half pension 24

moisturizer (cream) vochtinbrengende crème m/f

monastery klooster n 99

Monday maandag m/f 218

money geld n 139, 160; ~ order postwissel m/f

month maand m/f 218

moped brommer m/f 83

more meer 15, 67

more; I'd like some ~ … ik wil graag nog wat … 39; ~ slowly langzamer 94

morning; in the ~ 's morgens 221; good ~ goedemorgen 224

mosque moskee m/f 105

mosquito bite muggensteek m/f

mother moeder m/f 120

motion sickness reisziekte m/f 141

motor motor; ~bike motorfiets m/f 83; ~boat speedboot m/f 117; ~way snelweg m/f 92, 94

mountain berg m/f 107; ~ bike mountain bike m/f; ~ pass bergpas m/f 107; ~ range bergketen m/f 107

moustache snor m/f

mouth mond m/f 164, 166; ~ ulcer mondzweer m/f

move; to ~ zich bewegen 92; don't ~ him! verplaats hem niet! 92

movie film m/f 108; ~ theater bioscoop m/f 110

Mr. M.

A-Z

Mrs. Mevr.
much veel 15
mugged; to be ~ beroofd worden 160
mugging beroving m/f 159
mugs mokken m/fpl 148
mumps bof m/f
muscle spier m/f 166
museum museum n 99
music muziek m/f 112, 121
musician musicus m/f
must; I must ik moet
mustard mosterd m/f 38
my mijn 16
myself; I'll do it ~ ik zal het zelf wel doen

N name naam m/f 22, 36, 93, 118, 120; **my ~ is ...** mijn naam is ... 118; **what's your ~?** wat is uw naam? 118
napkin servet m/f 39
nappies luiers m/fpl 142
narrow smal 14
national nationaal
nationality nationaliteit m/f 23
native Nederlands 155; plaatselijk
nature natuur m/f; **~ reserve** natuurreservaat n 107; **~ trail** natuurpad n 107
nausea misselijkheid m/f
near dichtbij 12, 84; in de buurt 35; **~-sighted** bijziend 167; **~by** in de buurt 21, 87, 116; **~est** dichtstbijzijnde 80, 88, 92, 127, 130, 140
necessary nodig 112
neck nek m/f 147, 166
necklace halsketting m/f 149
need; I ~ to ... Ik heb ... nodig 18
nephew neef m
nerve zenuw m/f
nervous system zenuwstelsel n

never nooit 13; **~ mind** geeft niet 10
new nieuw 14
New Year Nieuwjaar n 219
New Zealand Nieuw-Zeeland 119
news nieuws n; **~agent** kiosk m/f 131; **~paper** krant m/f 150; **~stand** kiosk m/f 131, 150
next volgend 14, 68, 75, 78, 80, 81, 94, 100, 218; **~ stop!** volgende halte! 79; **~ to** naast 12, 95
nice fijn 14; leuk
niece nicht f
night; at ~ 's nachts 221
night; for two ~s (in hotel) voor twee nachten 22; **~club** nachtclub m/f 112
no nee 10; **~ one** niemand 16, 92; **~ way!** geen sprake van! 19
noisy lawaaierig 14, 24
non-alcoholic alcoholvrij
non-smoking niet-roken 36, 69
none geen/geeneen 15
nonsense! onzin! 19
noon twaalf uur 's middags 220
normal normaal 67
north ten noorden 95
nose neus m/f 166
not niet; **~ bad** niet slecht 19; **~ yet** nog niet 13
nothing niets 16; **~ else** verder niets 15
notify; to ~ op de hoogte brengen 167
November november 218
now nu 13, 32, 84
number nummer n 138; **~ plate** nummerbord n; **sorry, wrong ~** sorry, verkeerd verbonden
nurse verpleegster m/f
nylon nylon

O o'clock; it's ... ~ het is ... uur 220
occasionally bij gelegenheid

occupied bezet 14

October oktober 218

odds *(betting)* kansen m/fpl 114

of course natuurlijk 19

off-licence slijter m/f 131

off-peak buiten de spits

office kantoor n

often vaak 13

oil olie m/f 38

okay okee 10, 19

old oud 14; ~ **town** oude stadsgedeelte n 99

olive oil olijfolie m/f

omelet omelet m/f 40

on *(day, date)* op 13; ~ **foot** lopend 17, 95; ~ **the left** aan de linkerkant 12; ~ **the right** aan de rechterkant 12; **to be** ~ *(of film, etc.)* draaien 110; ~**/off switch** aan/uitknop

once één keer 217; ~ **a day** één keer per dag 76

one één; ~ **like that** zó één 16; ~~**way ticket** enkeltje n 65, 68, 74, 79

open open 14; **to** ~ opengaan 100, 132, 140, 152; **opendoen** (window) 77, 164; ~**air pool** openlucht zwembad n 117; ~**ing hours** openingstijden m/fpl 100

opera opera m/f 108, 111; ~ **house** operagebouw n 99

operation operatie

opposite tegenover 12, 95

optician opticiën m/f 131, 167

or of 19

orange *(color)* oranje 143; *(fruit)* sinaasappel m/f 158

orchestra orkest n 111

order, to bestellen 32, 37, 41, 135

organized hike/walk georganiseerde wandeling m/f

our ons/onze 16; ~**s** van ons 16

out uit; ~**door** openlucht; ~**side** buiten 12, 36

outrageous belachelijk 89

oval ovaal 134

oven oven m/f

over *(more than)* over; ~ **here** hierzo 157; ~ **there** daar 36; daarzo 157; **I've been** ~**charged** ik heb teveel betaald; ~**done** te gaar 41; **to** ~**heat** oververhit worden; ~**night** één nacht 23

owe; to ~ verschuldigd zijn 168; **how much do I** ~? hoeveel was dat?

own: on my own op mijn eentje 65, 120; **I'm on my** ~ Ik ben op mijn eentje 66

owner eigenaar m/f

P **p.m.** 's middags
pacifier fopspeen m/f

pack; to ~ inpakken 69

package pakje n 153

packed lunch lunchpakje n

paddling pool kinderbadje n 113

padlock hangslot n

pail emmertje n 155

pain pijn m/f; **to be in** ~ pijn hebben 167; ~**killer** pijnstiller m/f 141, 165

paint; to ~ verven

painter schilder m/f

painting schilderij n

pair; a ~ **of** een paar n 217

palace paleis n 99

palpitations hartkloppingen m/fpl

panorama panorama n 107

pants *(U.S.)* lange broek m/f 144

panty hose panty m/f 144

paper napkins papieren servetten m/fpl 148

paracetamol paracetamol m/f

paraffin paraffine m/f 31

paralysis verlamming m/f

parcel pak n 153

parents ouders m/fpl 120

park park n 96, 99, 107

parking; ~ lot parkeerplaats m/f 26, 87, 96; **~ meter** parkeermeter m/f 87

parliament building parlementsgebouw n 99

partner *(boyfriend/girlfriend)* partner m/f

party *(social)* feestje n 124

pass; to ~ *(a place)* langskomen 77

passport paspoort n 23, 66, 69, 160; **~ number** paspoortnummer n 23

pasta pasta m/f 38

pastry store banketbakker m/f 131

patch; to ~ verstellen 137

patient *(noun)* patiënt m/f

pavement; on the ~ op de stoep

pay phone telefooncel m/f

pay, to betalen 42, 136; **can I ~ in ...** mag ik in ... betalen 67

payment betaling m/f

peak bergtop m/f 107

pearl paarlemoer m/f 149

pebbly *(beach)* kiezelstrand n 117

pedestrian; ~ crossing voetgangersoversteekplaats m/f 96; **~ zone [precinct]** verkeersvrij gebied n 96

pegs wasknijpers m/fpl 148

pen pen m/f 150

people mensen m/fpl 92, 119

pepper peper m/f 38

per; ~ day per dag 30, 83, 86, 87, 116; **~ hour** per uur 87, 116, 153; **~ night** per nacht 21, 94; **~ round** *(golf)* per ronde 116; **~ week** per week 24, 30, 83, 86

perhaps misschien 19

period periode m/f 104; **to have a ~ (menstrual)** ongesteld zijn 167; **~ pains** menstruatiepijn m/f 167

perm permanent m/f 147

person persoon m/f 93

petrol benzine m/f 88; **~ station** het benzinestation n, pomp m/f 87

pewter tin m/f 149

pharmacy apotheek m/f 131, 140, 156

phone; to ~ telefoneren; **~ card** telefoonkaart m/f 127, 153

photo; to take a ~ fotograferen; **~copier** fotokopieerapparaat n 153; **~graph** foto m/f 98; **~grapher** fotograaf m/f

phrase zinnetje n 11; **~ book** idioomboekje m/f 11

pick up; to ~ ophalen 28

picnic picnic m/f; **~ area** picknickgebied n 107

piece stuk n 69; **a ~ of ...** een stuk ... 40

pill pil m/f 165; *(contraceptive)* pil m/f 167

pillow kussen n 27; **~ case** kussensloop m/f

pilot light waakvlammetje n

pink roze 143

pipe *(smoking)* pijp m/f

pitch *(for camping)* standplaats m/f

pizza pizza m/f 40

pizzeria pizzeria m/f 35

place plaats m/f 123; **to ~ a bet** wedden 114

plane vliegtuig n 68

plan; plans plannen m/fpl 124

plant *(noun)* plant m/f

plaster pleister m/f 141

plastic plastic; **~ bags** platic zakken; **~ wrap** huishoudfolie m/f 148

plate bord m 39, 148

platform perron n 76, 73, 77,

platinum platinum n 149

play; to ~ spelen 111, 114, 121; *(drama)* vertoond worden 110; *(movie, etc.)* draaien 110; *(noun)* toneelstuk n 108; **~ group** peuterspeelzaal m/f 113; **~ground** speeltuin m/f 113; **~ing field** sportterrein n 96; **~wright** toneelschrijver m/f 110

pleasant prettig 14

please alstublieft 10

plug plug m/f 148

pneumonia longontsteking m/f 165

point to; to ~ aanwijzen 11

poison gif n

police politie m/f 92, 159; **~ report** politierapport n 160; **~ station** politiebureau n 96, 131, 159

pollen count pollentelling m/f 122

polyester polyester m/f

pond vijver m 107

pop *(music)* popmuziek m/f 111

popcorn popcorn m/f 110

popular populair 111, 155

porcelain porselein n 154

port *(harbor)* haven m/f

porter kruier m/f 71

portion portie m/f 39, 40

possible: as soon as ~ zo snel mogelijk 161

post *(noun)* post; **to ~** versturen; **~ office** postkantoor n 96, 131, 152; **~age** posttarief n 152; **~box** brievenbus m/f 152; **~card** prentkaart m/f 152, 154

potato chips chips m/fpl 157

potatoes aardappels m/fpl 38

pottery aardewerk n 154

pound *(sterling)* pond m/f 67, 138

power; ~ cut stroomonderbreking m/f; **~ points** stopcontacten npl 30

practice praktijk m/f 161

pregnant; to be ~ zwanger zijn 163, 167

premium *(gas)* [super] super m/f 87

prescription recept n 140, 141; **to give a ~** een recept geven voor 165

present *(gift)* kado n

press; to ~ persen 137

pretty schattig

price prijs m/f 24

priest priester m/f

prison gevangenis m/f

produce store groenteboer m/f 131

profession beroep n 23

program programma n 108, 109

pronounce; to ~ uitspreken

Protestant protestants 105

pub café n

public *(noun)* publiek n 100

pump pomp m/f 83, 87

puncture platte band m/f 83, 88

puppet show poppenkast-voorstelling m/f

pure zuiver 145

purple paars 143

purse portemonnaie m/f 160

push-chair wandelwagentje n

put; to ~ *(to place)* zetten 22; **can you ~ me up for the night?** kan ik hier overnachten?; **where can I ~ ...?** waar kan ik ... neerzetten?

Q **quality** kwaliteit m/f 134
quarter; a ~ kwart n 217

queue; to ~ in de rij staan 112

quick snel 14

quickest; what's the ~ way? wat is de snelste weg?

quickly snel 17

quiet rustig 14, 126; **~er** rustiger 24

R **rabbi** rabbijn m/f
racetrack [race course] renbaan m/f 114

racket *(tennis, squash)* racket n 116

railway spoorweg m/f

rain; to ~ regenen 122;
~coat regenjas m/f 144

rape verkrachting
m/f 159

rapids stroomversnelling
m/fpl 107

rare *(steak)* kort gebakken; *(unusual)*
zeldzaam

rash uitslag m/f 162

razor scheerapparaat n; **~ blades**
scheermesjes npl 142

reading lezen n 121

ready; to be ~ klaar zijn 89, 137, 151

real *(genuine)* echt 149

rear achter 83

receipt kwitantie m/f 32, 42, 89, 168;
bon m/f 151; bonnetje n 136, 137

reception *(desk)* receptie m/f

receptionist receptionist(e) m/f

reclaim tag reclaim-kaartje n 71

recommend; to ~ aanbevelen 21, 37,
50; **can you ~ ...** kunt u ...
aanbevelen? 35, 97, 108, 112

record *(L.P.)* grammofoonplaat m/f
155; **~ store** platenwinkel m/f 131

red rood 50, 143; **~ wine** rode wijn
m/f 40

reduction korting m/f 24, 68, 74, 100

refreshments eten en drinken n

refrigerator koelkast m/f 29

refund geld terug 137

refuse bags vuilniszakken m/fpl 148

region regio m/f 106; **in the ~ of ...**
ongeveer 134

registered mail aangetekend 153

registration form inschrijfformulier
n 23

regular normaal 40, 87, 110

reliable betrouwbaar 113

religion godsdienst m/f

remember; I don't ~ ik kan het me
niet herinneren

rent huur m/f 83; **to ~** huren 86, 116,
117; **to ~ out** verhuren 29; **~al car**
huurauto m/f 160

repair; to ~ repareren 89; 137, 168;
repairs reparaties m/fpl 89

repeat; to ~ herhalen 94, 128; **please
~ that** kunt u dat herhalen? 11

replace vervangen 167

replacement part
vervangingsonderdeel n 137

report *(noun)* rapport n 160; **to ~**
melden 159

required, to be vereist zijn 111; nodig
zijn 112

reservation reservering m/f 22, 36,
68, 77, 112; **~ desk** reserveringsbalie
m/f 109

reserve; to ~ reserveren 21, 74, 81,
109; **I'd like to ~ ...** ik wil graag ...
reserveren 36

rest; to ~ uitrusten 106

restaurant restaurant n 35, 112

retired; to be ~ gepensioneerd
zijn 121

return ticket retourtje n 65, 68, 74

return; to ~ terugkomen 75, 81, 106;
(surrender) retourneren 86

reverse the charges; to ~ voor
rekening van de opgeroepene
bellen 127

revolting walgelijk 14

rheumatism reumatiek m/f

rib rib m/f

rice rijst m/f 38

right *(correct)* juist 14, 77, 79, 94; **~ of
way** voorrang m/f 93; recht van
doorgang n 106; *(side)* rechts;
on the ~ aan de rechterkant 76, 95;
that's ~ dat klopt

ring ring m/f 149

rip-off afzetterij m/f 101

river rivier m/f 107; **~ cruise**
rondvaart m/f 81

road weg m/f 94, 95; **~ map**
wegenkaart m/f 150

robbed; to be ~ beroofd worden 160

robbery diefstal m/f

rock music rock m/f 111

rolls *(bread)* broodjes npl 158

romantic romantisch 101

roof dak n; **~-rack** imperiaal n

room kamer m/f 21, 25

rope touw n

rosé rosé m/f 50

round rond 134; **~ neck** ronde nek
m/f 144; **~-trip** retourtje n 65, 79;
~-trip ticket retourtje n 68, 74

route route m/f 106

rowing roeien 115

rubbish *(trash)* vuilnis m/f 28

rucksack rugzak m/f

rude; to be ~ onbeleefd zijn

rugby rugby m/f 115

ruins ruïnes m/fpl 99

run; to ~ into *(crash)* inrijden op 93;
to ~ out of *(fuel)* niet meer hebben 88

rush hour spitsuur n

S **safe** *(lock-up)* safe m/f 27
safe *(not dangerous)* veilig 117;
to feel ~ zich veilig voelen 65

safety veiligheid; **~ pins**
veiligheidsspelden

salad salade m/f 38; sla m/f

sales *(job)* verkoop m/f 121; **~ tax**
verkoopbelasting m/f 24

salt zout n 38, 39

salty zout

same dezelfde/hetzelfde 75

sand zand n

sandals sandalen m/fpl 145

sandwich broodje n 40

sandy beach zandstrand n 117

sanitary napkin [towel] luiers
m/fpl 142

satellite TV satelliet-tv
m/f 22

satin satijn

**satisfied; I'm not ~ with
this** dat staat me niet
aan

Saturday zaterdag m/f 218

sauce saus m/f 38

sauna sauna m/f 22

sausage worst m/f 158

say; how do you ~ ...? hoe zeg je ...?

scarf sjaal m/f 144, 154

scheduled flight lijnvlucht m/f

sciatica ischias m/f 165

scissors schaar m/f 148

scooter autoped m/f

Scotland Schotland 119

screwdriver schroevendraaier
m/f 148

sea zee m/f 107; **~ front**
strandboulevard; **I feel ~sick** ik voel
me zeeziek

season ticket abonnementskaart m/f

seat (on train, etc.) plaats m/f 74, 77,
108, 109

second tweede 132, 217; **~ class**
tweede klas m/f 74; **~ floor** *(U.S.)*
eerste verdieping m/f; **~-hand**
tweedehands

secretary secretaris m/secretaresse f

sedative kalmerend middel n

see; to ~ zien 18, 24, 93, 124; **~ you
soon!** tot gauw! 126

self-employed; to be ~ voor jezelf
werken 121

self-service *(gas [petrol] station)*
zelfbediening m/f 87

sell; to ~ verkopen

send; to ~ versturen 153

senior citizen zestig-plusser m/f
74, 101

separated; to be ~ uit elkaar zijn 120

separately apart 42

September september 218

serious serieus

service *(church)* kerkdienst m/f 105; *(restaurant)* bediening m/f 42

serviette servet m/f 39

set menu dagmenu n 37

sex sex m/f

shady; too ~ te veel schaduw m/f 31

shallow ondiep

shampoo shampoo m/f 142; **~ and set** shampoo en versteviger m/f 147

share; to ~ *(room)* delen

sharp scherp 69

shaving; ~ brush scheerkwast; **~ cream** scheerzeep

she zij

sheath *(contraceptive)* condoom n

sheet *(bed)* laken n 28

ship schip n 81

shirt *(men's)* overhemd n 144

shock schok m/f

shoe schoen m/f; **~ repair** schoenreparatie m/f; **~ store [shop]** schoenenwinkel m/f 131; **shoes** schoenen m/fpl 145

shop assistant winkelassistent m/f

shopping; ~ area winkelcentrum n 99; **~ basket** winkelmandje n; **~ mall [centre]** winkelcentrum n 130; **~ cart [trolley]** winkelwagentje n; **to go ~** gaan winkelen

short kort 14, 144, 146, 147; **~-sighted** bijziend 167

shorts korte broek m/f 144

shoulder schouder m/f 166

shovel schepje n 55

show; to ~ laten zien 18; 94, 134; **can you ~ me that?** kunt u me dat laten zien? 106

shower douche m/f 21, 30; **~ room** douche m/f 26

shut dicht 14; **to ~** dichtgaan 132; **when do you ~?** wanneer sluit u?

shutter luik m/f 25

sick; I'm going to be ~ ik moet kotsen

side; ~ order bijgerecht n 38; **~ street** zijstraat m/f 95; **~s** *(head)* zijkant m/f 147

sights bezienswaardigheden m/fpl

sightseeing; ~ tour rondrit m/f 97; **to go ~** gaan bezichtigen

sign *(road)* verkeersbord n 93, 95; **~post** wegwijzer m/f

silk zijde

silver zilver n 149

silver plate zilverdoublé n 149; verzilverd vaatwerk n

singer zanger m/zangeres f 155

single *(ticket)* enkeltje n 65; eenpersoons 81; **~ room** eenpersoonskamer m/f 21; **~ ticket** enkeltje n 68, 74; **to be ~** ongetrouwd zijn 120

sink wastafel m/f 25

sister zus m/f 120

sit down, please gaat u zitten

sit; to ~ zitten 36, 77, 126

sixties jaren zestig m/f 111

size maat m/f 146

skin huid m/f 166

skirt rok m/f 144

sleep; to ~ slapen 167

sleeping; ~ bag slaapzak m/f 31; **~ car** slaapwagen m/f 77; **~ car [sleeper]** slaapwagen m/f 74; **~ pill** slaappil m/f

sleeve mouw m/f 144

slice; a ~ of ... een plakje ... 40

slippers sloffen m/fpl 145

slow langzaam 14; *(clock)* achter 221; **~ down!** rustig aan!; **to be ~** langzaam zijn

slowly langzaam 11, 17; **more ~** langzamer 128

SLR camera spiegelreflexcamera m/f 151

small klein 14, 24, 40, 110, 134; **~ change** klein geld n 138; **smaller** kleiner 134

smell; there's a bad ~ er hangt hier een luchtje

smoke; to ~ roken 126

smoking (adj.) roken 36; **~ area** roken 69

snack tussendoortje n; **~ bar** snackbar m/f 73

sneakers gymschoenen m/fpl

snooker biljarten n 115

snorkel snorkel m/f

snow; to ~ sneeuwen 122

soap zeep m/f 27, 142; **~ powder** zeeppoeder m/f

soccer voetbal m/f 115

socket stopcontact n

socks sokken m/fpl 144

soft drink frisdrank m/f 110, 157

sole (shoes) zool m/f

soloist solist m/f 111

soluble aspirin oplosbare aspirine m/f

some een paar

something iets 16; **~ to eat** iets te eten 70

sometimes soms 13

son zoon m 120, 162

soon gauw 13

sore; it's ~ het doet pijn; **~ throat** keelpijn m/f 141, 163

sorry! sorry! 10

soul music soul m/f 111

sour zuur 41

south ten zuiden 95

South Africa Zuid Afrika; **South African** (noun) Zuidafrikaan

souvenir souvenir m/f 98, 154; **~ guide** souvenirgids m/f 154; **~ store** souvenirwinkel m/f 131

space ruimte m/f 30

spade schepje n 155

spare reserve 28; extra

sparkling (wine) mousserend 50

speak; to ~ spreken 11, 18, 41, 67, 128; **to ~ to someone** met iemand spreken 128; **do you ~ English?** Spreekt u Engels? 11

special speciaal 86; **~ delivery** expres 153

specialist specialist m/f 164

specimen monster n 164

spectacles bril m/f

spell; to ~ spellen 11

spend; to ~ uitgeven

spicy pikant

sponge spons m/f 148

spoon lepel m/f 39, 41, 148

sport sport m/f 121; **~ing goods store** sportwinkel m/f 131; **~s club** sportvereniging m/f 116; **~s ground** sportterrein n 96

spot (place, site) plaats m/f 31

sprained; to be ~ verstuikt zijn 164

spring lente m/f 219

square vierkant n 134

squash squash 115

stadium stadion n 96

staff personeel n 113

stain vlek; **~less steel** roestvrij staal n 149

stairs trap m/f 132

stamp postzegel m/f 152, 150

stand staan: **to ~ in line** in de rij staan 112

standby ticket standby ticket n

start; to ~ beginnen 108, 112; *(car, etc.)* starten 88

statement *(police)* verklaring m/f 93

stationer's handelaar in kantoorbenodigdheden m/f

statue standbeeld n 99

stay *(noun)* verblijf n 32; **to ~** *(remain)* blijven 23, 65; *(spend the night)* logeren 123

sterilizing solution steriliseringsoplossing m/f 142

stiff neck stijve nek m/f

still; I'm ~ waiting ik wacht nog steeds

stockings kousen m/fpl 144

stolen; to be ~ gestolen worden 71, 160

stomach maag m/f 166; **~ ache** maagpijn m/f 163

stools *(faeces)* ontlasting m/f 164

stop *(noun)* halte m/f 79, 80; **to ~** stoppen 77, 98; **to ~ at** stoppen in 76; **~cock** plugkraan m/f 28

store winkel m/f; **~ guide** winkelplattegrond m/f 132

stormy; to be ~ stormen 122

stove fornuis n 28, 29

straight ahead rechtdoor 95

strained muscle spier verrekt 162

strange vreemd

straw *(drinking)* rietje n

strawberry *(flavor)* aardbeien 40

stream beekje n 107

streetcar tram m/f 79

strong sterk

student student m/f 74, 100, 121

study; to ~ studeren 121

style stijl m/f 104

subtitled; to be ~ ondertiteld zijn 110

subway metro; **~ map** metrokaart m/f 80; **~ station** metrostation n 80, 96

sugar suiker m/f 38, 39

suggest; to ~ voorstellen 123

suit pak n 144

suitable geschikt 140; **~ for** geschikt voor

summer zomer m/f 219

sun zon; **~ block** sun block m/f 142; **to ~bathe** zonnebaden; **~burn** zonnebrand m/f 141; **~glasses** zonnebril; **too sunny** te zonnig m/f 31; **~shade** parasol m/f 117; **I have ~stroke** ik ben verbrand 163; **~tan lotion** zonnebrandcrème m/f 142

Sunday zondag m/f 218

super *(gas)* super 87

superb voortreffelijk 101

supermarket supermarkt m/f 156

supervision toezicht n 113

supplement toeslag m/f 68, 69

suppositories zetpillen m/fpl 165

sure; are you ~? weet je het zeker?

surfboard surfplank m/f 117

surname achternaam m/f

sweater trui m/f 144

sweatshirt sweatshirt n 144

sweet zoet 50; **~s** snoep n 150

swelling zwelling m/f 162

swim; to ~ zwemmen 117; **~suit** zwempak n 144

swimming *(noun)* zwemmen n 115; **~ pool** zwembad n 22, 26, 117; **~ trunks** zwembroek m/f 144

swollen; to be ~ gezwollen zijn

symptom symptoom n 163

synagogue synagoge m/f 105

synthetic synthetisch 145

T **T-shirt** T-shirt n 144, 154

table tafel m/f 36, 112; **~ tennis** tafeltennis m/f 115

take, to nemen 24, 140; *(carry)* meenemen 71; *(medicine)* innemen 165; *(require)* gebruiken 86; *(time)* duren 78; **to ~ away** afhalen 40; **to ~ out** *(tooth)* uittrekken 168; **~ photographs** foto's nemen 98, 100; **I'll ~ it** ik neem hem 24, 135; **is this seat taken?** is deze plaats bezet? 77; **~ me to ...** kunt u me naar ... rijden? 84

talk; to ~ praten

tall lang 14

tampons tampons m/fpl 142

tan bruin worden

tap kraan m/f 25

taxi taxi m/f 32, 70, 71, 84; **~ stand [rank]** taxistandplaats m/f 96

tea thee m/f 40; **~ bags** theezakjes npl 158; **~ towel** theedoek m/f 154; **~spoons** theelepels m/fpl 148

teacher leraar m/f

team team n 114

teddy bear teddybeer m/f 155

telephone telefoon m/f 22, 92; **to ~** telefoneren 127; **~ bill** telefoonrekening m/f 32; **~ booth** telefooncel m/f 127; **~ call** telefoongesprek n 32; **~ number** telefoonnummer n 127

tell; to ~ vertellen 18; **can you ~ me ...?** kunt u me waarschuwen ...? 79

temperature temperatuur m/f 164

temporarily tijdelijk 168

tennis tennis m/f 115; **~ court** tennisbaan m/f 116

tent tent m/f 30, 31; **~ pegs** haringen m/fpl 31; **~ pole** tentstok m/f 31

terminus *(bus, etc.)* eindstation n

terrace terras n 35

terrible vreselijk 19, 122

terrific uitstekend 19

tetanus tetanus m/f 164

thank you dank u 10, 118

that dat 94; **~ one** die 16, 134, 157; **~'s all** dat is het 133; **~'s true!** dat is waar! 19

theater theater n 96, 99, 110, 111; *(hospital)* operatiezaal

theft diefstal m/f 160

their hun 16

theirs van hen 16

them hen 16

theme park pretpark

then *(time)* dan 13

there daar 17; **over ~** daar 76

thermometer thermometer m/f

thermos flask thermosfles m/f

these deze 134, 157

they zij

thick dik 14

thief dief m/f; **stop ~!** houd de dief! 224

thigh dij m/f 166

thin dun 14

think; I ~ ik geloof 42

third derde 217; **~ party insurance** aansprakelijkheidsverzekering m/f

thirsty; I am ~ ik heb dorst

this dit 84, 218; **~ evening** vanavond 36; **~ one** deze 16, 134, 157

those die 134, 157

thousand duizend 217

throat keel m/f 166

thrombosis trombose

through door

thumb duim m/f 166

Thursday donderdag m/f 218

ticket kaartje n 65

ticket ticket n 68, 69; kaartje n 74, 75, 79, 80, 81, 100, 108, 109, 114, 160; **~ office** loket n 73

tie das m/f 144

tight krap 146

tights panty m/f 144

A-Z

tiles tegels m/fpl 154
till receipt betalingsbewijs m/f
time tijd m/f 32; **is it on ~?** is hij op tijd? 76; **free ~** tijd vrij 98; **what's the ~?** hoe laat is het? 220; **~table** spoorwegboekje n 75
tin opener blikopener m/f 148
tint tint m/f 143
tire band m/f 83
tired; I'm ~ ik ben moe
tissue tissue n 142
to *(place)* naar 12
tobacco tabak m/f 150
tobacconist sigarenwinkel m/f 130
today vandaag 89, 124, 161, 218
toe teen m/f 166
toilet toilet n 25, 26, 29, 98, 113; **~ paper** toiletpapier n 25, 142
tomatoes tomaten m/fpl 157
tomorrow morgen 36, 84, 122, 124, 161, 218
tongue tong m/f 166
tonight vanavond 108, 110, 124
tonsilitis amandelontsteking m/f 165
tonsils amandelen m/fpl 166
too te 17, 41, 93, 135, 146; **~ much** te veel 15
tooth tand m/f 168; **~ache** tandpijn; **~brush** tandenborstel; **~paste** tandpasta m/f 142
top top; *(of head)* bovenkant m/f 147
torn; to be ~ *(muscle)* gescheurd zijn 164; **this is ~** dit is gescheurd
tough *(food)* taai 41
tour rondreis m/f 98; **~ guide** reisgids m/f 27; **~ operator** reisorgaisator m/f 26
tourist tourist; **~ office** VVV m/f 97
tow truck takelwagen m/f 88
towel handdoek m/f
tower toren m/f 99

town stad m/f 70; plaats m/f 94; **~ hall** stadhuis n 99;
toy speelgoed n 155
traffic verkeer n; **~ jam** verkeersopstopping m/f; **~ light** stoplicht n 95; **~ violation [offence]** verkeersovertreding m/f
trailer trailer m/f 30; *(caravan)* caravan m/f 81
train trein m/f 13, 73, 75, 77, 123; **~ station** station n 73, 84, 96
trained opgeleid 113
tram tram m/f 79
transfer overstappen
transit; in ~ tijdens het vervoer
translate; to ~ vertalen 11
translation vertaling m/f
translator vertaler m/f
trashcans vuilnisbakken m/fpl 30
travel; to ~ reizen; **~ agency** reisbureau n 131; **~ sickness** reisziekte m/f 141; **~'s check [cheque]** reischeque m/f 136, 138
tray plateau n
tree boom m/f 106
trim bijknippen 147
trip reis m/f 76, 78
trolley wagentje n 156
trousers lange broek m/f 144; **~ press** broekpers
truck vrachtwagen m/f
true; that's not ~ dat is niet waar
try on; to ~ *(clothes)* aanpassen 146
Tuesday dinsdag m/f 218
tumor tumor m/f 165
tunnel tunnel m/f
turn; to ~ down *(volume, heat)* lager zetten; **to ~ off** uitdoen 25; **to ~ on** aandoen 25; **to ~ up** hoger zetten
TV tv 22
tweezers pincet n
twice twee keer 217; **~ a day** twee keer per dag 76

twist; I've ~ed my ankle ik heb mijn enkel verstuikt

two-door car tweedeurs auto m/f 86

type soort n 109; **what ~ of …?** wat voor soort …? 112

typical typisch 37

tyre band m/f 83

U U.K. Groot-Brittannië 119

U.S. Verenigde Staten 119

ugly lelijk 14, 101

ulcer zweer n

umbrella parasol m/f 117

uncle oom m/f 120

unconscious; to be ~ bewusteloos zijn 92; **he's ~** hij is bewusteloos 162

under onder; **~done** niet gaar 41; licht gebakken; **~pants** onderbroek m/f 144

understand; to ~ begrijpen 11; **do you ~?** begrijpt u het? 11; **I don't ~** ik begrijp het niet 11, 67

undress; to ~ zich uitkleden 164

unemployed werkeloos

uneven (ground) ongelijk 31

unfortunately helaas 19

uniform uniform n

units (phone card) eenheden 153

United States Verenigde Staten

unleaded gas [petrol] loodvrije bezine m/f

unlimited mileage kilometers onbeperkt

unlock; to ~ openen

unpleasant vervelend 14

unscrew; to ~ losschroeven

until tot 221

up to tot aan 12

upper (berth) boven 74

upset stomach maagpijn m/f 141

urgent dringend 161

urine urine m/f 164

USA USA

use; to ~ gebruiken 139; **for my personal ~** voor mijn persoonlijk gebruik 67

V V-neck V-nek m/f 144

vacant vrij 14

vacation vakantie m/f 123; **on ~** op vakantie 66

vaccinated against; to be ~ ingeënt zijn tegen 164

vaginal infection vaginale infectie m/f 167

valet service valet service m/f

valid geldig 75

validate; to ~ bevestigen

valley vallei m/f 107

valuable waardevol

valve plugkraan m/f 28

vanilla (flavor) vanille 40

VAT BTW m/t 24; **~ receipt** BTW quitantie

vegan veganist m/f

vegetables groenten m/fpl 38

vegetarian vegetarisch 35, 39

vein ader m/f 166

venereal disease geslachtsziekte m/f 165

ventilator ventilator m/f

very heel 17; **~ good** heel goed 19

video game videospelletje n ; **~ recorder** videorecorder m/f; **~cassette** videocassette m/f 155

view uitzicht n; **with a ~ of the sea** met uitzicht op zee; **~point** uitkijkpunt n 99, 107

village dorp n 107

vinaigrette slasaus m/f 38

vinegar azijn m/f 38

visa visum n

visit *(noun)* bezoek n 66, 119; **to ~** bezoeken 123; *(hospital)* op bezoek komen bij 167; **~ing hours** bezoekuren m/fpl

vitamin pill vitaminetablet m/f 141

volleyball volleybal m/f 115

voltage voltage m/f

vomit; to ~ overgeven 163

W wait wachten 36, 41, 140; **to ~ for** wachten op 76, 89; **~!** wacht even! 98; **~ing room** wachtkamer m/f 73

Waiter! Meneer! m/f 37; **Waitress!** Mevrouw! m/f 37

wake wakker maken 70; **to ~ someone** iemand wakker maken 27; **~-up call** wekdienst

Wales Wales 119

walk; to ~ lopen; **to ~ home** naar huis lopen 65; **~ing boots** wandelschoenen m/fpl 145; **~ing route** wandelroute m/f 106

wallet beurs m/f 42, 160

ward *(hospital)* afdeling m/f 167

warm warm 14, 122; **~er** warmer 24

washbasin wasbak m/f

washing was m/f; **~ machine** wasmachine m/f 29; **~ powder** waspoeder m/f 148; **~-up liquid** afwasmiddel n 148

wasp wesp m/f

watch horloge n 149, 160

water water n 87; **~ bottle** waterfles; **~ heater** geiser m/f 28; **~ skis** waterski's m/fpl 117; **~fall** waterval m/f 107; **~proof** waterdicht; **~proof jacket** regenjack n 145

wave golf m/f

waxing wasbehandeling m/f 147

way weg; **I've lost my ~** ik ben de weg kwijt 94; **it's on the ~ to ...** het is op weg naar ... 83

we wij; **~'d like ...** wij willen graag ... 18

wear; to ~ dragen 159

weather weer n 122; **~ forecast** weerbericht n 122

wedding huwelijk n; **~ ring** trouwring m/f

Wednesday woensdag m/f 218

week week m/f 23, 97, 218

weekend weekend n 24, 218; **~ rate** weekendtarief n 86

weight gewicht n; **my ~ is ...** ik weeg ...

welcome to ... welkom in ...

well-done *(steak)* doorbakken

west ten westen 95

wetsuit duikerspak n

what? wat? 94, 104; **~ kind of ...?** wat voor ...? 106; **~ time ...?** hoe laat ...? 68, 76, 78, 81

wheelchair rolstoel m/f

when wanneer 13, 68, 78, 104

where waar 12, 73, 76, 78, 84, 88, 98; **~ is ...?** waar is ...? 80, 94, 99; **~ were you born?** waar bent u geboren? 119

which? welke? 16

white wit 50, 143; **~ wine** witte wijn m/f 40

who? wie? 16, 104

whose? van wie? 16

why? waarom? 15; **~ not?** waarom niet? 15

wide breed 14

wife vrouw m/f 120, 162

wildlife dieren in het wild m/fpl

wind wind m/f; **~breaker** windjek n 145; **~mill** molen m/f 154; **~screen** autovoorruit m/f; **to be ~y** waaien 122

window raam n 25, 77; *(shop)* etalage m/f 134, 149; **~ seat** plaats bij het raam m/f 69, 74

wine wijn m/f 40, 50, 158; **~ list** wijnkaart m/f 37

winery [vineyard] wijngaard m/f 107

winter winter m/f 219

wishes; best ~ beste wensen m/fpl 219

with met 17

withdraw; to ~ opnemen 139

within *(time)* binnen 13

without zonder 17, 38, 141

witness getuige m/f 93

wood bos n 107

wool wol m/f 145

work; to ~ *(function)* het doen 83; *(operate)* werken 28; **it doesn't ~** hij doet het niet 25, 137

worse slechter 14; **worst** ergst

write down; to ~ opschrijven 136

writing paper schrijfpapier n 150

wrong verkeerd 14, 95, 136; **there's something ~** er is iets mis 88

wrong number; to have the ~ verkeerd verbonden zijn 128

X Y Z

x-ray röntgenfoto m/f 164

yacht yacht n

year jaar n 119, 218

yellow geel 143

yes ja 10

yesterday gisteren 218

yogurt yoghurt m/f 158

you *(formal)* u 16; *(informal)* je/jij

young jong 14

your uw 16

yours *(formal)* uw 16; *(informal)* jouw

youth hostel jeugdherberg m/f 29, 123

zebra crossing zebrapad n

zero nul

zip(per) ritssluiting m/f

zoo dierentuin m/f 113

Dictionary
Dutch – English

This Dutch-English dictionary covers all the areas where you may need to decode written Dutch: hotels, public buildings, restaurants, shops, ticket offices, and on transportation. It will also help with understanding forms, maps, product labels, road signs, and operating instuctions (for telephones, parking meters etc.).
If you can't locate the exact sign, you may find key words or terms listed separately.

A

A-weg A-road
aan de toonbank betalen pay at counter
aanbellen a.u.b. please ring the bell
aanbevolen recommended
aangetekende brief registered letter
aanhangwagen trailer
aankomst arrivals
aanvullende cursus intermediate course
aanwijzingen directions (*map*)
abonnement season ticket
accommodatie accommodations
accommodatie verkrijgbaar available accommodations
achter barrière wachten a.u.b. please wait behind barrier
achternaam last name
advokaat lawyer (*title*)
afdeling department
afhaalmaaltijd take-out meal
afhankelijk van beschikbaarheid subject to availability
afloopdatum expiration date
afslag highway exit
after-lotion after-sun lotion
afval trash [rubbish]
afwasbak washbowl, sink
afzender sender
al naar gelang het seizoen according to season

alleen goederen freight only
alleen kranten newspapers only
alleen leveringen deliveries only
alleen met de hand wassen handwash only
alleen op weekdagen weekdays only
alleen parkeren voor vergunninghouders parking for permit holders only
alleen toegang voor inwoners access to residents only
alleen voor abonnees season ticket holders only
alleen voor inwoners residents only
alleen voor scheerapparaten shavers only
alleen voor tickethouders ticket holders only
alleen voor vergunningshouders permit holders only
alternatieve route alternative route
ambassade embassy
antiekwinkel antique store
ANWB (Algemene Nederlandse Wielrijders Bond) Royal Dutch Touring Club, automobile association
apart wassen wash separately
apotheek pharmacy
appartementsgebouw apartment building
april April

artikelen kunnen niet vergoed of geruild worden goods cannot be refunded or exchanged

a.u.b. please

augustus August

autodek car deck (*ferry*)

automatische deuren automatic doors

automatische openbare toilet automatic public toilet

autosnelweg highway [motorway]

autoverhuur car rental

avonddienst evening service

b.v. e.g.

B.V./N.V. Inc. [Ltd.] (*company*)

baai bay (*sea*)

babykleertjes babywear

badhuis baths

badkamer bathroom

badmutsen verplicht bathing caps must be worn

bagage niet zonder toezicht achterlaten do not leave baggage unattended

bagage-reclaim baggage [re-]claim

bagagecontrole baggage check

bagagekastjes luggage lockers

bakker baker

bakkerij bakery

balkon dress circle (*theater*)

banketbakker pastry shop

bankkosten bank charges

bebouwde kom built-up area

bediening service

bediening inbegrepen service included

bedieningsgeld service charge

begane grond first floor [ground floor]

begint om ... begins at ...

begint ... commencing ...

begraafplaats cemetery

behalve op ... except on ...

behandelingskamer treatment room

bel nummer ... dial number ...

belangrijk historisch kenmerk important historical feature

belastingvrije artikelen duty-free goods

belastingvrije winkel duty-free shop

bellen dial

beneden downstairs

benedenwoning (met tuin) garden apartment [flat]

benzinestation gas [petrol] station

beschermd gebied conservation area

bestemming/zone selecteren choose destination/zone

betaalbaar aan ... payable to ...

betaald paid

betaaltelefoon pay phone

beurs stock exchange

bevat geen ... contains no ...

bevroren frozen

bezoekersgalerij viewing gallery

bezoekuren visiting hours

bibliotheek library

bier beer

bij binnenkomst betalen pay as you enter

bij de meter betalen pay at the meter

bijeenkomsthal convention hall

bijgewerkt updated

binnen bereik van winkels/de zee within easy reach of stores/the sea

binnenste rondweg inner ring-road

bisschop bishop

bloedgroep blood group

bloemist florist

blusapparaat fire extinguisher

boarding boarding now (*airport*)

boarding-kaart boarding card (*airport*)

A-Z

boekwinkel bookstore
boerderij farm
bon bewaren in geval van ruilen of vergoeden keep your receipt for exchange or refund
bon/kaartje bewaren keep your receipt/ticket
boottocht boat trip
bos forest
boulevard boulevard
boven upstairs
branddeur fire door
brandstof fuel
branduitgang fire exit
brandweerkazerne fire station
brandweermannen firefighters
brievenbus post office box
Britse pond pound sterling
brood bread
brug bridge (*ship*)
buiten bereik van kinderen houden keep out of reach of children
buiten werking out of order
buitenlands foreign
buitenlandse valuta foreign currency
buitenste rondweg outer ring-road
buitenwijken suburbs
busbaan bus lane
bushalte bus stop
bushokje bus shelter
busroute bus route

C **cadeaubonnen bij de kassa kopen** buy a gift token at the cash desk
capsules capsules (*medication*)
centraal recherche team (CRT) criminal investigation department
check-in desk check-in desk (*airport*)
computers computers
conciërge caretaker
conferentiezaal conference room
conserveringsmiddelen preservatives
contanten cash

creditcard insteken insert credit card

D **dagschotel** dish of the day
dames ladies (*toilets*)
damesbladen women's magazine
dameskleding ladieswear
dank u voor uw bijdrage thank you for your contribution
de eigenaars kunnen geen verantwoordelijkheid aanvaarden voor eventuele schade of diefstal the owners can not accept responsibility for any damage or theft
delikatessen delicatessen
deltavliegen paragliding
deposito's en opnamen deposits and withdrawals
deur sluiten close the door
deuren worden … minuten na aanvang van voorstelling gesloten doors close … minutes after performance begins
deze bus gaat naar … this bus goes to …
deze machine geeft wisselgeld this machine gives change
deze trein stopt in … this train stops at …
Dhr. Mr.
dieet diet
dieetmenu diet menu
diepe deep end (*swimming pool*)
diepvriesprodukten frozen foods
diesel diesel
dinsdag Tuesday
discount-zaak discount store
dit bed moet worden opgemaakt this room needs making up
doe-'t-zelf winkel DIY store
dokken docks
dokter doctor
donderdag Thursday
doodlopende weg dead end

204

door de voor-/achterdeur binnenkomen enter by the front/rear door

door de voor-/achterdeur vertrekken exit by the front/rear door

doorlopende voorstelling continuous performance

doorrijhoogte ... headroom ... *(height restriction)*

dosering dosage

douane customs

douanecontrole customs control

douches showers

drankjes drinks

drijfzand quicksand

drinkwater drinking water

droge huid dry skin

droog haar dry hair

drukken om open te maken press to open

druppeltjes drops *(medication)*

duikplank diving board

duwen push

E € euro

eenennegentig octaan premium [super] *(gasoline)*

eenrichtingsstraat one-way street

Eerste Paasdag Easter Sunday

eerste klas first class

eerste verdieping second floor [first floor]

eerstehulp first aid

eetkamer dining room

EHBO (Eerste Hulp Bij Ongelukken) first aid

eigengemaakt homemade

einde inhaalverbod end of no-passing zone

einde parkeerverbod end of no-parking zone

einde vluchtstrook end of hard shoulder

einde werk in uitvoering end of roadwork

elektriciteitsmeter electric meter

elektrische artikelen electrical goods

Engels English

enkele reis one-way trip [journey]

evenement event

exact geld, geen wisselgeld exact fare, no change given

exact wisselgeld exact change

F **fabriekswinkel** factory outlet

februari February

fietsers cyclists

fietspad bicycle lane/path/track

file traffic jam

files: mogelijke vertragingen traffic jams: delays likely

film in originele versie film in original version

flatgebouw apartment building

fles met statiegeld returnable bottle

fooi tip

formele kleding formal wear

G **galerie** gallery

geannuleerd cancelled

gebeden prayers

geboortedatum date of birth

geboorteplaats place of birth

gebouw op monumentenlijst listed historic building

gebruik van claxon verboden use of horn prohibited

gebruiksaanwijzing instructions for use

gebruikte kaartjes used tickets

geen afval no littering

geen ankerplaats no docking

geen balspelletjes no ball games

geen creditcards no credit cards

geen doorgaand verkeer no acces

geen drinkwater no drinking water

A-Z

geen fotografie no photography
geen kinderen onder de ... no children under ...
geen kortingen no discounts
geen onvergezelde kinderen no unaccompanied children
geen pauzes no intermissions
geen staplaatsen no standing
geen statiegeld non-returnable
geen toegang no access/no entry
geen toegang tot fietsers en motorfietsers no access to bicyclists and motorcyclists
geen uitgang no exit
geen vuilnis storten no dumping
geen vuren/barbecues no fires/barbecues
geen waardevolle artikelen in uw auto achterlaten do not leave valuables in your car
geen zondagsdienst no Sunday service
geld in machine werpen en kaartje verwijderen insert money in machine and take ticket
geld wisselen currency exchange
geldautomaat ATM [cash machine]
geldopnamen withdrawals
gemaakt in ... made in ...
geopend open
geopend tot/op ... open until/on ...
gereduceerde prijzen reduced prices
gereserveerd reserved
gereserveerde rijbaan reserved lane
geschenken gifts
geschikt voor de magnetron microwaveable
geschikt voor vegetariërs/veganisten suitable for vegetarians/vegans
gesloten closed
gesloten voor renovatie closed for renovation
gesloten voor vakantie closed for vacation

gevaarlijke bocht dangerous turn
gevonden voorwerpen lost and found [lost property]
gevorderden advanced level
gezondheidscentrum health clinic
giften donations
gladde weg icy road
glasbak bottle bank
glutenvrij gluten free
goud gold
Gouden Gids yellow pages
gratis free
gratis geschenk free gift
groene kaart green (insurance) card
groenten vegetables
groentenboer produce store [greengrocer]
groepen welkom parties welcome
Groot-Brittannië (Verenigd Koninkrijk) United Kingdom
grot cave
grote weg highway [main road]

H

haardroger hairdryer
hal hall
half pension Modified American Plan [half board]
halte op verzoek request stop
halve prijs half price
haven harbor, port
hek dicht houden keep gate shut
helling incline
hengel fishing rod
hengelen angling
heren gentlemen (*toilets*)
herenkleding menswear
herfst fall [autumn]
het doek gaat op curtain up
het water niet drinken do not drink the water
heuvel hill
hier here
hier afscheuren tear here
hier te koop sold here

hier wordt Engels gesproken
English spoken

**historisch gebouw op
monumentenlijst** protected
historical building

hoofdweg main road

hoogspanning high voltage

hoogte boven zeepeil height above
sea level

hoorn opnemen lift receiver
(*telephone*)

horlogemaker watchmaker

houd afstand keep your distance

houdbaarheidsdatum sell-by
date/use by date

hout wood

huis te huur house to rent

huisarts general practitioner (G.P.)

hulplijn help line

huttendekken cabin decks

I **ijzerwarenwinkel**
hardware store

in aanbouw under construction

in contanten betalen pay cash

in de machine wassen machine
washable

in geval van brand ... in the event
of fire ...

**in geval van pech bellen met/contact
opnemen met ...** in case of
breakdown, phone/contact ...

in noodgevallen glas inslaan in case
of emergency break glass

in water oplossen dissolve in water

inbegrepen included (*in the price*)

inchecken check-in (*airport*)

industrieterrein industrial zone
[estate]

ingang entrance

ingang niet blokkeren do not block
entrance

inkoop van valuta tegen ...
currency exchanged at ...

inlichtingenbalie information desk

instructeur
instructor

intensive care intensive
care

intercity treinen intercity
trains

interferentie met andere medicijnen
interference with other drugs

inwoners van de EU EU citizens

J **jagen** hunting
januari January

jeugdherberg youth hostel

jongeren young adult/youth

juli July

juni June

juwelier jeweler

K **kaart insteken/munten
inwerpen** insert card/coins

kaartje ticket

kaartje/bon bewaren keep your
ticket/receipt

kaartje goldig voor metro ticket
valid for subway [metro]

kaartje insteken insert ticket

kaartje verwijderen take ticket

kaartjes voor vanavond tickets for
tonight

kaartjesbureau ticket agency

kaas cheese

kamers te huur rooms for rent

kamertarief room rate

kantoorboekhandel bookstore

kapper barber/hairdresser

kassa, hier betalen a.u.b. checkout,
please pay here

kassajuffrouw cashier

kasteel castle

... keer per dag ... times a day

kerk church

kerkdienst in uitvoering service in
progress

kermis fair (fun fair)

Kerstmis Christmas

A-Z

keuken kitchen
kies ... voor een buitenlijn dial ... for an outside line
kies... voor receptie dial ... for reception
kindbestendige dop childproof cap (bottle, etc.)
kinderen children
kinderzwembad children's pool
kiosk newsstand
klanteninformatie customer information
klantenparkeerplaats customer parking lot [car park]
klantenservice customer service
klein small
kleurecht colorfast
klif cliff
kliniek clinic
kloppen voordat u binnenkomt knock and enter
knooppunt highway interchange [motorway junction]
kookadvies cooking suggestions
koopjes bargains
korting discount
koud cold
kraan water faucet [tap]
kruidenierswinkel produce store [grocer]
kruising intersection [junction]
kuilen potholes
kust coast
kwaliteitsstandaard quality standard

L laantje lane
laat uw kaartje afstempelen validate/punch your ticket
laatste benzinestation vóór de autosnelweg last gas [petrol] station before the highway [motorway]
laatste oproep last call
laatste toegang om ... uur latest entry at ... p.m.

ladingslimiet load limit
lang voertuig long vehicle
lang/kort parkeren long-/short-term parking
langzaam rijden slow down
langzaam rijdend verkeer slow traffic
leer leather
legitimatiebewijs ID card
lente spring
levensgevaar danger of death
lichten use headlights
lichtingstijden times of collection
liefst gekoeld opdienen best served chilled
lift elevator [lift]
ligstoel deck chair
links houden keep to the left
linnen linen
logies-ontbijt bed and breakfast
loodvrij regular/unleaded (gasoline)
losse steenslag loose shavings [chippings]
loterij lottery
lucht air (gas station)
luchthaven airport
luchtpomp air pump (gas station)

M maak uw veiligheidsriem vast fasten your seat belt
maandag Monday
maandelijks monthly
maart March
makelaar estate agent
makkelijk te openen ampullen easy-to-open ampules
manager manager
mandjeskassa express checkout
markt market
maximumsnelheidslimiet maximum speed limit
medische nooddienst emergency medical service
meer lake
mei May

meisjesnaam maiden name
menu van de dag menu of the day
met airconditioning air conditioned
met badkamer with bathroom
met de hand gemaakt handmade
met de hand genaaid hand-sewn
met douche with shower
met maaltijden with food/meals
met statiegeld returnable
met uitzicht op zee with sea view
metro subway
metroconducteur subway ticket inspector
meubilair furniture
Mevr. Mrs.
middag: 's middags p.m.
middelbare school high school [secondary school]
middernacht midnight
minimum (vereiste) minimum (requirement)
minimum/standaard prijs minimum/standard price
... minuten vertraging ... minutes delay
mist fog
mistgevaar risk of fog
moeder mother
moeras swamp, marsh
mogelijke vertragingen waarschijnlijk delays likely
morgen tomorrow
moskee mosque
multipak multipack
munt inwerpen insert coin
munten worden geaccepteerd coins accepted
museum museum
muur wall
muziekwinkel record store
Mw. Miss

N na de maaltijd innemen take after meals (*medication*)
naaktstrand nudist beach

naam van echtgenoot(ote) name of spouse (male/female)
nacht night
nachtapotheek all-night/duty pharmacy
nachtbel night bell
nachtportier night porter
nagesynchroniseerd dubbed
nationale verzekeringskaart national insurance card
natte verf wet paint
nettogewicht net weight
netwerk network
neveneffecten side effects
niet aan zonlicht blootstellen do not expose to sunlight
niet duiken no diving
niet inbegrepen not included (*in the price*)
niet inhalen no passing
niet inwendig in te nemen not to be taken internally
niet met de bestuurder praten do not talk to the driver
niet oraal in te nemen not to be taken orally
niet oversteken do not cross
niet rennen no running
niet roken no smoking
niet roken op autodekken no smoking on car decks
niet stoppen no stopping
niet storen do not disturb
niet strijken do not iron
niet uit het raam leunen do not lean out of windows
niet vissen no fishing
niet-EU inwoners non-EU citizens
niets aan te geven nothing to declare
nieuw verkeerssysteem in werking new traffic system in operation
nieuwe titels new titles/new releases

Nieuwjaar New Year
Nieuwjaarsdag New Year's Day
nieuws news
non-stop naar ... non-stop to ...
noodgeval emergency
noodrem emergency brake
nooduitgang emergency exit
noord(elijk) north(ern)
normaal haar normal hair
normale huid normal skin
nummer in noodgevallen emergency number
N.V./B.V. Inc. [Ltd. public/private] *(company)*

O ochtendmis morning mass
ochtend: 's ochtends a.m.
olie oil *(gas station)*
onbevoegde voertuigen worden weggesleept unauthorized vehicles will be towed away
ondergoed lingerie/underwear
ondergrondse garage underground garage
ondertiteld subtitled
ondiepe shallow end
ontbijt breakfast
ontbijtkamer breakfast room
onthoud het nummer van uw parkeerplaats note your parking space number
ontmoetingsplaats meeting place [point]
ontruim uw kamer vóór ... vacate your room by ...
ontvangstcentrum reception center
oorlogsmonument war memorial
oost(elijk) east(ern)
op bestelling gemaakt made to order
op een koele plaats bewaren keep in a cool place
op-/afritten ramps

opdieningssuggesties serving suggestions
openbaar gebouw public building
openbaar park public park
openbare feestdag national holiday
openbare tuinen public gardens
openingstijden business hours [opening hours]
openlucht outdoor
openlucht zwembad outdoor swimming pool
ophaalbrug drawbridge
opheffingsverkoop closeout [closing-down] sale
op maat gemaakt custom made
oprit snelweg expressway entrance
opruiming clearance [sale]
opruimingsartikelen kunnen niet geruild worden sale items cannot be exchanged
opstaan voor iemand misstaat niemand please give up this seat to seniors and the disabled
opticiën optician
Oudejaarsavond New Year's Eve
overdekt zwembad indoor swimming pool
overdekte markt covered market
overgewicht excess baggage
overmorgen the day after tomorrow
overstappen in ... change at ...
overweg railroad [level] crossing

P paardrijden horseback riding
pad path
pakket package, parcel
Palmzondag Palm Sunday
paperback paperback *(book)*
parallelweg service road
parasollen umbrellas [sunshades]
parkeer en reis park and ride
parkeergarage multistory parking lot [car park]
parkeermeter parking meter
parkeerschijfzone disc parking zone

parkeerticket parking ticket
parkeerverbod no parking
parkeren toegestaan parking permitted
parkeren voor treinpassagiers parking for train users
parochie parish
particulier eigendom private property
pas op caution
pas op de hond beware of the dog
pas op het trapje watch the step
Pasen Easter
paskamer fitting room
passagiers eerst laten uitstappen let passengers off first
paviljoen pavilion
pension guest house
per dag per day
per expres express mail
per expres pakjespost express parcel post
per week per week
perron platform
picknickgebied picnic area
pillen pills
plaats bij het gangpad aisle seat
plaats bij het raam window seat
plaatsnummer seat number
plein square
plezierboten pleasure craft
polikliniek outpatients (*hospital department*)
politie,brandweer, ambulance emergency services (*police, fire, ambulance*)
politiebureau police station
populair-wetenschappelijke literatuur non-fiction (*section in bookstore*)
postkantoor post office
postwissels money orders
postzegels stamps
pretpark amusement park
prijs per liter price per liter
prijsverlaging discounts

prijzen drastisch verlaagd prices slashed
privé private

R recept prescription
rechtbank courthouse
rechts houden keep to the right
rechtstreekse verbinding direct service
reddingsboten life boats
reddingsgordel life preserver [belt]
reformprodukten health foods
reformwinkel health-food store
reisbureau travel agent
reisbus bus [coach]
renbaan racetrack [race course]
reparaties repairs (*car, etc.*)
reparatiewerkplaats repair shop / workshop
reservoir reservoir
rij row
rijbewijs driver's license
rivier river
rivierboten river boats
rivieroever river bank
roken smoking
romans fiction (*section in bookstore*)
rondtocht round-trip
rondvaarten cruises, boat trips
rondweg bypass (*road*)
room service room service
rotonde traffic circle [roundabout]
rustgebied rest area

S sauna sauna
's morgens a.m.
's avonds in the evening
schaal 1:100 scale 1:100
schaatsen ice-skating
schaatsen skates
schip ship
schoenen shoes
schoenmaker shoemaker

schokbestending shockproof
schoonheidsverzorging beauty care
secundaire weg secondary road
slager butcher
slagveld battle site
slecht wegdek rough/uneven road surface
sleutels bij receptie achterlaten leave keys at reception
sleutels slijpen terwijl u wacht keys made while you wait
's middags p.m.
smaakstof flavoring
smalle weg narrow road
snel-klaar quick-cooking
snelheid verminderen reduce speed
snelheidslimiet speed limit
snoepwinkel candy store [confectioner]
souterrain basement
spaarbank savings bank
speelgoed toys
speelgoedwinkel toy store
speelhal amusement arcade
spelletjeskamer game room
spreekkamer consulting room (doctor)
staal steel
stadhuis town hall
stadion stadium
stadscentrum downtown area
stadsmuur city wall
stalles orchestra [stalls] (theater)
steegje alley
steward/stewardess flight attendants (male/female)
stilist stylist
stomerij dry-cleaner/steamer
stoplichten traffic lights
stoptrein local train
stortplaats dumping ground/site
straat street

strandhuisje cabana, bathing (beach) cabin
strandmeester lifeguard (beach)
stripverhaal comics (magazines)
stromend water running water
stroom stream
suiker sugar
suikervrij sugar-free
sun-block sun-block cream
surfplank surfboard

T tabletten tablets
tafellinnen en beddegoed household linen (table and bed linen)
tandarts dentist
taxistandplaats taxi stand
te huur for rent [for hire]
te kauwen chewable (tablets, etc.)
tegenliggers oncoming traffic
telefonist(e) telephone operator (male/female)
telefoongesprek op rekening van de ontvanger collect call [reverse-charge call]
telefoongids directory (telephone)
telefoonkaart phone card
tenminste houdbaar tot ... best before ... (date)
terminal air terminal
thuisadres home address
ticket bij vooruit plaatsen place ticket on windshield [windscreen]
tijdens overtocht geen toegang tot autodekken no access to car decks during crossing
tijdschriften magazines, periodicals
toegang vrij admission free
toegestane bagage luggage allowance
toeristenbureau tourist office
toets uw PIN in dial your PIN
tol toll
tolhuisje toll booth
tolroute toll route

tolweg toll road

tot until

trekken voor alarm pull for alarm

trottoir sidewalk [pavement]

tuincentrum garden center

Turks bad Turkish bath

tussen ... en ... between ... and ... (*time*)

twaalf uur 's middags noon

twee halen, één betalen buy two, get one free

Tweede Paasdag Easter Monday

tweede etappe second leg

tweedehandswinkel secondhand store

U **uit de diepvries koken** cook from frozen

uiterst langzaam dead slow

uitgang exit, way out

uitkijkpunt view point

uitrit vrachtwagens truck exit

uitschakelen switch off

uitsluitend only

uitverkocht sold out

... uren vertraging ... hours delay

uur hour

uw auto in de eerste versnelling achterlaten leave your car in first gear

uw geld/kaart verwijderen take your money/card

uw kentekenbewijs laten zien show your registration documents

uw tassen hier achterlaten leave your bags here

V **vaatwasmachinebestendig** dishwasher-safe

vacatures vacancies

vakantiehuisje/-appartement vacation cottage/apartment

vakantierooster vacation timetable

valhelm crash helmet

valhelmen verplicht crash helmets obligatory

vallende rotsen falling rocks

valuta wisselen currency exchange

van te voren boeken advance reservations

van ... tot ... from ... to ... (*time*)

vanavond this evening

vandaag today

vanmiddag this afternoon

vanmorgen this morning

vast menu voor ... euro's set menu for ... euros

veld field

verbeterd improved

verbinding verbroken disconnected

verboden forbidden

verboden op het gras te lopen keep off the grass

verboden toegang keep out

verboden voor motorfietsen no entry for motorcycles

verdieping floor (*level in building*)

vereist required

Verenigde Staten United States

vergeet niet om ... don't forget to ...

vergeet niet om uw kaartje te laten afstempelen don't forget to validate your ticket

vergeet niet uw gids een fooi te geven remember to tip your guide

ver gevorderden very advanced level

vergoeding refund

verkeer uit tegenovergestelde richting oncoming traffic

verkeersdrempels speed bumps

verkeerspolitie traffic police

verkoop van valuta tegen ... currency sold at ...

verliest zijn vorm niet will not lose its shape
verpleegsters nurses
verplichte route voor gevaarlijke stoffen compulsory route for hazardous goods
vers fresh
versnaperingen refreshments available
vertraagd delayed
vertraging delay
vetgehalte fat content
vet haar greasy hair
vette huid oily skin
vetvrij fat-free
vierbaansweg dual highway [carriageway]
vijf ampère five amp
vijf artikelen of minder five items or less
vijver pond
vissen toegestaan fishing permitted
visstalletje fish stall
vliegtuig plane
vliegveld airport
vlooienmarkt flea market
vluchtinformatie flight information
vluchtnummer flight number
vluchtstrook hard-shoulder
vochtinbrengende crème moisturizer
voeten vegen a.u.b. please wipe your feet
voetgangers pedestrians
voetgangersgebied traffic-free zone
voetgangersoversteekplaats pedestrian crossing
voetpad footpath
vol full up
volgende lichting om ... next collection at ...
volpension American Plan [full board]
voor ... before ...
voor ... dagen for ... days

voor de maaltijd before meals
voor gebruik uw dokter raadplegen consult your doctor before using
voor inlichtingen, zie ... for inquiries, see ...
voorrang right of way
voorrang geven yield [give way]
voorstelling performance
voor tanken benzine betalen pay for gas before filling tank
voor twee personen for two
voor verkeer gesloten closed to traffic
voor vertrek uw tassen laten zien show your bags before leaving
voorzichtig rijden drive carefully
vraag om assistentie please ask for assistance
vrachtwagen truck
vrachtwagenroute truck route
vragen bij de receptie ask at reception
vreemde talen foreign languages
vrij vacant
vrij houden keep clear
vruchtensappen fruit juices
vuurtoren lighthouse
vuurwerk fireworks

WX Y Z
waarschuwing warning
wacht op de kiestoon wait for the tone
wacht op uw kaartje wait for your ticket
wachten a.u.b. please wait
wachtkamer waiting room
wagentjes carts [trolleys]
wandelen walking, hiking
wandelpad walkway, path
warenhuis department store / general store
warm hot (*water, tap*)
wasserette laundry
water niet drinken don't drink the water

waterskiën waterskiing
wedstrijd contest
weekdagen weekdays
weerbericht weather forecast
weg road
weg gesloten road closed
weg in aanbouw road under construction
wegenkaart road map
wegenwacht breakdown services
wegomlegging detour [diversion]
wekelijks weekly
welkom! welcome!
west(elijk) west(ern)
wij accepteren creditcards credit cards accepted
wij kopen en verkopen ... we buy and sell ...
wijnproeven wine tasting
windmolen windmill
windsurfen windsurfing
winkelcentrum shopping mall [centre]
winkelmandje shopping basket
winkelplattegrond store guide
wisselkantoor currency exchange office
wisselkoers exchange rate
woensdag Wednesday
wol wool
woninginrichting home furnishings
woonerf residential zone
woonwijk housing estate
zachte berm soft edge [verge]
zakengebied business district
zaterdag Saturday
zebrapad crosswalk [pedestrian crossing/zebra crossing]
zee sea
zeepeil sea level
zeilinstructeur sailing instructor
zeilvereniging sailing club
zelfbedieningsrestaurant self-service restaurant

zet uw motor af turn off your engine
ziekenhuis hospital
zijde silk
zitkamer lounge
zitplaatsen boven seats upstairs
zomer summer
zomer-/winterrooster summer/winter schedule
zondag Sunday
zonder maaltijden without food
zonnedek sun deck
zout salt
zuid(elijk) south(ern)
zuivel dairy
zuivelprodukten dairy products
zware truck met oplegger heavy goods vehicle
zwemmen swimming
zwemmen onder toezicht supervised swimming
zwemvesten life jackets

A-Z

Numbers

GRAMMAR

The Dutch use a comma for a decimal point and a period [full stop] or space to indicate '000s. For example: 4.575,50; 3 467; €4,95. Larger numbers are built up in a similar way to English:

2.567.498   **twee miljoen, vijfhonderd zevenenzeventig duizend, vierhonderd achtennegentig.**

0	**nul** _nool_		15	**vijftien** _fayf_teen
1	**één** _ayn_		16	**zestien** _zes_teen
2	**twee** _tvay_		17	**zeventien** _zay_vernteen
3	**drie** _dree_		18	**achttien** _akh_teen
4	**vier** _feer_		19	**negentien** _nay_khernteen
5	**vijf** _fayf_		20	**twintig** _tvin_terkh
6	**zes** _zes_		21	**eenentwintig** _ayn_entvinterkh
7	**zeven** _zay_vern		22	**tweeëntwintig** _tvay_entvinterkh
8	**acht** _akht_		23	**drieëntwintig** _dree_-entvinterkh
9	**negen** _nay_khern		24	**vierentwintig** _feer_entvinterkh
10	**tien** _teen_		25	**vijfentwintig** _fayf_entvinterkh
11	**elf** _elf_		26	**zesentwintig** _zes_entvinterkh
12	**twaalf** _tvaalf_		27	**zevenentwintig** _zay_vernentvinterkh
13	**dertien** _dehr_teen		28	**achtentwintig** _akht_entvinterkh
14	**veertien** _fayr_teen			

29	**negenentwintig** *naykhernentvinterkh*	fourth	**vierde** *feerder*
30	**dertig** *dehrtikh*	fifth	**vijfde** *fayfder*
31	**eenendertig** *aynendehrtikh*	once	**één keer** *ayn kayr*
32	**tweeëndertig** *tvayendehrtikh*	twice	**twee keer** *tvay kayr*
40	**veertig** *fayrtikh*	three times	**drie keer** *dree kayr*
50	**vijftig** *fayftikh*	a half	**een helft** *ayn helft*
60	**zestig** *zestikh*	half an hour	**een half uur** *ayn half uwr*
70	**zeventig** *zayverntikh*	half a tank	**een halve tank** *ayn halver tangk*
80	**tachtig** *takhtikh*	half eaten	**half opgegeten** *half opkherkhaytern*
90	**negentig** *naykherntikh*		
100	**honderd** *hondert*	a quarter	**een kwart** *ayn kvart*
101	**honderd één** *hondert ayn*	a third	**een derde** *ayn dehrder*
102	**honderd twee** *hondert tvay*	a pair of ...	**een paar ...** *ayn paar*
200	**tweehonderd** *tvayhondert*	a dozen ...	**een dozijn ...** *ayn doozayn*
500	**vijfhonderd** *fayfhondert*	1999	**negentien negenennegentig** *naykhernteen naykhernennaykherntikh*
1,000	**duizend** *doaizernt*		
10,000	**tienduizend** *teendoaizernt*	the 1990's	**de jaren negentig** *der jahrern naygherntigh*
1,000,000	**één miljoen** *ayn milyoon*	the year 2000	**het jaar tweeduizend** *het jahr twaydoaizernt*
first	**eerste** *ayrster*	2001	**tweeduizend één** *tvaydoaizernt ayn*
second	**tweede** *tvayder*	the Millennium	**het Millennium** *het milehnneeyuhm*
third	**derde** *dehrder*		

217

Days Dagen

Monday	**maandag** _maandakh_
Tuesday	**dinsdag** _dinsdakh_
Wednesday	**woensdag** _voonsdakh_
Thursday	**donderdag** _donderdakh_
Friday	**vrijdag** _fraydakh_
Saturday	**zaterdag** _zaaterdakh_
Sunday	**zondag** _zondakh_

Months Maanden

January	**januari** _yanuwaaree_
February	**februari** _faybruwaaree_
March	**maart** _maart_
April	**april** _april_
May	**mei** _may_
June	**juni** _yuwnee_
July	**juli** _yuwlee_
August	**augustus** _oakhuhstuhs_
September	**september** _september_
October	**oktober** _oktoaber_
November	**november** _noavember_
December	**december** _daysember_

Dates Data

It's ...	**Het is ...** _het is_
July 10	**tien juli** _teen yuhlee_
Tuesday, March 1	**dinsdag, één maart** _dinsdakh, ayn maart_
yesterday	**gisteren** _khisterern_
today	**vandaag** _fandaakh_
tomorrow	**morgen** _morkhern_
this .../last ...	**deze .../vorige ...** _dayzer/foarikher_
next week	**volgende week** _folkhernder vayk_
every month/year	**elke maand/elk jaar** _elker maant/elk yaar_
on [at] the weekend	**in het weekend** _in het weekend_

Seasons Jaargetijden

spring	**de lente** der _lente_r
summer	**de zomer** der _zoa_mer
fall [autumn]	**de herfst** der herfst
winter	**de winter** der _vin_ter
in spring	**in de lente** in der _lente_r
during the summer	**tijdens de zomer** _tay_derns der _zoa_mer

Greetings Groeten

Happy birthday! — **Gefeliciteerd met uw verjaardag!**
kherfaylisitayrt met _uw_er fer_yaar_dakh

Merry Christmas! — **Vrolijke Kerst!** _froa_liker kehrst

Happy New Year! — **Gelukkig Nieuwjaar!**
kher_luhk_kikh _noo_yaar

Happy Easter! — **Prettige Paasdagen!**
_prett_ikher _paas_daakhern

Congratulations! — **Hartelijk gefeliciteerd!**
_hart_layk kherfeleeseetayrt

Good luck! / All the best! — **Succes! / Het allerbeste!**
suhk_ses_ / het _aller_bester

Have a good trip! — **Goede reis!** _khoo_der rays

Give my regards to … — **Doe de groeten aan …**
doo der _khroo_tern aan

Public holidays Openbare feestdagen

1 January	**Nieuwjaarsdag**	New Year's Day
30 April	**Koninginnedag**	Queen Mother's Birthday
4 May	**Dodenherdenking**	Remembrance Day, World War II (_shops open_)
5 May	**Bevrijdingsdag**	Liberation Day (_shops open_)
25 / 26 December	**Eerste Kerstdag / Tweede Kerstdag**	Christmas Day / Boxing Day
Movable dates		
Good Friday	**Goede Vrijdag**	(_shops open_)
Easter	**Pasen**	
Easter Sunday / Easter Monday	**Eerste Paasdag / Tweede Paasdag**	
Ascension Thursday (_May_)	**Hemelvaartsdag**	
Whitsuntide	**Pinksteren**	
Whit Sunday / Whit Monday (_May_)	**Eerste Pinksterdag / Tweede Pinksterdag**	

Time De tijd

In everyday conversation time is expressed as below, with the addition of **'s morgens/'s ochtends** (in the morning), **'s middags** (in the afternoon) or **'s avonds** (in the evening). Times of trains, however, are expressed using the 24-hour clock, for example 14.45 (**veertien uur vijfenveertig**).

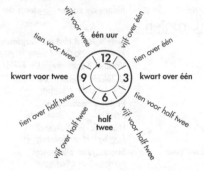

Excuse me, can you tell me the time?	**Meneer/mevrouw, weet u ook hoe laat het is?** *mer<u>nayr</u>/mer<u>frow</u>, vayt uw oak hoo laat het is*
It's …	**Het is …** *het is*
five past one	**vijf over één** *fayf <u>oa</u>fer ayn*
ten past two	**tien over twee** *teen <u>oa</u>fer tvay*
a quarter past three	**kwart over drie** *kvart <u>oa</u>fer dree*
twenty past four	**tien voor half vijf** *teen foar half fayf*
twenty-five past five	**vijf voor half zes** *fayf foar half zes*
half past six	**half zeven** *half <u>zay</u>vern*
twenty-five to seven	**vijf over half zeven** *fayf <u>oa</u>fer half <u>zay</u>vern*
twenty to eight	**tien over half acht** *teen <u>oa</u>fer half akht*
a quarter to nine	**kwart voor negen** *kvart foar <u>nay</u>khern*
ten to ten	**tien voor tien** *teen foar teen*
five to eleven	**vijf voor elf** *fayf foar elf*
twelve o'clock (noon/midnight)	**twaalf uur (twaalf uur 's middags/ middernacht)** *tvaalf uwr (tvaalf uwr s<u>mid</u>dakhs/<u>mid</u>dernakht)*

at dawn	**bij dageraad** *bay daakheraat*
in the morning	**'s morgens** *smorkherns*
during the day	**overdag** *oaferdakh*
before lunch	**voor de lunch** *foar der luhnsh*
after lunch	**na de lunch** *naa der luhnsh*
in the afternoon	**'s middags** *smiddakhs*
in the evening	**'s avonds** *saafonts*
at night	**'s nachts** *snakhts*
I'll be ready in five minutes.	**Ik ben over vijf minuten klaar.** *ik ben oafer fayf minuwtern klaar*
He'll be back in a quarter of an hour.	**Hij komt over een kwartier terug.** *hay komt oafer ayn kvarteer truhkh*
She arrived half an hour ago.	**Ze is een half uur geleden aangekomen.** *zer is ayn half uwr kherlaydern aankherkoamern*
The train leaves at …	**De trein vertrekt om …** *der trayn fertrehkt om*
13:04	**dertien uur vier** *dehrteen uwr feer*
00:40	**twaalf uur veertig** *tvaalf uwr fayrtikh*
The train is ten minutes late/early.	**De trein is tien minuten te laat/te vroeg.** *der trayn is teen minuwtern ter laat/ter frookh*
It's five minutes fast/slow.	**Hij gaat vijf minuten voor/achter.** *hay khaat fayf minuwtern foar/akhter*
from 9:00 to 5:00	**van negen tot vijf** *fan naykhern tot fayf*
between 8:00 and 2:00	**tussen acht en twee** *tuhssern akht en tvay*
I'll be leaving by …	**Ik vertrek niet later dan …** *ik fertrehk neet laater dan*
Will you be back before …?	**Komt u voor … terug?** *komt uw foar … truhkh*
We'll be here until …	**We zijn hier tot …** *vay zayn heer tot*

NORTH SEA

Netherlands

Groningen
Leeuwarden
Assen
Den Helder
Zwolle
Haarlem □ Amsterdam
The Hague Utrecht Apeldoorn Enschede
Delft Gouda
Rotterdam Arnhem
Dordrecht Nijmegen
Breda
Vlissingen Tilburg
Roosendaal Eindhoven

Germany

Belgium

Maastricht

NORTH
SEA

Netherlands

Knokke
Ostend Bruges Antwerp
Gent
Kortrijk
Schaerbeek
Brussels
Liège
Verviers
Mons Charleroi Namur

Belgium

France

Luxembourg

Quick reference
Beknopt naslaggedeelte

Good morning.	**Goedemorgen.**	_khoodermorkhern_
Good afternoon.	**Goedemiddag.**	_khoodermiddakh_
Good evening.	**Goedenavond.**	_khoodernaafont_
Hello.	**Hallo.**	_hallo_
Good-bye.	**Dag.**	_dakh_
Excuse me. (getting attention) (male/female)	**Meneer/Mevrouw.**	_mernayr/merfrow_
Excuse me? [Pardon?]	**Pardon?**	_pardon_
Sorry!	**Sorry!**	_sorree_
Please.	**Alstublieft.**	_alstuwbleeft_
Thank you.	**Dank u.**	_dangk uw_
Do you speak English?	**Spreekt u Engels?**	_spraykt uw engils_
I don't understand.	**Ik begrijp het niet.**	_ik berkhrayp het neet_
Where is …?	**Waar is …?**	_vaar is_
Where is the bathroom [toilet]?	**Waar is het toilet?**	_vaar is het twalet_

Emergency Noodgevallen

Help!	**Help!**	_help_
Go away!	**Ga weg!**	_khaa vekh_
Leave me alone!	**Laat me met rust!**	_laat mer met ruhst_
Call the police!	**Bel de politie!**	_bel der poaleetsee_
Stop thief!	**Houd de dief!**	_howt der deef_
Get a doctor!	**Haal een dokter!**	_haal ayn dokter_
Fire!	**Brand!**	_brant_
I'm sick.	**Ik ben ziek.**	_ik ben zeek_
I'm lost.	**Ik ben verdwaald.**	_ik ben ferdvaalt_
Can you help me?	**Kunt u me helpen?**	_kuhnt uw mer helpern_

Fire/Police/Ambulance: ☎ 06-11
Tourist Medical and Dental Service: ☎ 664 2111 (24-hour)

Embassies/Consulates

UK:	**(020) 676 43 43**	Australia:	**(070) 310 82 00**
USA:	**(020) 575-5309**	Eire:	**(070) 363 09 93**
Canada:	**(070) 361 41 11**		